CW00969398

A HISTORY OF THE

BRISTOL BRITANNIA

The Whispering Giant

A HISTORY OF THE

BRISTOL BRITANNIA

The Whispering Giant

DAVID LITTLEFIELD

HALSGROVE
PRESS

First published in Great Britain in 1992 by Halsgrove Press

British Library Cataloguing in Publication Data

Littlefield, David J. A.
History of the Bristol Britannia:
Whispering Giant
I. Title
629.133

ISBN 1-874448-01-9

First published to celebrate the 40th anniversary
of the Bristol Britannia, 1952–1992

Kim – I dedicate this book to you
with all my love.

FRONT COVER PHOTOGRAPHS

Main Picture:

G-ANBA the first production series 100 Britannia – a Variant 102
(BRITISH AEROPLANE CO. LTD)

Inside bottom left

'Every tail tells a story', two of these three Britannias have been preserved.
Which ones? Read through to find out.
(TOM SINGFIELD)

Inside bottom right

G-AOVF preserved in BOAC livery at the Aerospace Museum, RAF Cosford.
(AUTHOR)

Halsgrove Press
1 Chinon Court
Lower Moor Way
Tiverton
Devon EX16 6SS
Tel: 0884 243242
Fax: 0884 243325

Designed for Halsgrove Press by
Topics Visual Information
397, Topsham Road
Exeter EX2 6HD
Tel: 0392 876800

Typeset by ICON · Exeter

Printed and bound in Great Britain by The Bath Press

CONTENTS

FOREWORD by Sir Peter Masefield 7

PREFACE 9

ACKNOWLEDGEMENTS 10

INTRODUCTION 11

PART ONE

Evolution of the Whispering Giant 13

Britannia Order Book 24

Production Breakdown 25

The Britannia is Accepted 25

The Engine Flame-out Tests of 1956 26

PART TWO

Bristol Britannia General Details 29

Britannia Series and Variants 35

PART THREE

Three View Plan of 100 Series 37

Technical Specifications, Series 100 37

Series 100 Aircraft Histories 38

PART FOUR

Technical Specifications, Series 250 49

Three View Plan of 250 Series 50

Series 250 Aircraft Histories 52

PART FIVE

Technical Specifications, Series 300 65

Comparison Three View Plan of 100 & 300 Series 65

Cutaway Plan and Key to Variant 312 66–67

Series 300 Aircraft Histories 69

PART SIX

Technical Specifications, Series 305 71

Series 305 Aircraft Histories 72

PART SEVEN

Technical Specifications, Series 310 77

Series 310 Aircraft Histories 78

PART EIGHT

Technical Specifications, Series 320 99

Three View Plan of 320 Series 100

Series 320 Aircraft Histories 101

PART NINE – APPENDICES

APPENDIX 1 Preserved Britannias 120

APPENDIX 2 Britannia Association 121

APPENDIX 3 Company Fleet Lists 122

APPENDIX 4 Registration Cross Reference 128

APPENDIX 5 Registration List 130

APPENDIX 6 Aircraft Quick Reference Tables 133

Index 156

FOREWORD

By Sir Peter G. Masefield

(Managing Director of Bristol Aircraft Limited, 1955–60)

Just a few of the long line of the world's major transport aircraft stand out as significant steps forward in the history of air transport – along that bumpy path which still stretches into the misty future. Those historic aircraft range from the Handley Page W-8 and the Vickers Vimy Commercial of 1919, to Concorde and the Boeing 747-400 of only seventy years or so later – but a whole age forward in aircraft evolution.

One of the outstanding aircraft of those first seventy years of air transport was the Bristol 175 Britannia; the worlds first long-range turbo-prop airliner, the 'Whispering Giant'.

The Britannia prototype – G-ALBO – made its first flight at Filton on 16 August, 1952. Despite the subsequent four and a half years of difficult 'de-bugging' before a production Britannia 102 flew its first airline service with BOAC (from London to Johannesburg on 1 February, 1957), the Britannia will be remembered with affection not only by its pilots, to whom it was 'a gentleman's aeroplane', by its passengers, to whom it was a spacious, quiet (except in the front row of passenger seats), and stolid aeroplane, but also because it was the first aircraft in the world to have a genuine all-the-year-round ability to operate regular air services non-stop across the North Atlantic.

The elegant 84-tonne Britannia, born out of the second Brabazon Committee of 1944, built up a solid reputation for reliability in a service life of thirty-two years. Its place in history spans the evolutionary slot between the last of the piston-engine transport monoplanes (the DC-7c) and their eventual successors, the long-range jets. The Britannia remained in production at Filton and Belfast for twelve years, between December 1948 and the end of 1960, and in its operational life with 96 different airline operators, and the Royal Air Force Transport Command, Britannias flew a total of more than 3.2 million aircraft hours and some 620 million aircraft miles (at an average block speed of some 310 miles an hour) while carrying more than 37 million passengers for in excess of half a million individual flights.

In the end – and largely because of the protracted time required to eliminate the Proteus engine-icing problems (simple when we found out how, by means of a miniature television camera inserted down the air intake), the Britannia was not ready to take full advantage of international airline requirements for a new long-range passenger aeroplane in the few years between the piston-powered types and the early jets. Hence, only 85 Britannias were built. There were two prototypes, 17 of the initial Britannia 100s, 45 of the larger, long-range, Britannia 300 series, and 23 of the military Britannia 250s. Such relatively small production numbers were, of course. a disappointment to all concerned. The problems had been that the Bristol Type 175 was, to a large extent, an adventure into the unknown, not only on the part of both the Bristol Aeroplane Company and Bristol Aero Engines, but also for many of its component and systems designers and suppliers. Nor had the relatively small Bristol Aeroplane Company either sufficient funds or productive capacity available, nor the background of civil aircraft and turbine aero-engine experience in manufacture and development, to bring all that was needed to such a formidable task 'on the frontiers of knowledge'.

Even so, but for the wholly unexpected (and, at first, intractable) engine-icing problems (which took nearly three critical years to solve), the Britannia would have sold to the airlines of the world in much greater and worthwhile numbers – especially in the United States where, in 1957, Howard Hughes, the owner of TWA, would have placed a substantial order had quick deliveries been possible.

Those of us who spent intensive years of our lives devoted to the Britannia, and gained much hard won experience in the process, remember the aircraft and its times with a mixture of affection and pride, of frustration and exasperation and of sadness that so much endeavor from a dedicated team fell short of the world-wide success which was so nearly won.

David Littlefield has well covered all these aspects of the Britannia's life in his deeply researched, and well-produced, book *The Whispering Giant*. He records the individual history of every one of the 85 Britannias which were flown. I commend most warmly this important contribution to transport aircraft history.

Notable Britannia achievements during its service life included, in July 1957, the first non-stop flight ever made from Europe to the Pacific Coast of North America. The distance of 4090 nautical miles (Great Circle) from Heathrow to Vancouver, was covered in 14 hours 40 minutes at a block speed of 279 knots (321 mph). That was followed, on 19 December, 1957 by a non-stop flight of 4930 nautical miles (G.C.) by EL-AL from New York to Tel Aviv in 15 hours 35 minutes at a block speed of 316 knots (364 mph) with some help from a tailwind. At the time it was a world's distance record for a civil transport aeroplane.

Nor should we forget that the Britannia begat two derivatives in Canada, built by Canadair Limited. The first was a maritime-reconnaissance version, the Canadair CL-28 Argus. Thirty-three of them were delivered to the Royal Canadian Air Force between September 1957 and July 1967. There was also a lengthened version of the Britannia 250 – the CL-44 – of which 39 were built, 12 for the RCAF and 27 for civil operators.

Additional projects – which remained no more than design studies – were to be built around the 4000 ehp Bristol BE-25 Orion turbo-prop engine. That advanced power plant, regrettably, was cancelled by the Ministry of Supply in January 1958 after encouraging flying trials in the prototype Britannia G-ALBO. There are also designs for a Bristol Type 187 Britannia 410 with four Orion engines which would have had a cruising speed of some 450 mph, together with the Bristol Type 189 maritime-reconnaissance variant of the Britannia with four Napier Nomad engines – intended as an Avro Shackleton replacement. None of those were built. But they were followed by the Bristol Type 195 high-wing freighter (intended initially for the Royal Australian Air Force but eventually built as the Short Belfast 'heavy loader'). And finally there came – in 1956 – a last Britannia project with laminar-flow wings and four Orion engines – the Bristol 197 – a very advanced turbo-prop of outstanding potential economy; overtaken by the jets.

Initially priced at £700 000 for the 90-passenger Britannia 102, the 114-passenger Britannia 300 was eventually sold at double that price – and good value at it. In all, Britannias earned a total of more than £80-million worth of sales – a substantial proportion for export. All of this is well covered, aeroplane by aeroplane, in David Littlefield's Britannia story.

Worthy of remembering, too, are the names, and the high endeavour, of those who laboured so hard and so long to bring the Britannia into safe and profitable service. All too often only the inanimate objects – the aircraft – receive deserved applause, while the men, and the women, who laboured to give them life, are forgotten.

The Britannia's roll of honour must begin with the Rt Hon. The Lord Brabazon of Tara – the first Baron Brabazon – that remarkable ebullient character and aeronautical pioneer who sparked off the Britannia by way of the initial specification for the 'Brabazon Type 3'. In due course, that was translated into Ministry of Supply specification 2/47 for a 'Medium-Range Empire' Aircraft – the MRE – to be powered with four Bristol Centaurus piston-engines. That was later enlarged and extended to a 'Long-Range Empire Aircraft' – the LRE – still with Centaurus engines, and to be made capable of non-stop Atlantic range.

By 1950, however, the then promising, Proteus turbo-prop engine was substituted, the name Britannia adopted and the design adapted for 90-passenger seats, six abreast.

In all this, three government departments had been involved – though often at loggerheads. They were headed, at the Ministry of Civil Aviation by Sir Henry Self (the Permanent Secretary), at the Ministry of Supply by Sir Cyril Musgrave (the Under-Secretary [Air]), and at the Air Ministry by Air Chief Marshal Sir William Coryton (Controller of Supplies [Air]).

At BOAC – which began to clothe the Brabazon requirement with detail – there was, first, Lord Knollys (Chairman) and then Sir Harold Hartley, followed by Sir Miles Thomas. They were well supported by Whitney Straight, Managing Director and Chief Executive; by his Operations Development Director, Alan Campbell-Orde; by his Engineering Director, Charles Abell and by his Chief Project Engineer, Clifford Jackson.

At the Bristol Aeroplane Company the Britannia project was set in hand to follow the great Brabazon-1 as a major civil design, development and production enterprise; later to be supplemented from Short Brothers and Harland in Belfast where the Admiral Sir Matthew Slattery was the driving force.

The enterprising and imaginative Bristol mainspring of Britannia endeavours was led by Sir Reginald Verdon-Smith, with Dr (later Sir) Archibald Russell in charge of the design team.

To name, just a few, of the additional Bristol team (in alphabetical order):

Godfrey Auty *(Deputy Chief Test Pilot)*, Chris Barnes *(Head of Technical Publications)*, Peter Bates *(Deputy Commercial Manager)*, Frank Britton *(Aero Engines)*, R.S. Brown *(Works Director)*, Ron Davies *(Economic Charts)*, Richard Day *(Public Relations)*, Paul Falconer *(Assistant Test Pilot)*, Bill Farnes *(Sales Director)*, David Farrar *(Chief Structural Engineer)*, George Gedge *(Deputy Works Director)*, Walter Gibb *(Chief Test Pilot)*, Howard Giddings *(Chief Development Engineer)*, Phillip Gordon-Marshall *(Manager, Public Relations)*, Stanley Haggett *(Overseas Sales – Canada)*, James F. Harper *(General Manager)*, Jack Harrington *(General Service Manager)*, K. Hayward *(Works Manager)*, Fred Higginson *(Military Liaison Officer)*, Stanley Hooker *(Technical Director and Chief Designer Bristol Aero-Engines)*, Trevor Hoyle *(Technical Sales)*, John Jefferies *(Assistant General Manager)*, Peter King *(Publicity Manager)*, Geoffrey Knight *(Commercial Manager)*, David Lawrence *(Charts and Statistics)*, Margaret Lawrence *(Secretariat and Tours Administrator)*, Ken Marshall *(Sales Engineering)*, Tom Pritchard *(Company Secretary)*, Doug Scoffham *(Sales Engineering)*, Hugh Statham *(Deputy Chief Test Pilot)*, Alec Symon *(Design Manager)*, Bill Thomas *(Manager Chart Room)*, Bill Todd *(Flight Engineering)*, Eric Warlow-Davies *(Chief Engineer, Bristol Aero Engines)*, Roger White-Smith *(Service Manager)*, Mick G. Wilde *(Chief Aerodynamicist)*, Mike Wilson *(Technical Sales)*, David Woodward *(Aero Engines)*.

That skilled and splendid team, dedicated to the Britannia in all its aspects, brought into airline service an aeroplane – the Britannia – which, in the words of Sir Stanley Hooker built up 'a reputation of being the fastest, smoothest, quietest and safest propeller aircraft in the world which gave many years of service to BOAC, the RAF and a small number of other operators ... For the Proteus, the years of toil and tears receded as it established itself as a reliable and efficient engine (which likewise), pioneered two non-aero uses for powerful gas turbines; propelling warships and generating electricity.'

So, may I commend all that the Britannia and the Proteus engine stood for, so well inscribed between the covers of this book. Behind the story lies infinite toil, tribulations and some triumphs. They were, hardly 'days of wine and roses'. But they were, indeed, the stuff of aeronautical history, of high endeavour and – in the end – solid achievement.

Sir Peter Masefield, Reigate
APRIL 1991

PREFACE
'In Memoriam'

The late Steve Pearcey and Cubana crew with CUT669 at Luton.

This historical record of the Bristol Britannia is written as a tribute to the memory of the late Stephen Piercey, whose enthusiasm for prop-aircraft inspired many to record on film the exciting but sometimes forgotten world of the prop-liner.

In early seventies Steve was a regular visitor to Monarch Airlines Operations at Luton where I was then working. At the time, Monarch was scrapping two of its venerable Britannias. It was Steve who persuaded me to venture through the Managing Director's door with the suggestion that Monarch should preserve a Britannia for posterity. To my surprise, after many hours of gentle negotiation, our goal was achieved when, on 25 June 1975, I was privileged to fly into Duxford on G-AOVT, resplendent in Monarch Airlines livery, where to this day she remains as part of Duxford's airliner collection.

This was really the seed which has grown into the Britannia Aircraft Preservation Trust, and this book stands as a memorial to Steve, my friend, and founding father of Britannia aircraft preservation.

Roger Hargreaves
20 MAY 1992

ACKNOWLEDGEMENTS

To all the people and companies who have taken the time and trouble to read and reply to all my letters seeking the remotest Britannia related material, I extend my most sincerest thanks and gratitude.

Sir Peter Masefield; Brian Stainer (Aviation Photo News); David H Kirkman (Flightlines International); David Cox (Licensing Manager of Britannia Airways); Peter R March; Jim Oughton; Richard Tomlinson (Aircraft Photographic); Martin Street (Martin Street Photography, Honiton); Brian Pickering (Military Aircraft Photographs); Rev. Tony Furlong; Roger Hargreaves (Proteus Aero Services and Bristol Aero Collection); Peter Rushby; William Green and Gordon Swanborough (Greenborough Associates); Ron "Ginge" Giblin (Monarch Engineering Ltd); Gerard Glaister (BBC "Buccaner series" producer); Andy Anderson; David Berry (Royal Air Force and Britannia Association); Andy Rodger; Alison Rodger; Julia Tolman; The Exmouth Journal; Rod Smith (A&AEE Boscombe Down); Peter J Bish; Roger Wasley; Waller Studios Luton; Aeroprints; A D Nettle (Galaxy Aircraft Photos); Roy Wyer (Monarch Engineering Ltd); W J Wilcox (Royal Air Force); L V Haynes (Monarch Airlines); Invicta International Airlines Ltd; Redcoat Air Cargo Ltd; Michael Hayles (Managing Director) and P M E Rooley (of Heavylift Cargo Airlines); A L Veitch (Scotpic); Patrick Carter; Duxford Aviation Society; John Francis of Aerospace Museum, Cosford; John Roach (co-author of Turbo-prop airliner production list); British Aerospace, Commercial Aircraft Division; Bristol Aeroplane Company Ltd; Fred Huntly of British Airways Archives and Museum, Heathrow Airport for allowing access to all the neccessary BOAC (British Airways) files required; Adrian Meredith (Adrian Meredith Photography, Heathrow Studios); Ian MacLean; John Carr & Bert Hard of Luton Airport Fire Service; David J Charlton (Chief Photographer British Aerospace, Commercial Aircraft, Airbus Division); Public Relations Manager – Short Bros, Belfast; Ken Ford (Director Cabin Services – Monarch Airlines); Peter Page (Duxford Displays Ltd; Guy Holman; Peter Pavey (Rolls-Royce Plc Filton); Tony Merton-Jones (Propliner); Tom Singfield; Mr and Mrs R. Piercey; Fred Hounslow; Tony De Bruyn; Westcountry Books; and Andy Jones. And if I've missed anybody out, my deepest thanks.

AUTHOR'S NOTE

Whilst every care has been taken to ensure all the information is correct, any inaccuracies found are accidental, and for these I apologise.

INTRODUCTION

My first encounter with the Britannia was back in 1962 when my father, who was serving with the Royal Air Force, was posted to Singapore. We were at London (Heathrow) Airport and I remember the aircraft which was then part of BOAC's fleet.

We left for Singapore in the evening and I recall seeing the flames shooting out of the Proteus exhausts and vanishing into the dark as each engine in turn started up. This was my first experience of flying.

We spent three years in Singapore, where I saw many aircraft coming and going at RAF Seleter, and at Changi. None of them caught my attention as much as the Bristol Britannia and I was absolutely delighted to find that for our return to England we would once again be flying on a Britannia.

We arrived at Paya Leba Airport on a bright sunny day, and as the bus drew nearer to the airport terminal building we all saw the large red and black tail of a Britannia with a large white 'E' in the centre. It was one of British Eagle International's fleet, a variant 312, registered G-AOVM, named 'Team Spirit'. She was to be ours for the long journey home.

In the hot tropical sunshine she looked magnificent, especially against the palm strewn background. She caught the eye of everyone on the bus and fired my imagination for a life-long obsession with this beautiful craft.

The journey home to England followed a route from Paya Leba to Bombay, then on to Istanbul before landing at London (Heathrow) Airport. Once back in England I didn't see another Britannia until I joined the Air Training Corps, based at RAF Bicester, Oxfordshire.

This particular aircraft was an RAF variant 252, or in RAF terms a C.Mk2, serialled XN-398 and named 'Altair'. We were to have an air experience flight from RAF Brize Norton, and as with normal RAF transport aircraft, this one was fitted with rearward facing seats, which took me some time to get used to.

When you look at a Britannia, even when the paint is worn and the once pristine metal finish has been covered with grey paint, you can still see the graceful lines this aircraft has, its enormous size and streamlined engine nacelles hiding the powerful Bristol Proteus powerplants.

The 'Whispering Giant' as the Britannia became affectionately known was, and will always be a truly wonderful turbo-prop passenger airliner. British built, it was found serving

G-AOVM in the same livery at the same airport, almost as if I had taken the photograph myself. (Flightlines International)

areas of the world from America to Australia and almost anywhere in between.

With the addition of freight doors to some of the civilian versions (but initially in all the RAF fleet), the Britannia was kept employed, because although passenger carrying was taken over by jet and newer smaller propeller-driven aircraft, the Britannia became a real winner with the freight airlines and smaller operators.

Because of early problems experienced with the engine icing, the up-and-coming Britannia was overshadowed by the dawn of the jet age, which the Britannia had to contend with from the start. The new aircraft like the de Havilland Comet and the Boeing 707 proved more tempting, due to their speed, and the Britannia was to find it a difficult task to enter many of the airlines it had hoped to capture.

What really kept the Britannia employed once passenger carrying had ceased? Well I would say the large freight door that was fitted to some aircraft made the Britannia extremely useful in freight operations, especially the ex-RAF aircraft that were made available following the disbandment of Nos. 99 and 511 squadrons. Obviously none of the short-fuselaged types had the door and so this hastened their demise as they were replaced by new propeller aircraft and, in most cases, jet aircraft such as the BAC 111, and Boeing 727 and 737. The Britannia continued to be a workhorse, carrying freight around the world from all sorts of destinations on either charter operations or ferrying coffee beans, livestock, construction equipment, computers and in some cases the odd passenger or two. In many cases ex-RAF Britannias were purchased, not to fly but to keep another one flying as the spares inventory was a valuable asset due to a very small production run.

Everything about the Britannia is truly British, most of all its determination to carry on flying and outpace its original rivals and to continue giving sterling service to whoever has been lucky enough to operate this fine aircraft. Every Britannia built either at Filton or Belfast is covered within this book, and between them they have operated in 205 different registrations and have worn over 110 liveries, including variations. Although this book only covers the Bristol 175 Britannia it must not be forgotten that from the Britannia there evolved other aircraft such as the Canadair CL-28 Argus maritime aircraft, the Canadair CL-44, the Canadair Yukon, and the Short Belfast heavy transport.

This book is intended as a tribute to everyone who was associated with the Britannia. After all they have a lot to be thanked for!

David J.A.Littlefield.
Exmouth, Devon.
MAY, 1992.

ABOUT THE AUTHOR

At the early age of 7 years, David Littlefield flew for the first time on board a BOAC 102 series Britannia. Something magical about this aircraft has kept him spellbound ever since.

Over the years he has followed with interest every aspect of the Britannia's career and kept photographic records, memorabilia, models, paintings, souvenirs from the aircraft and of course gathered information regarding individual histories – in fact, any Britannia related item is eagerly acquired for his life long collection.

His ultimate ambition was to record the entire production run built between Filton and Belfast and encase it within the covers of this book for future generations to see. That ambition has been achieved with 15 years hard work behind it.

David, now 36, shares his interest with his family and their home is adorned with Britannia aircraft paintings.

David is actively involved with Britannia aircraft preservation. He is a trustee of the Britannia Aircraft Preservation Trust, an associate member of the Britannia Association, a member of the Rolls-Royce Heritage Trust and a team member of the Bristol Aero Collection, and although he was too young to be involved with the Bristol Britannia in its early days, he has certainly made sure he's involved with it at the end of its days.

PART ONE

Whispering Giant

The evolution of the Bristol Britannia.

The evolution of the Bristol Britannia started as far back as November 1944 under the direction of the Brabazon Committee which had stated that there was a requirement for an aircraft capable of flying BOAC's post-war Empire Routes. Under the designation 'The Brabazon Type III' the aircraft was to be powered by four engines, and had an all up weight of approximately 100 000lb, and was to be designed to fly for 2500 statute miles at a speed of 250 mph.

Following further examination of the requirements of BOAC by the Civil Aircraft Requirements Committee, the initial Ministry of Supply draft specification 2/47 was put forward during January 1947. The aircraft was to be piston engined and the all up weight at the slightly lower 90 000lb was envisaged. Seating for 32 passengers was proposed and at stage lengths of 1500 statute miles, the aircraft would be capable of carrying 2750lb of freight.

Coinciding with this proposal were two other considerations which involved the Lockheed Constellation airliner. The first of the two ideas was the Constellation, licence-built and powered by Bristol Centaurus 662 engines, known as the Project Y.

The other proposal was again the Constellation airliner but although already on order for BOAC, it would have been adapted to take the Bristol Centaurus engine and came under the name of Project X. Both these proposals were in fact rejected by the Treasury because of the Government of the day implementing dollar restrictions.

By 6 February 1947, several aircraft manufacturers had tendered for the contract to supply BOAC with an aircraft capable of fulfilling their requirement for a Medium Range Empire (MRE), later upgraded to a Long Range Empire (LRE), passenger transport. Three months were given for a decision to be made from the proposals put forward, and on 6 August 1947, BOAC decided on the type 175 put forward by the Bristol Aeroplane Company Ltd. BOAC wrote to the Ministry of Civil Aviation on 8 August 1947 stating its intention of supporting an improved version of the Bristol 175.

The draft prototype specification prepared by the Bristol Aeroplane Company, in conjunction with BOAC and the Ministry of Supply, was completed by December 1947 but had then been amended by March 1948 to provide the possibility of a later version being powered by either the Napier Nomad or the Bristol Proteus engines.

On 5 July 1948 the Bristol Aeroplane Company had received written confirmation to proceed with their design and supply three prototype Bristol 175 aircraft under Ministry of Supply ownership to be given the registrations VX-442 which became G-ALBO, VX-447 later G-ALRX, and VX-454 which was never built as the third prototype, the airframe being instead used as a functional mock-up.

Following numerous projected design features, weights etc., they were to be powered by four Bristol Centaurus 663 radial engines, with a wingspan of 130ft, and capable of carrying 42 passengers, with an all up weight of 104 650lb. At a later date it was proposed to equip with the newer Bristol Proteus turbo-prop engines.

Artist's impression of the Bristol 175 with Centaurus 663 engines. (Author)

Avro Lincoln SX972 powered by two Bristol Proteus engines at Filton in June 1949.
(Bristol Aeroplane Co/British Aerospace)

On 8 July 1948 BOAC decided to authorise the placing of a production order for 25 Bristol 175 aircraft subject to further negotiations on price. On 10 November 1948 BOAC's board amended this to read '25 140 C.P. version of the Bristol 175 aircraft', a decision which was then communicated to MCA on 17 November. On 24 November 1948 discussions took place with the Parlimentary Secretary MCA for the purpose of agreeing action with regard to expenditure and instruction to proceed with the production order.

MCA approval for an order of 25 aircraft was given in July 1949 but in view of the fact that the price of the aircraft had not been agreed, the board then decided not to give an instruction to proceed to the Bristol Aeroplane Company. On 20 July 1949 it was resolved to conclude a contract with Bristols for 25 Bristol 175 aircraft and the contract was duly signed on 28 July 1949.

During the previous month an Avro Lincoln (SX-972) commenced flight testing of the Bristol Proteus engines following the bench testing previously carried out. With respect to the flight control systems, an Avro Lancaster (RE-131) was fitted with the servo-tab controls and test flown and later in 1951 a Bristol Freighter Mk IIA (G-AICT) was fitted with a Britannia tail fin, rudder and tail plane at a scale of $\frac{7}{10}$ths and flown to survey the characteristics of the Britannia's servo-tabs and artificial feel system. During the test flights, this Bristol Freighter carried the 'G' class registration G-18-40. Another aircraft, an Airspeed Ambassador (G-AKRD), was fitted with two Proteus engines and together with Britannia type airscrews was test flown during 1954.

Eleven aircraft were due for delivery between April and December 1954, with a further 14 between January and October 1955. It was decided that the first six aircraft were to be powered by the Centaurus engines. On 12 October 1949 BOAC was informed through the Technical Committee (minute 175) that there was every indication that there would be a delay in the development of the Bristol Proteus II engine and that BOAC might need to take a greater number of Centaurus powered aircraft than was originally intended.

But in March 1950 following the Cabinet Air Transport Committee's direction, the Ministry of Supply cancelled the development contract for the Centaurus 663, and the Bristol Aeroplane Company was notified that BOAC did not require the Centaurus engined version of the Bristol 175.

On 13 April 1950 the Chairman of BOAC reported that they had been required to reduce the number of aircraft under the contract to 15, all of which were to be powered by the Bristol Proteus engine, and to this effect a modified agreement, dated 29 December 1950, was written giving BOAC an option to reduce the number of aircraft on order from 25 down to 15.

Proteus engine test platform showing a standard production test prop – in this case a 16 foot De Havilland hollow 'Paddle' prop which was not used for production engine tests. The engine test beds (213 and 214) are now displayed in their original positions fully restored and form part of the Rolls-Royce Heritage Trust's display at Filton, Bristol, complete with a mounted Proteus engine.
(Rolls-Royce PLC)

The delivery programme for the first six aircraft was affected but not by more than a month for any aircraft. The agreement provided that if the delivery dates were to be exceeded they should no longer attract rejection of the aircraft or damages. Delivery dates which would attract rejection or

G-ALBO a variant 101. The first prototype seen at Filton conducting the first taxiing trials. (Bristol Aeroplane Co Ltd)

damages could not be assessed until the Bristol Proteus engine development had reached the stage which would enable the manufacturing programme for the Proteus engines to be established and assumed that the engines of the Proteus series could be made available for installation in the first aircraft within 20 months of the date of the type approval. In fact type approval for the Bristol Proteus 705 was obtained in August 1954.

In November 1951 BOAC's board agreed in principle that in view of changes in international policy their plans envisaged the operation of more than 15 Bristol 175s and, subject to the consent of the Capital Issues Committee, they should not exercise their option to reduce the number of aircraft on order from 25 to 15 in which event it would be essential for materials for the last ten aircraft to be ordered without delay to ensure continuity of production.

Named the Britannia in 1952 following agreement between BOAC and the Ministry of Supply, the plane was built in two lengths, 114ft 0ins and 124ft 3ins. Progressive increases in fuel capacities and the raising of pressure differentials in the cabin brought about further classifications. (It was also hoped to equip later Britannia variants with the Bristol BE.25 Orion engines which in fact did not take place, except for one unit being fitted to G-ALBO).

Each major Britannia variant was allocated a group basic series number, while production variants, which differed depending on customer requirements, would have a further number in that basic series.
In each series the prototype aircraft was always allocated the number 1 on the end of the series designation, e.g.

Britannia series 300 – Basic series.
Britannia variant 311 – Prototype aircraft.
Britannia variant 312 – Production aircraft (BOAC).

Basic series numbers were only altered when major changes were made to the airframe or powerplants.

The 100 series was the basic designation for the short fuselage Britannia. It was powered by the Bristol Proteus 705 engine (3780ehp). The medium range fuel capacity of 6690 imperial gallons and a cabin pressure diferential of 7.2lb sq.in. giving 8500ft at 35 000ft were allocated. Two aircraft designated variant 101 were built, the first, G-ALBO flew the Britannia's maiden flight from Filton on 16 August 1952 powered by non-production Bristol Proteus 625 engines.

G-ALBO flew originally without the upturned wingtips that became so familiar and with the engine exhaust outlets half way down the engine nacelles. To help with lateral stability the wingtips were adjusted to an upturned configuration and after repositioning the exhaust outlets to the rear of each nacelle it was found that they actually helped with the forward momentum by way of the extra jet reaction which amounted to about 1000lbs of thrust per engine. In 1953 G-ALBO appeared at the Farnborough Air Show with these alterations.

In July 1953 BOAC requested from the Ministry of Supply a development contract to cover the cost of 5000 hours operational flying on the Britannia which it was considered would be necessary before the type could be put into service. They also suggested that the Certificate of Airworthiness should not be granted until this period of flying had been completed.

G-ALBO in flight showing to advantage the original wingtips and engine exhausts halfway along the engines. (Bristol Aeroplane Co Ltd/British Aerospace)

On 12 November 1953 the Bristol Aeroplane Company informed BOAC of the intended acceleration to their production programme and that the aircraft would be delivered earlier than expected. During the following months BOAC's Chairman had referred to indications of the satisfactory progress of the development of the aircraft.

G-ALBO in the prototype livery. (Peter R March)

The second prototype G-ALRX first flew on 23 December 1953 but after only 51 hours 10 minutes of flight testing logged was written off on 4 February 1954 following a broken turbine disc, after an engine overspeed which caused an oil fed fire in No.3 engine. G-ALRX was put down on the frozen foreshore of the River Severn, but despite valiant attempts to rescue her was destroyed by the incoming tide.

In February 1954, the Chairman of BOAC reported that negotiations were proceeding with Bristols for eight Long-Range Britannia 300 aircraft and reported the untimely loss of G-ALRX.

The production variant of the series 100 was the variant 102 of which 15 aircraft were built. These were ordered by BOAC and equipped with the production version of the Bristol Proteus 705 engines, and registered from G-ANBA to G-ANBO inclusive. No other 100 series Britannias were built. The first production Britannia G-ANBA, was used on Bristol's development flights, after the loss of the second prototype G-ALRX. G-ANBA was accompanied on these flight test programmes by G-ANBB and G-ANBC, between them flying from Johannesburg to Khartoum in March 1955, thus completing the tropical trials originally started by the prototype 100 series Britannia, G-ALBO.

Deliveries should have begun in May 1954 but in July 1954, owing to the limited C of A flying which the Bristol Aeroplane Company had been able to complete, they offered to deliver 8 aircraft between May and December 1955. The 15th aircraft was not offered before June 1956 – a year later than Bristol's previous indication. Since it was understood that the revised dates contained no contingency element, it was considered prudent to assume for planning purposes that deliveries would be deferred 12 months beyond the revised dates quoted by the Bristol Aeroplane Company.

Because of accidents which occurred to the Comet 1 between May 1953 and April 1954, BOAC decided to insist on Britannia aircraft being subjected to tests similar to a Comet 2 before the carriage of passengers was granted. Arising out of this requirement, Bristol's put forward a revised delivery programme which should have resulted in the delivery of the first ten series 100 by the end of 1955 and the whole fleet of series 100 and the ten series 300 by the end of 1956. This information was received in October 1954 when Bristol's request for BOAC to provide aircrew to carry out a test and route proving flying was considered and approved subject to certain conditions.

In March 1955, the Bristol Aeroplane Company had submitted guaranteed delivery dates for the series 100 and 300 aircraft on the assumption that the C of A for the series 100 aircraft would be granted by August 1955. The C of A aircraft G-ANBC made its first flight on 29 June 1955 and in September it was stated that the date of the first flight of the series 300 was to be February or March 1956. On 10 August 1955 BOAC's chairman signed two agreements covering the purchase of 15 series 100, eight series 300 and ten 300LR Britannia aircraft.

Although a full C of A had not been granted, BOAC,

Variant 102 Britannias in Filton's production hangar during manufacture on 7 July 1954. All of these aircraft were ordered by BOAC. (Bristol Aeroplane Co Ltd/British Aerospace)

The production hangar on 20 November 1955 shows G-ANBL (nearest to camera on the right) during one of the many stages of manufacture. The Britannia just above her is fitted with one of her Bristol Proteus 705 engines, while the aircraft to her right is in the process of having her fuselage sections joined. (Bristol Aeroplane Co Ltd/British Aerospace)

accepted two series 100 aircraft, designated variant 102 G-ANBC and G-ANBD on 30 December 1955. An immediate programme of performance test flying and instructor refresher flying was instituted at London (Heathrow) Airport until 9 January 1956 when both aircraft were flown to Hurn Airport to begin the conversion flying programme.

The first BOAC proving flight to Johannesburg left London (Heathrow) Airport on 29 March 1956 and the fading of all engines was experienced when the aircraft encountered the inter-tropical front. Urgent discussions were held with the manufacturers to determine the cause, since that and certain other defects had to be cured before scheduled services were commenced – and this was provisionally delayed from 1 July to 1 August 1956.

The engine flame-outs (as they were known) kept reoccurring, delaying the Britannia's service with BOAC for another nine months. The flame-outs were eventually traced to dry ice being picked up while flying through Cu-Nim cloud at heights in excess of 16 000 feet in extremely low temperatures. The dry ice was actually forming within the engine intake ducting, causing it to build up to such a degree that once it parted as slush it was ingested into the combustion chambers causing complete flame-outs. Once this had happened, the only way to restart the engines was to carry out a manual relighting drill.

Flame-out trials on variant 102, G-ANBH at Entebbe had been carried out by 15 June 1956 and Bristols indicated that the cause had been discovered to be 'ice ingestion' with a modification programme instituted without further delay. But in July 1956 the introduction of scheduled services was put back until 1 October 1956.

G-ANBH flew to Entebbe for further flight tests on 16 July returning to the UK on 30 July 1956. Modifications suggested by the tests were incorporated on G-ANBC which left the UK on 29 August 1956 with the purpose of proving the worth of these modifications. The results were disappointing and the engines were unacceptable in their condition at that time. Accordingly in September 1956 it was decided that BOAC should suspend commercial operations of the Britannia 102 for the time being.

After lengthy flight testing using G-ANBH under the command of Walter Gibb, Bristols' Chief Test Pilot, who had taken over the position previously held by Bill Pegg, modifications began to take effect.

Following further modification work, a new type of plug was devised which would help to prevent the loss of combustion if and when any more ice managed to get through. Four glow plugs were fitted to each Proteus engine which would restore any loss to combustion immediately and, by way of their design, would do the job automatically. Designed jointly by Bristol Aero Engines Ltd, and the company KLG Sparking Plugs Ltd, these plugs would actually glow incandescent within the alternate flame tubes with the heat from the combustion. If the mixture of air and fuel was interrupted by way of melting ice particles, the automatic relight glow plugs, as they were then known, would immediately relight the air and fuel mixture.

Other refinements to the air intake tunnels followed and, with the addition of deflector plates, test flights operated by Bristol's and BOAC proved the modificationas successful.

In May 1956, the Bristol Aeroplane Company gave the dates for delivery of the 18 variant 312 as being between May 1957 and April 1958 and in the meantime tests continued on the 102 and 312 fatigue and static test specimens.

In November 1956 the encouraging results of tests with the newly designed Platinum Glowplugs were received and BOAC took the view that ten hours of flying in icing conditions was desirable before a final judgement was made. The danger of damage to the entry guide vanes by ice in the air intakes was still considered to be serious.

In December 1956 it having been decided that all obstacles to the operation of the Britannia aircraft had been removed, it was prudent to introduce the variant 102 into passenger service with effect from 1 February 1957 and services to South Africa did in fact start on that day and to Australia on 1 March 1957. Also during February it was decided to increase the order for the 312 to 18 aircraft by substituting the 312 for the previously ordered 300s.

As a result of releasing the Britannia 300, the Bristol Aeroplane Company was able to obtain an order from the American airline, Northeast Airlines, and the initial delivery dates for the Britannia 312 was delayed by at least four months.

The Britannia 200 was initially reserved by BOAC and was intended to have been the first of the long fuselage freighter version of the Britannia. An order for five aircraft was originally considered but was replaced by orders for the Britannia 310 series. Had the series 200 gone into production, it would have been powered by the Bristol Proteus 755 engines and been equipped with the medium range fuel capacity.

The series 250 Britannia had the long fuselage designed to carry freight in the forward upper deck in addition to the lower freight holds. The floor was strengthened with cargo tie-down points and a large freight door was fitted to the forward fuselage on the port side. The powerplant was the Proteus 755 (4120ehp) engines. Cabin pressure differential of 8.3lb sq.in gave 6000 feet at 35 000 feet. The series 250 was preceded in development and production by the series 300 and 310. Originally it was intended to equip the 250 series with the medium range fuel capacity of 6690 imperial gallons, but this was not to be as all 250 series aircraft were instead equipped with the long range fuel capacity of 8490 imperial gallons. With this fuel capacity the provisional designation 250LR was allocated but later withdrawn. All the series 250 aircraft were scheduled for manufacture at Short Brothers and Harland at Belfast.

A Britannia 250 prototype was never built due to the experience gained with the series 300 and 310 prototypes. Three production aircraft were built within the 250 series designation. The variant 252 was ordered by the Ministry of Supply, intended for civilian operators on lease or charter, also for air trooping, freight carrying, etc., they were built with a wooden floor for forward freight stowage, and equipped with forward toilets.

The three variant 252s were intially registered as G-APPE, G-APPF, G-APPG prior to delivery to the Royal Air Force where they were serialled XN-392, XN-398 and XN-404 respectively, and in RAF service known as the C.Mk2.

Another 250 series variant was the 253, built for the Royal Air Force. These had a metal freight floor but no forward toilets. The Proteus powerplant was the 755 (4120ehp) engine, within RAF service re-designated the Proteus 255. These Britannia 253 (C.Mk1) aircraft conformed to the requirements laid down by the Ministry of Supply specification C.176P issue II. A total of 23 series 250 Britannia aircraft were manufactured, three 252s were built at Belfast alongside 15 253s. The five remaining 253s were built at Filton, these being XM-498, XM-517, XM-518, XM-519 and XM-520.

The Britannia 300 L.R. was the designation initially given to the long fuselage Britannia which was to have been equipped with the long-range fuel capacity of 8490 imperial gallons. No Britannias were built to this designation as the series was instead completed as the series 310 during production.

The Britannia 300 was the basic designation of the first long fuselage Britannia. Proteus 755 (4120ehp) turbo-prop engines were fitted as was the medium range fuel capacity of 6690 imperial gallons. The cabin differential of 7.25lbs sq.in. gave 8500 feet at 35 000 feet. The series 300 was regarded as the intermediate step between the series 100 and the series 310, all of which were built at Belfast except for the prototype. The series 300 prototype G-ANCA was built at Filton and flown for the first time on 31 July 1956. Used initially as a test aircraft and powered by the Proteus 755 (4120ehp) engines, it was later to have been equipped with the Bristol Orion engine. Sadly the aircraft crashed on 6 November 1957.

Two 302 designation Britannias were originally purchased by Aeronaves De Mexico, registered XA-MEC and XA-MED. A design study into the variant 303 and 304 was not completed and no production aircraft were built.

The variant 305 ordered by Capital Airlines, was later cancelled, then ordered by Northeast Airlines of the United States, but again cancelled due to financial problems, and although originally ordered by BOAC, who did not take delivery, was sold to other airlines. It had increased fuel capacity which brought it into line with the long range tankage of 8490 imperial gallons. The first variant 305 flew on 1 June 1957 from Belfast and was delivered to Filton for modification. Two of the variant 305s were converted to 307 and sold to Air Charter Ltd of London, becoming British United Airways in 1960. These aircraft were later converted to variant 307F aircraft. Two other 305s were sold to Transcontinental S.A. and were converted to variant 308 prior to delivery, and later converted to freighter configuration. The final variant 305 went to Ghana Airways as the sole variant 309.

Only eight of the 300 series Britannias were built at Belfast, the exception, the prototype G-ANCA, being built at Filton.

The next series was the 310, of which 35 aircraft were built, inclusive of the prototype. The cabin pressure differential was raised to 8.3lb sq. in. giving 6000 feet at 35 000 feet. The powerplant was the Proteus 755 (4120ehp) engine and the fuel capacity was 8490 imperial gallons. The prototype aircraft G-AOVA first flew from Filton on 31 December 1956. Originally designated a 311 this aircraft caused some confusion as she was also the first aircraft in a series for BOAC and given the variant 312, meaning that G-AOVA was a prototype and production aircraft together. G-AOVA was later converted to the sole variant 319. BOAC had ordered 18 variant 312 Britannias which were registered as G-AOVA to G-AOVS, excluding G-AOVQ which was not allocated to the Britannia fleet. G-AOVA was not part of BOAC's fleet and was replaced by G-AOVT because of the amount of test flying that had already been carried out by G-AOVA.

On 29 January 1957 the first 312 (actually built as a variant 311 Prototype) G-AOVA flew direct from Prestwick to Winnipeg for cold weather trials and in March that year it was understood that the tests were satisfactory. Instead of delivering the first variant 312 in April it was decided to

G-ANCF
during construction. G-ANBA and G-ANBB are also receiving modifications and overhaul. (Short Bros. Belfast)

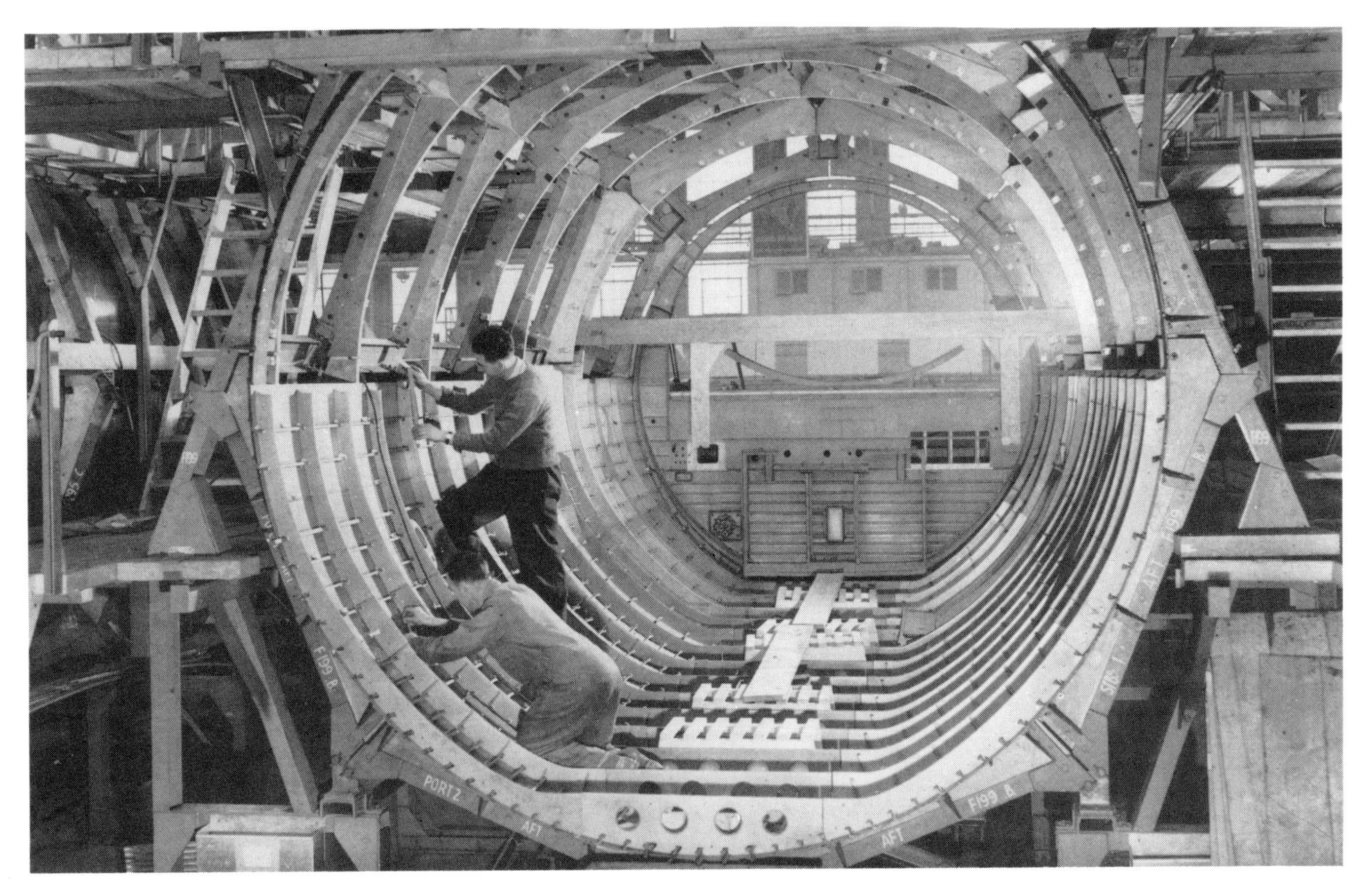

One of the prefabricated forward fuselage sections under construction at Belfast. (Short Bros. Belfast)

deliver two aircraft on 25 May 1957. Because of strike action by Bristol's employees, delivery was rescheduled for 25 June 1957.

A board meeting in May 1957 (Technical Minute 701) referred to recurrences of engine 'flame-outs' on the variant 102 and to the possibility that the 312 might not meet specification in relation to specific fuel consumption to the drag and empty weight. In June 1957 it was further noted that delivery dates of the last of the variant 102 had slipped back a month so that the last one was not expected until mid-August, 1957 but was in fact delivered on 12 August 1957.

The first 'real' variant 312 G-AOVB was delivered on 10 September 1957. The C of A, though legally unrestricted, contained a recommendation regarding the avoidance of prolonged flight in icing conditions. G-AOVB flew to the USA on 28 September 1957 and engine tests were subsequently carried out in the Miami area. After about 4½ minutes in cloud numbers 2 and 4 engines failed and the aircraft had to land using only engines 1 and 3, one of which experienced a 'bump' just after leaving the cloud. G-AOVB remained at Miami to await the delivery of 4 modified engines. This incident revealed a new problem for the Britannia engines: when rapid cooling was experienced the compressor casing contracted causing the compressor blades to rub.

The first passenger service on the Britannia 312 operated on 19 December 1957 with a flight from London (Heathrow) Airport and New York. The eighteenth and final Britannia 312 was delivered to BOAC on 31 December 1958.

On 6 June 1955 the Israeli airline El-Al ordered three series 310 Britannias designated as 313s and on 18 July 1958 placed an order for a fourth. The registrations allocated were 4X-AGA, 4X-AGB, 4X-AGC and 4X-AGD. Canadian Pacific Airlines ordered six variant 314s, which took up the Canadian registrations of CZ-CZA to CZ-CZD and CF-CZW and CF-CZX. The variant 315 was a design study for Capital Airlines, USA although not taken up. The Britannia 301 prototype flew in Capital's livery initially until being modified following the cancellation of their order.

The variant 316 was a design study for Qantas Empire Airways of Australia but not taken up. The variant 317 was purchased by Hunting Clan, two aircraft were built at Filton, and the first flew on 10 October 1958. Both aircraft remained on the British register and carried the registrations G-APNA and G-APNB. The 4 variant 318s were supplied to Compania Cubana de Aviacion, from December 1958 onwards.

In July 1956 the 324 (1) design study was put forward for Swissair but not taken up and following this Bristol offered the 324 (2). Canadian Pacific Airlines ordered two 324 variant Britannias nicknamed the 'Americanised version'. These were powered by the Proteus 765 giving 4445ehp. Accepted by Canadian Pacific Airlines during October and November 1959, these aircraft received the registrations CF-CPD and CF-CPE.

These were the last Britannias built and they saw the close of Britannia production at Filton and Belfast. Although other Britannia variants were discussed they never reached production, except for derivatives built by Canadair (the CL-28 Argus Maritime patrol aircraft and its civilian counterpart the CL-44 which was also used by the Canadian armed forces under the name 'Yukon' designated CC 106), and the British built Short Belfast which at one time was known as the 'Britannic'.

The Britannia 321 was a designation allocated for a prototype aircraft but not built. The Britannia 322 was a design study for BOAC, the Britannia 323 was a design study for BEA, and the Britannia 324 was a design study for Swissair, all not taken up.

The Britannia 410 was the basic series designation for the long fuselage, long-range Britannia developed from the series 310 and powered by the Bristol Orion (BE.25) engines. Basically the aircraft would have been similar to the series 310 built with the Orion powerplant and the fuel capacity increased to 8840 imperial gallons. An aircraft built under this designation as a prototype would have been the variant 411 but, as the series was not built, there was no prototype. The Britannia 412 was a design study for BOAC, but not built.

G-ALBO in later years powered by a Bristol Orion BE.25. in the No.1 position whilst in the No.4 position is a Bristol Proteus 755. No.2 position is fitted with a Proteus 765 and No.3 is fitted with a Proteus 705. (Peter R March)

The Britannia 420 was to have been the designation for the long fuselage, long-range Britannia that would have been developed from the series 410. An internally revised wing with integral tankage, gave a total capacity raised to 9840 imperial gallons. Other details were similar to the series 410, but the Bristol Orion engines would have given greater shaft power and the propellors would have had a higher activity factor.

The Britannia 422 was a design study for BOAC, which was also studied with a fuselage length extended a further 82 inches bringing its total length up to 131 feet 1 inch from the previous 124 feet 3 inches. The Britannia 430 was the basic series designation for the 'stretched' long fuselage, long-range Britannia which would have been powered by the Bristol Orion engines. It would also have had an additional 10 feet 3 inch extension to the fuselage to allow two extra rows of seats which in effect would have given an overall fuselage length of 134 feet 6 inches.

The Britannia 432 was another design study for BOAC, and again not taken up. The Britannia 450 was the basic series designation for a long fuselage, long-range Britannia powered by Bristol Orion engines and was basically developed from the series 250 Britannia. The Britannia 453 was a design study for the Royal Air Force Transport Command which proceeded no further.

The Britannia 520 was the basic series designation for the long fuselage, long-range Britannia powered by the Bristol Orion engine and was a development of the series 420 incorporating a stiffened airframe. The Britannia 522 was a design study for BOAC but not taken further.

The final series was the Britannia 600, which was the basic series designation for the Bristol Type 187 Britannia which was to have been developed with a new high speed wing and incorporating a 'Double Bubble' fuselage allowing seating for 200 passengers and powered by the Bristol Orion engines. Like the previous designated series this too proceeded no further due to the reluctance of the Treasury and the Orion's development ceased. The Rolls Royce Tyne powerplant was instead investigated and completed.

A Canadair CL-28 Argus, which was allocated the designation CP-107. Pictured is a Mark 1 variant. (Aviation Photo News)

Other proposals were put forward and included a Britannia equipped for air to air refuelling and was designed as a replacement for the KC97 tanker. With 12 335 imperial gallon tanks, it would have been able to deliver 500 gallons per minute via a drogue and probe system.

A Britannia 200 series built as a maritime reconnaisance aircraft was proposed as a competitor to the CL-28 in April 1953 and would have been fitted with a Boulton Paul nose turret, but no tail turret, and would have been able to cruise at 175 mph for eight hours, with a range of 1150 statute miles. Both of these proposals were never built.

Although the Britannia production line ceased following the manufacture of 85 aircraft, there was another production line building a Britannia derivative. In 1953 the Canadian Department of Defence selected the Bristol Britannia airframe for use as the basis for a long-range maritime patrol aircraft to equip the Royal Canadian Air Force.

In April 1954 the Canadair Division of the General Dynamics Corporation were given the responsibility for building 13 aircraft, later increased to 25. Close co-operation between Bristol Aircraft and Canadair of Montreal saw the roll-out of the first completed aircraft on 28 December 1956 from Canadair's Plant 1. The first flight of the prototype CL-28 was on 28 March 1957. The aircraft was coded VN-710 and its serial number was 20710.

The main difference between the Britannia and the CL-28, Argus (as the type became known) was the power plant, of which the Canadian aircraft was equipped with four American 18 cylinder two-row Wright Cyclone R-3350-34W compound engines, giving 3500 h.p. Other dissimilarities included the provision of small spoilers in the wings to meet the military requirements laid down for high rates of roll.

Due to the different engines it was possible to have an undercarriage that did not need to fold flat before entering the rear of the engine nacelles as it did on the Britannias. Fuel capacity was increased from 6690 imperial gallons (Britannia) to 6800 imperial gallons. Within the large chin radome the aircraft was fitted with search radar; the mark 1 aircraft had the larger radome housing the American built APS-20 radar whereas the mark 2 Argus had the smaller radome with the British built ASV Mk21 radar. In the tail section within the large boom was the Magnetic Airborne Detector (MAD). This gave an overall fuselage length of 128 feet 3 inches.

A crew of 15 was accommodated in the unpressurised fuselage, and within the lower fuselage, separated by the wing torsion-box, were two weapon bays containing the various types of mine, sonobouy, depth-charge, anti-submarine bombs, homing torpedoes and air-to-air surface missiles.

The type was given the Royal Canadian Air Force designation CP-107 Argus, and 33 aircraft were supplied which were made up with 13 Mk 1 and 20 Mk 2 variants.

In June 1957 work commenced on building the Canadair CL-44-6, which was based on the Britannia but stretched and intended as a passenger and freight carrying aircraft. Powered by four Rolls Royce Tyne R-Ty 12 turbo-props developing 5730ehp each, the aircraft was given the RCAF designation CC-106 and was fitted with two freight doors on the port fuselage, one forward and one rear of the main wing. The flight deck retained the Britannia type windscreens, but had six eye-level windows above.

Twelve CC-106 aircraft were built, the first flying the type's maiden flight on 15 November 1959 and in service with the RCAF were allocated the name 'Yukon'. In 1971 these aircraft

The CL-44-6 was named Yukon inRCAF service and designated CC-106. This aircraft is pictured in the lease markings of ALAS of Uraguay and with whom she was written off during a hard landing at Montevideo, Uraguay on 10 October 1979. (Aviation Photo News)

A CL-44D4-1 with the swing tail is seen while on lease to BOAC who were waiting for their first Boeing 707 cargo freighters. The aircraft crashed at Da Nang, South Vietnam on 24 December 1966 during a lease to Flying Tiger Line. (Aviation Photo News)

were retired from military service and passed to civilian operators as freighters under the designation CL-44-6, but like the CL-44D-4, the CL-44-6 was never fitted with the swing tail.

The CL-44D-4 of which 27 were built had the swing tail fitted for 'straight in' loading and is similar in design to the CL-44-6 but was fitted with seven high visibility windscreens and no eye-level windows above.

Four CL-44D-4's were stretched to 151ft 10in and designated CL-44J for the Icelandic airline Loftleider. With this configuration, they were used as high density passenger aircraft allowing seating for 189 passengers and an absolute maximum of 214.

The CL-44-O is an unusual adaption to the basic fuselage of the CL-44D-4 by the addition of a larger top fuselage 'tube'

A CL-44D4-8 which following conversion to CL-44J standard in March 1966 is pictured with the Irish registration EI-BRP and owned by Heavylift Cargo Airlines. (Heavylift Cargo Airlines)

which allows the carriage of large outsize cargo loads, such as aircraft parts or construction equipment, and many other varied loads.

Nicknamed 'Skymonster', this aircraft was originally converted by Conroy Aircraft Ltd, for use in carrying Rolls Royce RB-211 aircraft engines. This aircraft is now owned by Heavylift Cargo Airlines of London, Stansted Airport. Registered EI-BND she is the only CL-44 aircraft built to what Heavylift Cargo call the 'Guppy' configuration. Along with five Short SC5 Belfasts, and a CL-44J (now scrapped at Southend) she makes up a fleet of Britannia-derived freight aircraft accommodating heavy/awkward cargoes.

Specifications appertaining to the Britannia derivatives are shown below.

CANADAIR CL-28 ARGUS	**Mk 1**	**Mk 2**
WINGSPAN:	142ft. 2in.	142ft. 3in.
LENGTH:	122ft. 1in.	128ft. 3in.
HEIGHT:	36ft. 8in.	36ft. 9in.
WING AREA:	2075sq. ft.	2075sq. ft.
CRUISE SPEED:	290mph.	290mph.
MAXIMUM RANGE:	4000st.miles.	4000st.miles.
CREW:	15	15
TOTAL BUILT:	13	20

CANADAIR CL-44-6 YUKON

WINGSPAN:	142ft. 3.5in.
LENGTH:	136ft. 7in.
HEIGHT:	36ft. 8in.
WING AREA:	2075sq. ft.
ALL UP WEIGHT:	205 000lb.
WEIGHT EMPTY:	88 850lb.
MAX' PAYLOAD:	60 480lb.
MAX' PAYLOAD RANGE:	2360st.miles.
MAX' RANGE:	4490st.miles.
CRUISE SPEED:	380mph.
CREW:	4 to 6
PASSENGERS:	134
CARGO CAPACITY:	6900cu.ft.
TOTAL BUILT:	12

CANADAIR CL-44D-4. CL-44J. CL-44-O (GUPPY).

WINGSPAN:	142ft. 3.5in.
LENGTH:	136ft. 7in.
LENGTH: (CL-44J)	151ft. 10in.
HEIGHT:	37ft. 6in.
WING AREA:	2075sq. ft.
ALL UP WEIGHT:	210 000lb.
WEIGHT EMPTY:	88 872lb.
MAX' PAYLOAD: (GUPPY.)	56 000lb.
MAX' PAYLOAD RANGE:	3320st.miles.
MAX' RANGE:	5660st.miles.
MAX' RANGE: (CL-44J)	5260st.miles.
CRUISE SPEED:	402mph. max.
CRUISE SPEED: (CL-44J)	380mph. max.
CREW:	3 to 7
PASSENGERS:	160
PASSENGERS: (CL-44J)	189 or 214
CARGO CAPACITY:	7430cu.ft.
CARGO CAPACITY: (CL-44J)	8637cu.ft.
CARGO CAPACITY: (GUPPY.)	13 000cu.ft.
CARGO HOLD CAPABILITY:	
MAX' LENGTH:	98ft. 0in.
MAX' HEIGHT:	11ft. 4in.
MAX' WIDTH:	14ft. 0in.
TOTAL BUILT:	27

The total production of the Britannia derivative, built by Canadair is CL-28 (CP-107, Argus) 33 aircraft, (CL-44-6, CC-106, Yukon) 12 aircraft, CL-44 (CL-44D-4, CL-44J, CL-44-O) 27 aircraft.

SHORT SC5 BELFAST (C.1. in RAF service).

WINGSPAN:	158ft. 10in.
LENGTH:	136ft. 5in.
HEIGHT:	47ft. 0in.
WEIGHT EMPTY:	130 000lbs.
MAX' PAYLOAD:	80 500lbs.
MAX' PAYLOAD RANGE:	1000 nautical miles.
MAX' RANGE EMPTY:	3500 nautical miles.
CRUISE SPEED:	275 knots.
CREW:	4
MAX' TAKE-OFF WEIGHT:	230 000lbs.
MAX' LANDING WEIGHT:	215 000lbs.
CARGO CAPACITY:	11,350cu.ft.
CARGO HOLD CAPABILITY:	
MAX' LENGTH WITH RAMP DOWN:	90ft. 0in.
MAX' HEIGHT:	13ft. 4in.
MAX' WIDTH:	16ft. 1in.
TOTAL BUILT:	10

As 1992 sees no Britannia aircraft operating and the type obviously will not be flying on its 40th Anniversary, it is ironic to find that it may well be the job of the derivatives to see in this rather important milestone for the Bristol Britannia, and although built in Canada, the CL-44-O (Guppy) and the Belfast built, Short SC5 Belfast will actually fly the flag under British ownership of Heavylift Cargo Airlines.

BRITANNIA ORDER BOOK

DATE ORDERED	ORDERED BY	VARIANT	NO. ORDERED	NO. CANCELLED	FIRST D/D	LAST D/D	BUILT
2.2.48	Ministry of Supply	–	3	–	PROTOTYPES	Filton	
5.7.48	Ministry of Supply	101	2	3	PROTOTYPES	Filton	
28.7.48	B.O.A.C.	102	25	–	Order amended Dec. 1950		
Dec. 1950	B.O.A.C.	102	–	10	30.12.55	12.8.57	Filton
Dec. 1950	B.O.A.C.	300	10	–	Re-order August 1955		
Feb. 1955	Ministry of Supply	252	3	–	12.11.58	8.4.59	Belfast
8.6.55	EL AL	313	3	–	12.9.57	28.11.57	Filton
Aug. 1955	B.O.A.C.	300	–	10	Amending previous order		
Aug. 1955	B.O.A.C.	302	8	–	Amended Dec. 1955 and Feb.1956		
Aug. 1955	B.O.A.C.	300LR	10	–	Amended Dec. 1955 and Feb.1956		
18.10.55	Canadian Pacific Airlines	314	3	–	9.4.58	31.5.58	Belfast
Nov. 1955	Royal Air Force	253	6	–	4.6.59	30.11.59	Belfast
Dec. 1955	B.O.A.C.	302	–	1	Sold to Ministry of Supply		Filton
Dec. 1955	B.O.A.C.	312	1	–	Replacement for above		Filton
Dec. 1955	Ministry of Supply	301	1	–	Prototype 300 series		Filton
Feb. 1956	B.O.A.C.	302	–	5	Change of type		Belfast
Feb. 1956	B.O.A.C.	305	5	–	See later cancellation		
Apr. 1956	Canadian Pacific Airlines	314	2	–	29.6.58.	3.7.58.	Belfast
May 1956	Royal Air Force	253	4	–	30.9.59	5.2.60	Filton
Dec. 1956	Royal Air Force	253	3	–	23.12.59	19.3.60	Filton & Belfast
Dec. 1956	Hunting Clan	317	2	–	2.12.58	11.12.58	Filton
Dec. 1956	B.O.A.C.	302	–	2	Released for re-sale		Belfast
Dec. 1956	B.O.A.C.	305	5	5	Released for re-sale		
Dec. 1956	B.O.A.C.	312	8 (19)	–	Replacement for above		
					10.9.57	1.1.59	Filton
Dec. 1956	Northeast Airlines (USA)	305	5	–	Cancelled June 1958		Belfast
Apr. 1957	Canadian Pacific Airlines	314	1	–	7.8.58		Filton
24.5.57	Cubana de Aviacion	318	2	–	15.12.58	56.2.59	Filton
31.5.57	Aeronaves de Mexico	302	2	–	1.11.57	15.12.57	Belfast
Oct. 1957	Royal Air Force	253	7	–	1.2.60	2.12.60	Belfast
Jun. 1958	Northeast Airlines (USA)	305	–	5	Order cancelled		
18.7.58	EL AL	313	1	–	7.3.59		Filton
July 1958	Cubana de Aviacion	318	2	–	15.5.59	22.8.59	Filton
28.7.58	Air Charter Ltd	307	1	–	12.9.58		Belfast
Feb. 1959	Air Charter Ltd	307	1	–	24.3.59		Belfast
24.8.59	Transcontinental S.A.	308	2	–	16.12.59	17.12.59	Belfast
Sept. 1959	Canadian Pacific Airlines	324	2	–	16.10.59	13.11.59	Filton
May 1960	Ghana Airways	309	1	–	27.7.60		Belfast
Early 1960	B.O.A.C.	312	–	1	Prototype released for re-sale		
July 1960	Ghana Airways	319	1	–	8.11.60		Filton

Number Ordered 124 — Total Production 85 — Number Cancelled 39

Production at Filton 55

Production at Belfast 30

BRITANNIA PRODUCTION BREAKDOWN

SERIES	VARIANT	NUMBER BUILT	OPERATOR	DATE INTRODUCED INTO SERVICE
100	101	2	Ministry of Supply	
100	102	15	BOAC	February 1957
300	301	1	Ministry of Supply	–
300	302	2	Aeronaves de Mexico	December 1957
305	307	2	Air Charter (BUA)	September 1958
305	308	2	Transcontinental S.A.	December 1959
305	309	1	Ghana Airways	November 1960
310	311/312 319	1	Bristol Aircraft sold to Ghana Airways	December 1960
310	312	18	BOAC	December 1957
310	313	4	EL AL (Israell A/Ls)	December 1957
310	314	6	C. Pacific Airlines	June 1958
310	317	2	British & Commonwealth Shipping Co. (Aviation) Ltd. Later BUA	January 1959
310	318	4	Cubana (one aircraft leased to Cunard Eagle Airways 1960)	December 1958 April 1960
320	324	2	C. Pacific Airlines (leased to Cunard Eagle Airways February 1961)	October 1959
250	252	3	Ministry of Supply; Operated by RAF Transport Command as the Britannia C.2	April 1959
250	253	20	RAF Transport Command Britannia C.1	June 1959
	TOTAL	85		

In addition four functional mock up and ground test aircraft were constructed.

SERIES	VARIANT	NUMBER	DESCRIPTION
100	101	1	Full-scale 'Functional Mock-up' used at Filton
100	102	1	Static test aircraft for use in the water-tank at RAE. Farnborough
310	312	1	Static test aircraft for use in the water-tank by Bristol Aircraft at Filton
310	312	1	Systems mock-up used at Filton

MANUFACTURERS' DETAILS.

TYPE: 175, BRISTOL BRITANNIA (all variants.)

MANUFACTURERS:

THE BRISTOL AEROPLANE COMPANY LIMITED
and the BRISTOL AIRCRAFT LIMITED
(FILTON, BRISTOL).

SHORT BROTHERS & HARLAND, LIMITED,
QUEENS ISLAND, BELFAST,
NORTHERN IRELAND.

BRITANNIA DERIVATIVES:

CANADAIR LIMITED, CARTIERVILLE,
MONTREAL, CANADA.

SHORT BROTHERS & HARLAND, LIMITED,
QUEENS ISLAND, BELFAST,
NORTHERN IRELAND.
(SHORT BELFAST.)

The Bristol Britannia is accepted.

BOAC received its first two Bristol Britannia series 100 aircraft when they were handed over by the manufacturer's, the Bristol Aeroplane Company Limited at a ceremony at London (Heathrow) Airport on 30 December 1955. Just a few hours earlier they had been granted their Certificates of Airworthiness by the Air Registration Board.

The two aircraft, registered G-ANBC and G-ANBD, were flown from the manufacturers base at Filton to London (Heathrow) Airport by Captain A.S.M. Rendall, Flight Superintendent of the Britannia fleet, and Captain F.W. Walton, Training Captain of the Fleet.

Each aircraft was laid out with different interiors, G-ANBC was equipped as a 94 seat tourist aircraft, while G-ANBD was equipped with a 54 seat layout for 1st class travel and also incorporated a horseshoe lounge bar amidships.

During the flight both aircraft carried senior members of the Bristol Aeroplane Company and a considerable number of Press representatives.

Sir Reginald Verdon Smith (right) hands over the log books for G-ANBC and G-ANBD to Sir Miles Thomas, at London (Heathrow) Airport. (British Airways via Adrian Meredith Photography)

The handover ceremony took place on the south side of the Headquarters Building, between Sir Reginald Verdon Smith, Chairman of the Bristol Aeroplane Company, and Sir Miles Thomas, Chairman of BOAC. During the ceremony the log books for each aircraft were handed over from Sir Reginald to Sir Miles.

Sir Reginald paid tribute to the collaboration which existed between the two Companies throughout the Britannia development programme and said that they had benefitted greatly from the co-operation between his company and BOAC.

Sir Miles Thomas declared that this was indeed a memorable day and represented a great contribution to British trade. 'We are going to go ahead as fast as we can with our training programme,' and he added 'When we get some more aircraft we shall lose no time in pushing ahead on our route to Johannesburg.' Sir Miles said that calls to Cairo and Nairobi would probably also be made on the flight to Johannesburg. After the Britannias started to operate on this route the aircraft would then be progressively placed on routes to the Far East and Australia.

He mentioned in particular the Britannia's quiet performance which earned the name 'Whispering Giant'. In fact the Britannia was named as such following the landing at Johannesburg after the first record flight. The local newspaper *The Daily Rand* was so amazed at the Britannia's quiet arrival that instead of the expected thundering elephant, they reported the arrival of the 'Whispering Giant', and to this day the Bristol Britannia has quite rightly kept this complimentary nickname.

It is of interest to note that following official noise-level tests, it was found that during the Britannia's take-off run only 81 decibels were recorded from ground level, and that it proved that the Britannia was actually quieter than other four-engined aircraft by between 20–25 decibels.

The engine 'flame-out' tests of 1956

Following the record breaking flight to Johannesburg by G-ANBH in March 1955, the South African Service was the first to be operated by the Britannia 100 series.

It was only when regular services were being operated throughout the monsoon season at heights of 25 000–30 000 feet that reports began to filter back of engine flame-outs. In order to carry out urgent tests G-ANBH was assigned to this work straight off the production line.

After its initial test flights G-ANBH was fitted out as a research aircraft, with normal airframe and engine instrumentation, but with special meteorological instruments.

Very little was known about thunderstorms in detail except that some of those on board had vivid memories of violent results from flying through them in South East Asia during the war. Obviously it was necessary to analyse storms in detail and that was the brief for the first series of sorties at the beginning of June 1956. It was first necessary to measure temperatures, ice particle sizes, up and down air current forces and in particular the critical heights at which the Britannia had to operate to be fuel efficient. In order to gather this information G-ANBH carried a flight crew to operate the

G-ANBH's cabin interior showing seating and camera panel. (Peter Rushby)

Two observers with Automatic Observer Instrument Panel. (Peter Rushby)

aircraft in the normal manner, a meteorological crew to carry out weather observations, flight test observers and a photographer, plus all the necessary ground and repair crew.

A series of flights entering clouds at varying heights soon set the pattern for subsequent tests and very quickly showed how serious the problem could be. Indeed on one flight during an extremely rough patch came the cry 'I say boys, do you realise we're flying the biggest glider you've ever seen!!' All four engines had flamed-out and owing to the high power requirements needed to start the early Proteus engines, only one engine could be started at a time and it was not known at the time if they could be 'windmilled'. It was decided to have an engineer standing in a harness with the sole job of restarting the engines as they cut out.

The strain on the aircraft and crew was tremendous and a rest was needed after each storm. Any equipment not well lashed down would break loose and quite frequently crew members were to be seen draped across valuable loosened equipment. Large quantities of 'kwells' were consumed, and the aircraft, frequently struck by lightning suffered damage to the nose containing the weather radar. Leading edges of the wings, tailplane, and tailfin were considerably modified by hail. Pieces of ice that had been recovered from the engine cowlings after very rapid descents to base, were measured and photographed and it soon became evident that the air intakes held the key to the problem.

Entebbe had turned out to be a good base for operations, well within range of the monsoon storm lines and sufficiently well equipped for the necessary repairs. After two weeks of punishment trials, it was time to return in order to try and solve the problem. Over the next month G-ANBH was repaired, each of the four engines fitted with a different modification to the air intakes and film and close circuit television cameras were fitted inside the engine cowlings allowing those onboard to observe the build up of ice and the effect of any heaters. During the next series of flights from Entebbe it was obvious that the shape of the actual air entry

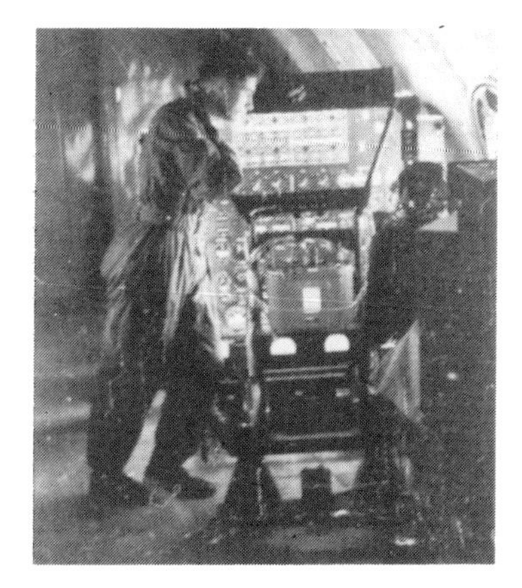

Camera panel and flight test observers. (Peter Rushby)

Observer with Vinten Camera and panel. (Peter Rusby)

G-ANBH flight deck set up for Stick Force and 'G' Measurements. (Peter Rushby)

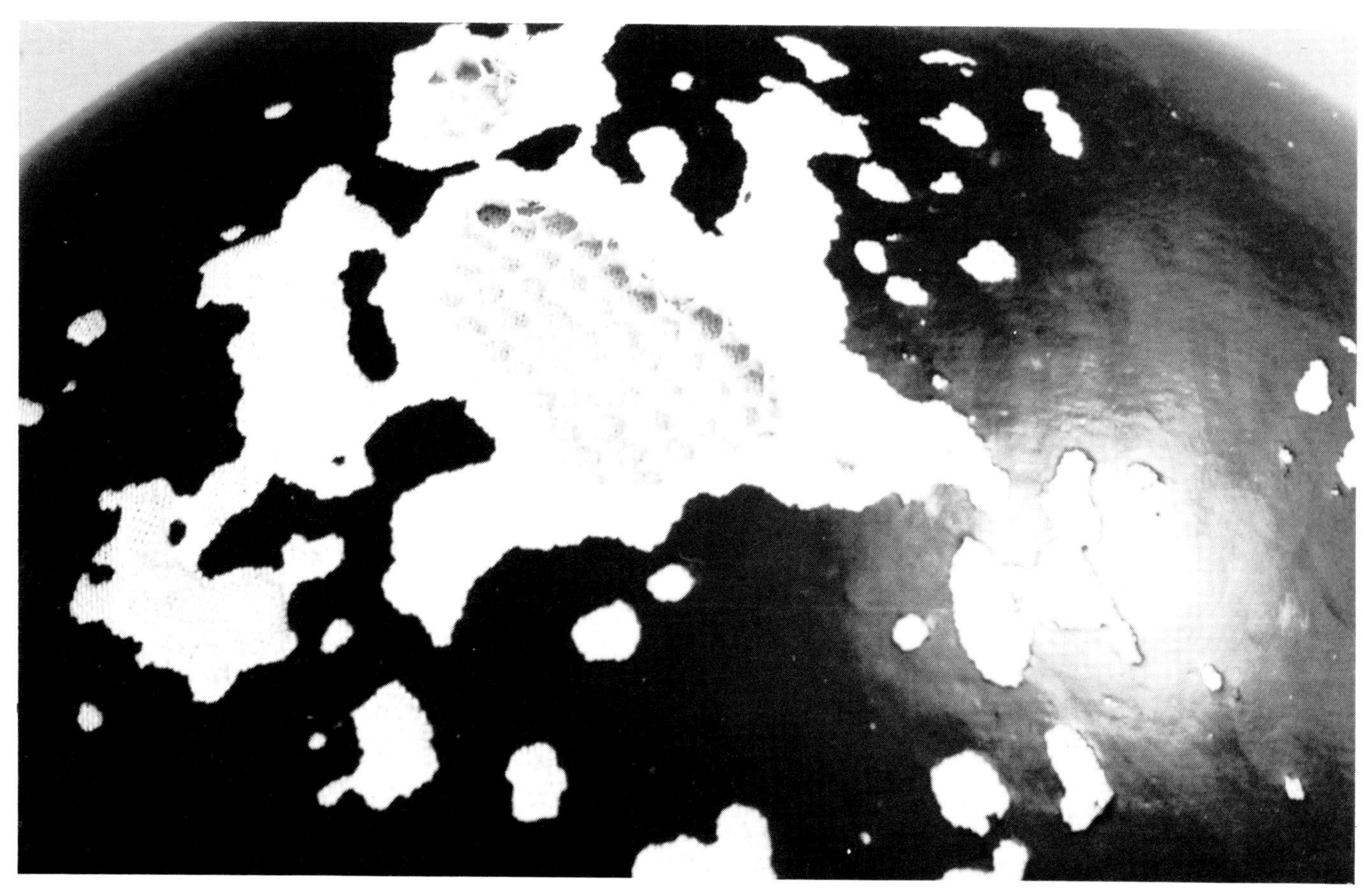

G-ANBH's nose cone damaged by hail during the 'flame-out' trials over Entebbe in July 1956. (Peter Rushby)

passages to the engines was critical. The eventual result was the 'rabbit warren' air intake. This virtually solved the problem after many attempts and a lot of damage to the aircraft which had to be almost rebuilt before going into service.

All this was carried out in the early days of aircraft instrumentation: indeed a whole book could be written on the life and work of a flight test observer. The instrumentation techniques have developed from the days when a few bright-eyed young men watched the pilot's instruments and wrote down the results, to a modern breed of highly qualified and trained university graduates using the latest in electronic and optical instruments, measuring every parameter of the airframe, engines and performance. Much of this improvement came about with missile development.

The Britannia's instrumentation recording was mostly done by photographing panels containing perhaps 100 instrument dials at regular intervals with F24 wartime aerial cameras, or 35mm cine cameras. Rudimentary continuous paper recorders, and wire recorders were used for straingauging, and still much reliance was placed on visual observation and the feelings of the crew. 'The days of telemetry and video came too late for our beloved Britannia'.

PART TWO

Bristol 175 Britannia

General details

The Bristol Britannia is a conventional low wing monoplane, powered by four Bristol Proteus turbo-prop engines, (specified under their respective technical details).

The fuselage is 12ft in diameter and of semi-monocoque construction, sealed for pressurisation through the majority of its length. The cabin floor which is situated below the centre line of the fuselage extends the full length of the pressurised area. Access to the two freight holds are on the starboard side of the aircraft below the floor line. Both holds are pressurised so that live animal cargoes may be carried.

On the port side of the fuselage are the two main access doors to the cabin, one forward of the wing for crew access, which slides rearwards, and one behind the wing for passenger access which also slides rearwards.

On all RAF Britannias and certain civil ones, a large freight door is fitted to the port forward fuselage which incorporates the front crew access door. Some Britannias have smaller emergency doors near the tailplane, one on the port side and two on the starboard side. Some variant 102s were fitted with an additional emergency door forward of the starboard tailplane and all Britannias have overwing emergency exits mounted as pairs on each side which can be removed quickly. The early 102 variants had five of these exits on each side. A crew ditching hatch is fitted above the cockpit area. The dorsal fin and fin stub form part of the fuselage structure. The tail fin and tailplane are both detachable and are basically built in the same way as the main plane. The tail rudder and the tailplane elevators are finished with a metal surface.

The main plane consists of a box spar forming the central area of which the leading and trailing edge sections are

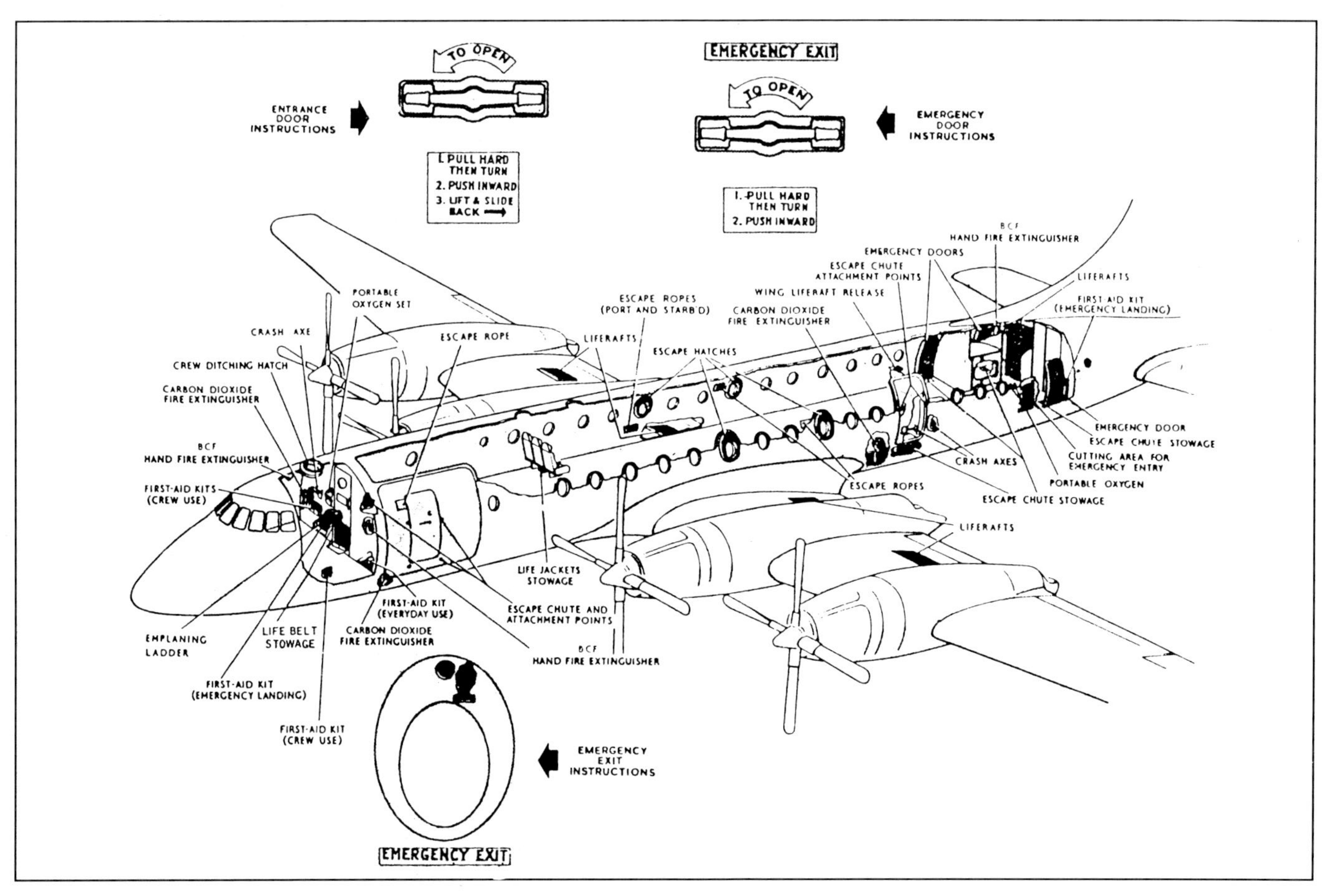

The emergency facilities are similar on all Britannias and are shown here on a variant 253. (Manufacturer's)

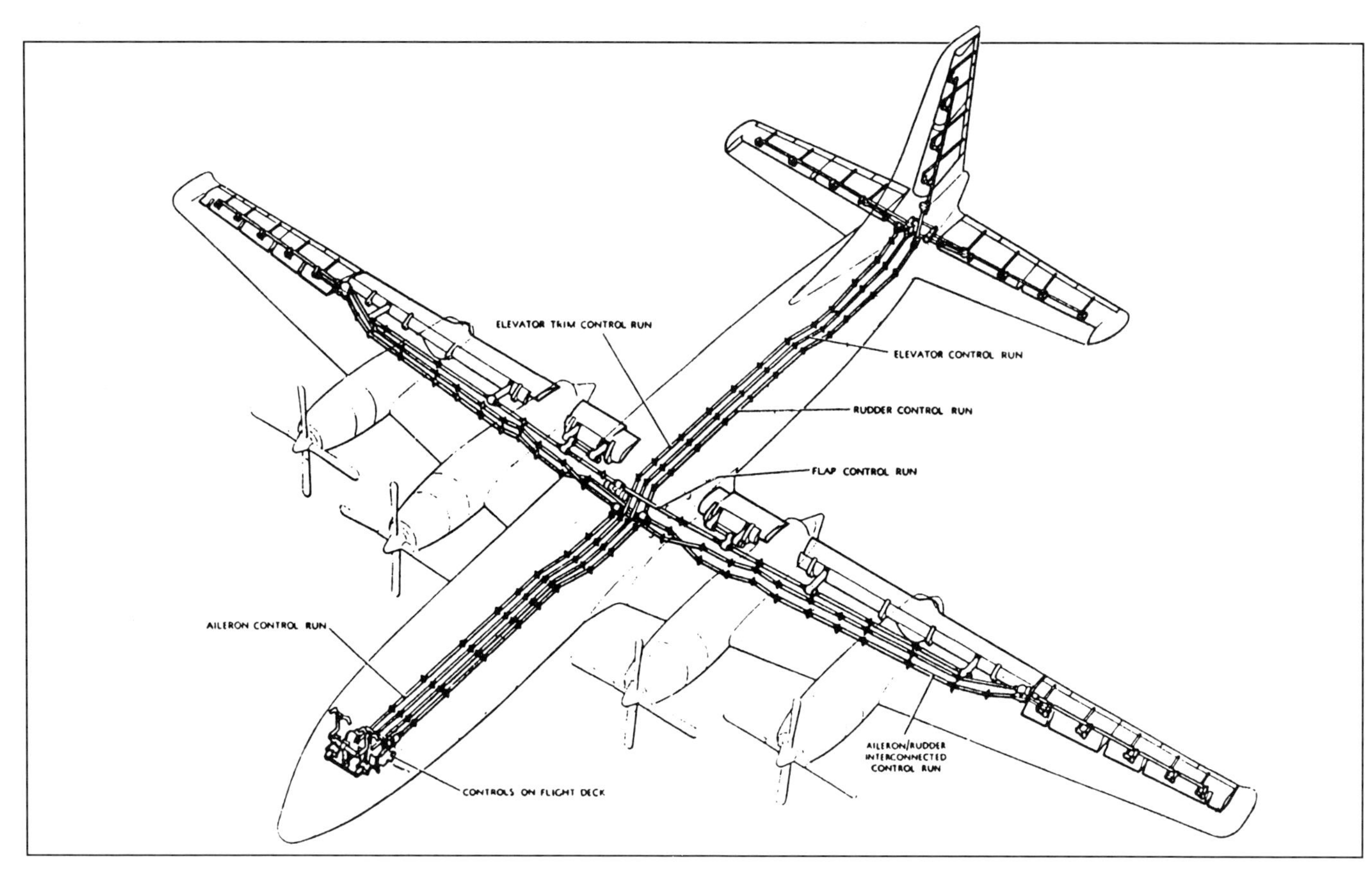

The internal layout of the control runs from the flightdeck to the primary flight surfaces are shown in this manufacturers drawing. (Manfacturer's)

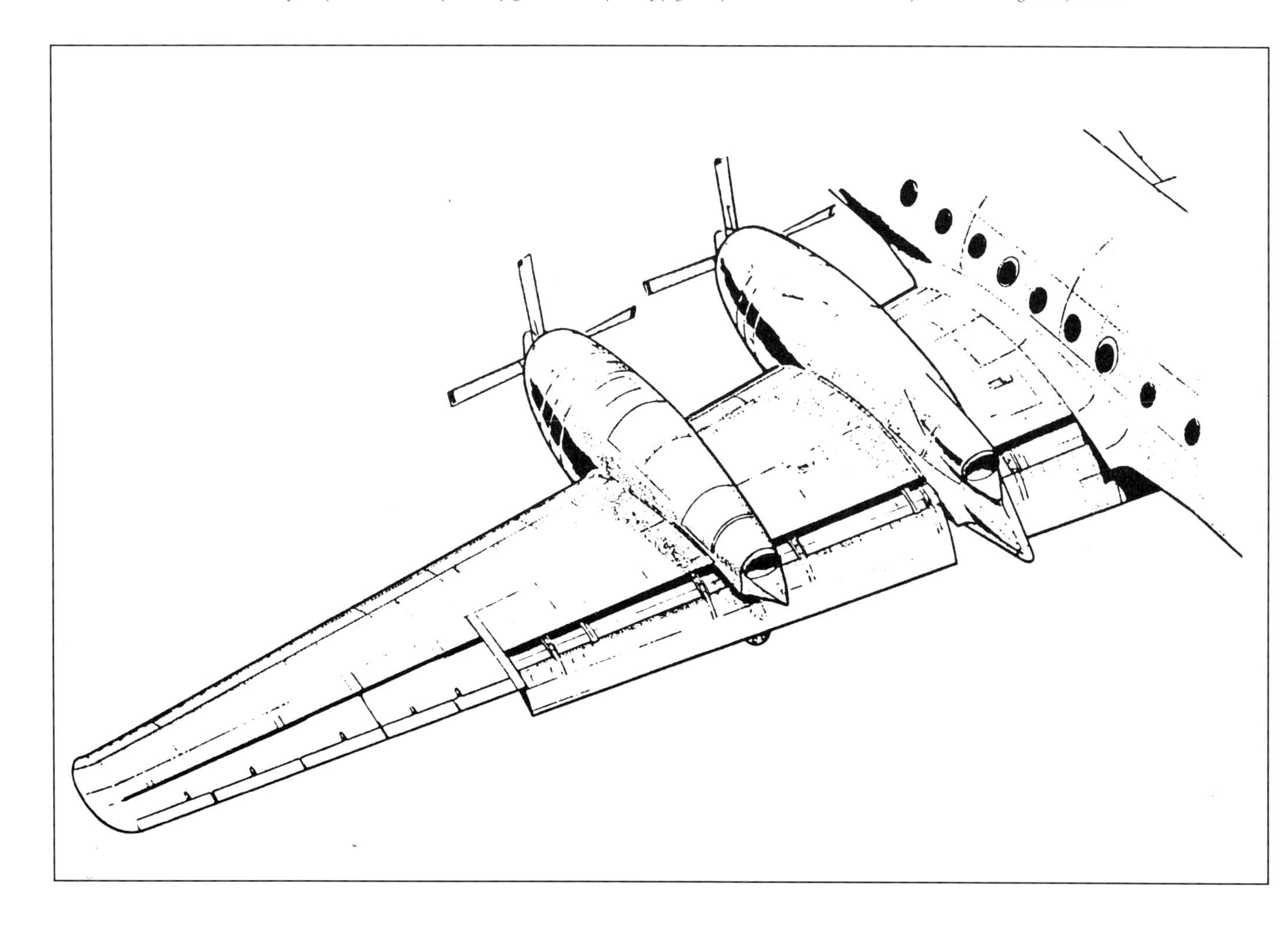

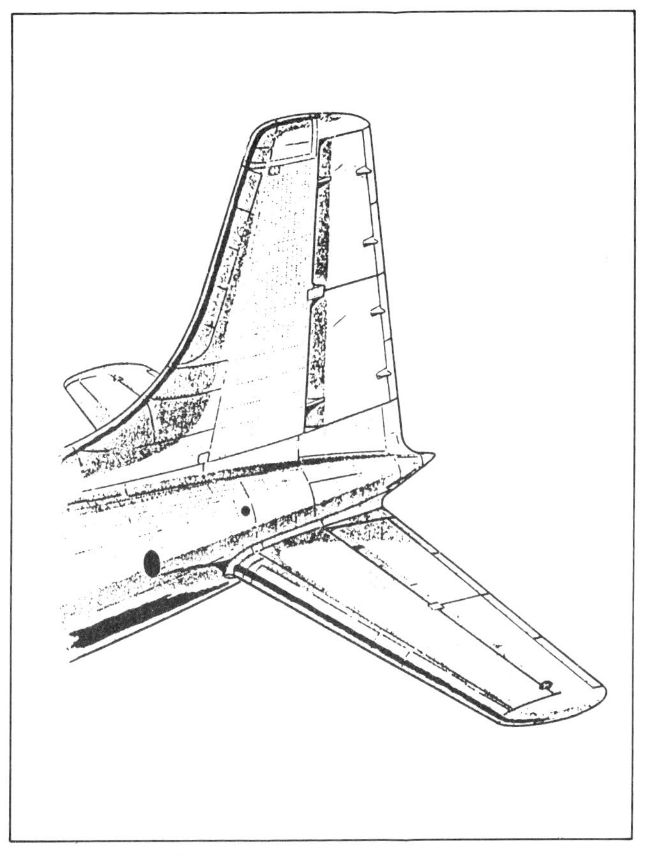

The constant chord servo tabs are shown to advantage at the trailing edges of the ailerons, elevators and rudder. Also the double slotted flaps can be seen. (Manufacturer's)

attached, the leading edge section being removable. It was constructed in four sections, the inner, the outer, and the port and starboard, all of which were not designed to be broken down for dismantling and are an integral part of the aircraft's structure.

Passing through the unpressurised part of the aircraft, the box spar carries the attachments for the ailerons, flaps and main undercarriage units. The four engine nacelles which fall in behind the firewall were designed to be part of the aircraft's main plane structure.

Each engine drives a de Havilland four-bladed, constant-speed feathering and reversable propeller. The undercarriage is of the tricycle configuration, and the tail fin is a single unit with a low tail plane. An unusual feature with regard to the flying surfaces is that the pilot does not have direct control over them but activates small servo tabs on the ailerons, the rudder and elevators.

The double slotted flaps (Fowler flaps were originally planned and Youngman flaps were originally proposed for the Bristol 175 Mk1) are also finished with a metal covering, and when extended to maximum cover an area of 401 square feet. They are electro-mechanically operated and, as outer and inner pairs, span the trailing edge of the main wing from the ailerons to the fuselage. The ailerons are at the outer end of each main wing and are split into two sections, the inner and outer, and are also finished with a metal covering.

The primary control surfaces are operated by constant-chord servo-tabs, mechanically connected to the pilot's dual controls. There is an artificial 'feel' device which is incorporated into the control circuits with the trimming of the rudder and ailerons included.

The undercarriage consists of two main units, each one consisting of four wheel bogies complete with hydraulically operated brakes for each wheel. The nose unit consists of two wheels side by side which are steerable. During retraction the main undercarriage units are raised hydraulically in a rearward direction into the rear of each inner nacelle after each bogie has turned through 90 degrees enabling them to lie parallel with the back of the oleo strut. The reason why the two rear wheels on each bogie are spaced further apart is to allow this operation.

The front unit, also hydraulically operated, retracts into its bay in a forward direction, and although within the main fuselage this bay is not pressurised.

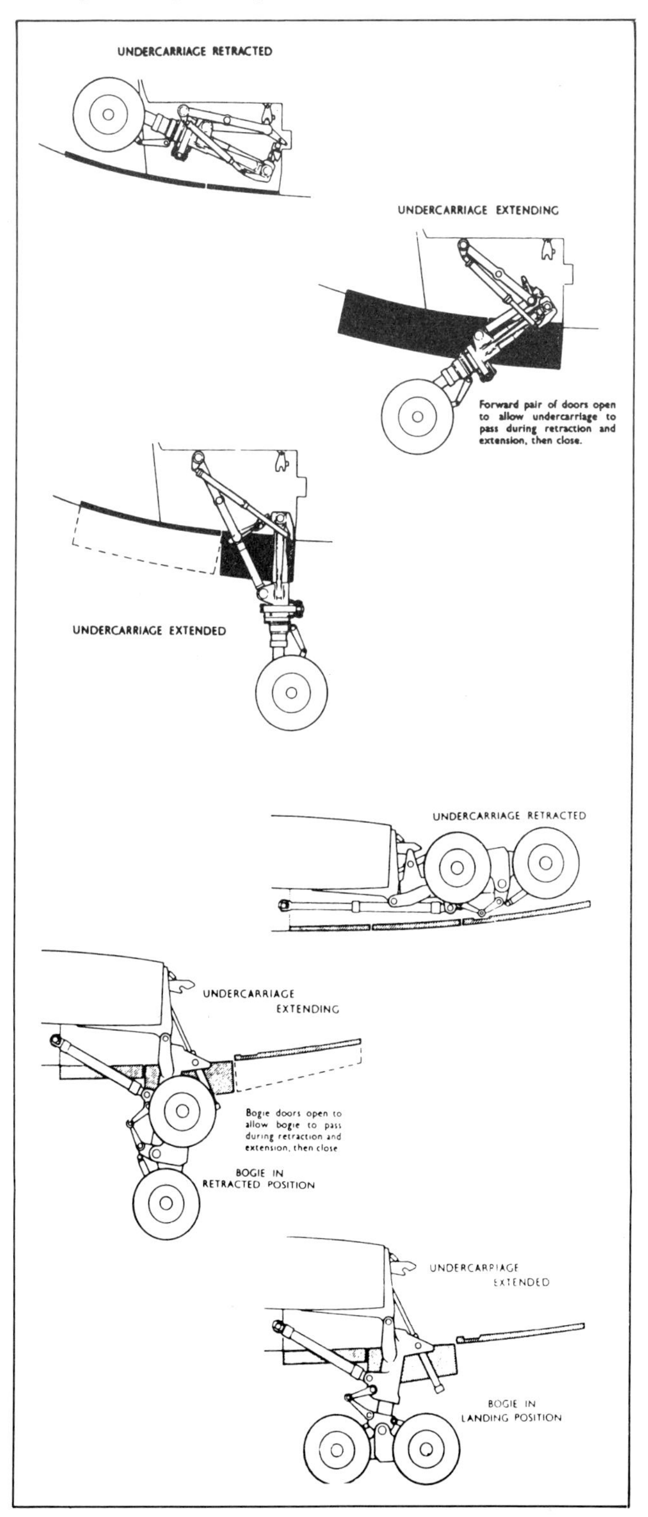

The Britannia's undercarriage retraction sequence is shown in simplified form. (Manufacturer's)

The Britannia's fuel load is stored in four main bags of a flexible design, the main outer ones being number one and four, with the main inner bags being number two and three. In addition to these bags there are two outer transfer tanks which supply their adjacent tank of number one and four, plus a centre transfer tank which is able to transfer fuel to either one, or both, of number two and three tanks.

The main tanks are fitted with booster pumps to enable adequate fuel supply during the ever-changing flight attitudes. Each of the transfer tanks are fitted with two fuel transfer pumps. Fuel can be loaded either by gravity or pressure loading, and also off loading, plus the ability to jettison when required.

The Britannia's air conditioning system is fitted with an ancillary humidification system and can heat, cool humidify and pressurise the air within the confines of the aircraft, from the passenger cabin to the flightdeck area and also the toilet areas, the dressing rooms, and the freight holds.

Air to the air conditioning system is supplied from the compressor of each of the four engines, and is designed to maintain a cabin altitude of between 5000 to 6000 feet at all of the flight altitudes up to a maximum of 35 000 feet.

The hydraulic system of the Britannia supplies power for undercarriage retraction and lowering. It also powers the wheel braking operations, control surface locking and the steering of the nose wheels. In an emergency the undercarriage can be lowered, with the power taken from a separate electrically operated pump unit or, if need be, by a hand pump. The windscreen wiper units, elevator artificial 'feel', the elevator control damper and, in some Britannia variants, the upper freight door lifting jack, are all operated by a totally different self-contained hydraulic system.

The de-icing system on the Britannia consists of ram air from the engine air intakes which has passed through the heat exchange units, operated by exhaust gas, this is then channelled to heat the leading edge of the main plane. As for the tail fin and tail plane leading edges, these are heated continuously by electrically heated mats. There are also areas just aft of the leading edge which are cyclica"y de-iced by electric mats. All four propellers are cyclically de-iced and six of the flightdeck windows are heated electrically with warm air to the remaining four.

The power plant of the Britannia is designed into a unit known as an Engine Change Unit (ECU), this means that everything forward of the fireproof bulkhead can be replaced as one complete unit, and each unit can be interchanged between any of the four engine nacelles on one aircraft or into nacelles on other Britannias. They are located behind hinged panels which form the engine intake ducts. The oil system forms an integral part of each engine change unit. Each of the engine mountings is a welded tube structure, and is attached at four points to the airframe. The engine throttle and propellor controls are operated electrically.

The electrical system of the Britannia consists of four 50 KVA self-exciting engine driven generators which supply the power for the electrical systems within the aircraft. Each of the generators has three 3-phase outputs; one at 208 volts, one at 65 volts and one, from an integral booster, at 104 volts. The 208 volt ac supplies are used for driving the hydraulic pumps, search radar and de-icing. The 104 volt outputs are rectified to give 112 volt dc supplies for the medium voltage services. The 65 volt outputs are rectified and transformed to give 28 volt dc supplies for low voltage services. A secondary supply system at 115 volts 400 cps constant voltage and frequency, is provided by inverters connected to the 122 volt bus bars, for instruments and controls.

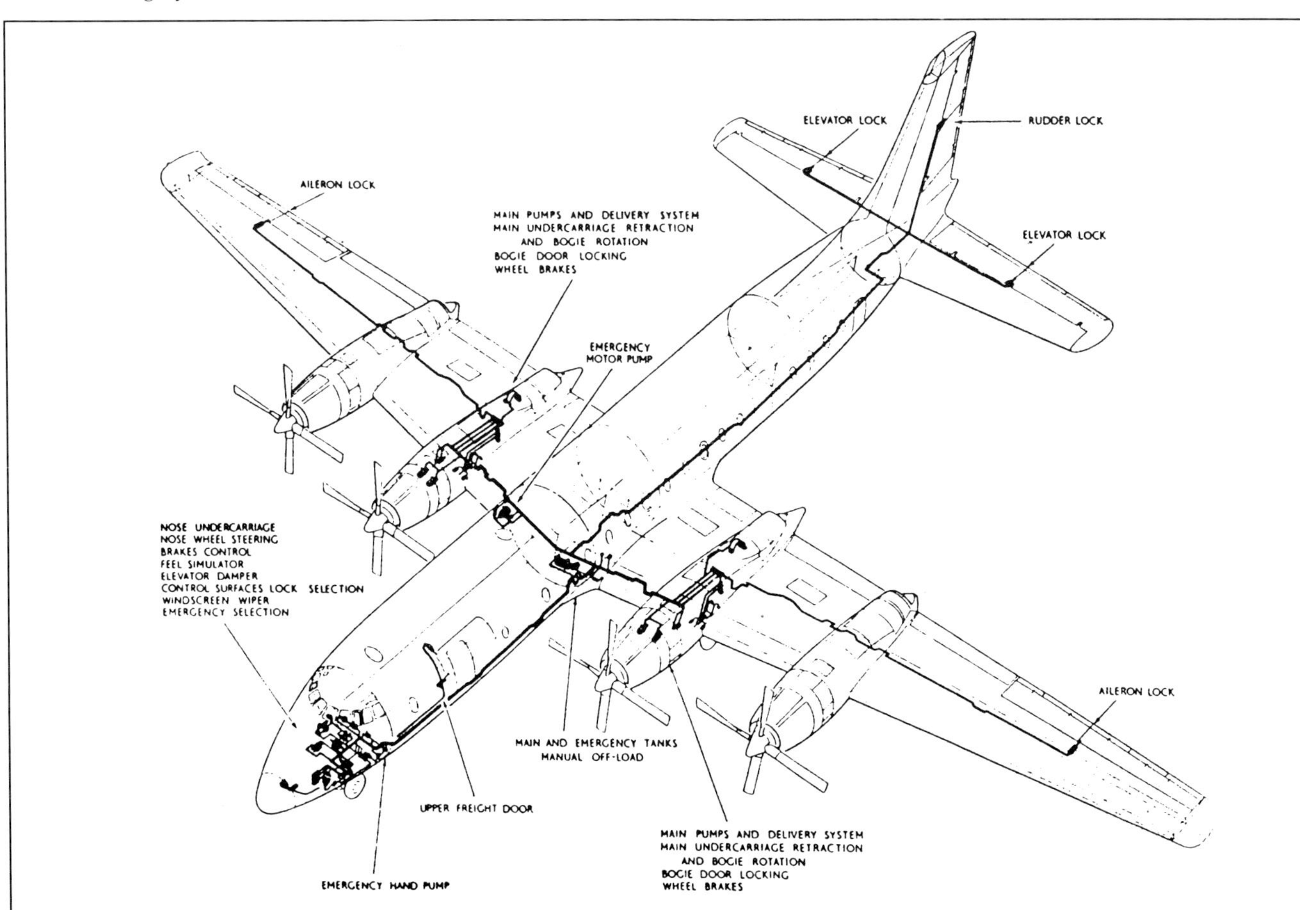

The hydraulic systems, showing the areas operated. (Manufacturer's)

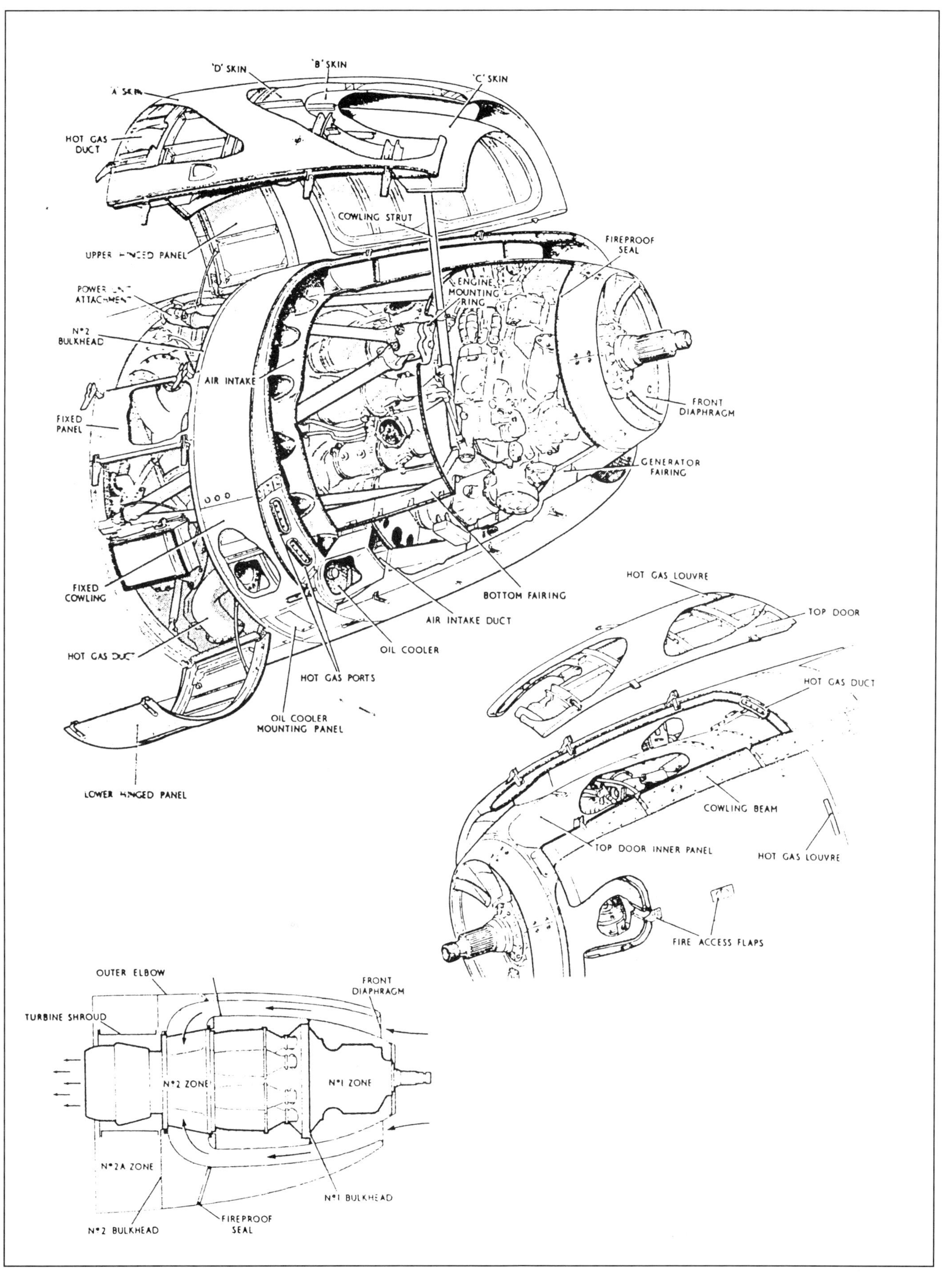

An Engine Change Unit, in this case a Bristol Proteus 755. (Manufacturer's)

Table showing the details of the structural components of the Britannia

Main plane:	
Dihedral	3 deg
Incidence	3 deg.at root + 0.6 deg. at tip.
Wash-out	2.4 deg.
Root section	N.A.C.A.25017
Tip section	N.A.C.A.4413 modified
Area, gross	2075sq ft.
Flaps (total)	401sq ft.
Aileron (each including tabs)	70sq ft.
Aileron movement	21 deg. up; 15 deg. down
Taper ratio	3.43
Sweepback	Nil at 80% chord.
Aspect ratio	9.76
Root chord (centre line)	271.385"
Tipchord	79.21"
Standard mean chord	176.148"
Flap movement	45 deg.
Fuselage:	
Long fuselage . . . Gross surface area	3802sq ft.
Maximum diameter	144"
Passenger door height	70"
Passenger door width	31.5"
Cargo door height	30"
Cargo door width	51"
Rear emergency doors	48"×24" (3 doors)*
Overwing exits	19"×26" (4 exits)*

* excluding the 100 series

Tail plane and elevators:	
Dihedral	Nil
Incidence	Nil
Area, gross	588sq ft.
Elevators (each including tabs)	85sq ft.
Elevator movement	30 deg. up; 15 deg. down
Tail fin and rudder:	
Area, clear of fuselage (including rudder and dorsal fin)	356.4sq ft.
Rudder (including tabs)	92.2sq ft.
Dorsal fin	41sq ft.
Rudder movement	16 deg. each way
Alighting gear:	
Track, main gear	31 feet.
Track, bogie	20.2" forward 29.8" aft
Wheelbase, nose to main gear	42'1.4"
Wheelbase, bogie	4 feet
Main wheel and tyre (4)	40"×12"–18"
Nose wheel and tyre (2)	32"x8.8"–16"
Minimum turning radius	57.5 feet.
Minimum propellor clearances:	
To ground, static	17" (180,000lbs)
To fuselage	19"
Between propellors	2" (projected on one plane)
Between adjacent propellors	42"

Bristol Britannia all series

Series 100	C/N	REGISTRATION
variant: 101	12873/4	G-ALBO and G-ALRX
102	12902 to 12916	G-ANBA to G-ANBO

Series 250	C/N	REGISTRATION
variant: 252	13450 to 13452	G-APPE to G-APPG
253	13397 to 13400	XL-635 to XL-638
	13434 to 13436	XM-489 to XM-491
	13448/9	XL-639 and XL-640
	13454 to 13457	XL-657 to XL-660
	13508 to 13410	XM-496 to XM-498
	13511 to 13414	XM-517 to XM-520

Series 300	C/N	REGISTRATION
variant: 301	12917	G-ANCA
302	12918/19	G-ANCB and G-ANCC
307	12920/1	G-ANCD and G-ANCE
308	12922/3	G-ANCF and G-ANCG
309	12924	G-ANCH

Series 310	C/N	REGISTRATION
variant: 311	13207	G-AOVA*
12	12925/6	G-AOVH and G-AOVI
	13230/1	G-AOVB and G-AOVC
	13235 to 13238	G-AOVD to G-AOVG
	13418 to 13424	G-AOVJ to G-AOVP
	13427	G-AOVT
	13429/30	G-AOVR and G-AOVS
313	13232 to 13234.	4X-AGA to 4X-AGC
	13431.	4X-AGD
314	13393 to 13396	CF-CZA to CF-CZD
	13428	CF-CZX
	13453	CF-CZW
317	13425/6	G-APNA and G-APNB
318	13432/3	CU-P668 and CU-P669
	13437	CU-P670
	13515	CU-P671
319	13207	G-AOVA

Series 320	C/N	REGISTRATION
variant: 324	13516/7	CF-CPD and CF-CPE

** 13207. G-AOVA was built as a variant 311, later converted to a variant 312 before finally being upgraded to a series 320 and sold as a variant 319.*

Bristol 175 Britannia
Main contract dates and details concerning the 102 and 312 aircraft for BOAC.

Contract No. 6/Acrft/2460/CB10(b) – 5 July, 1948. Medium Range Empire (Bristol type 175) specification 2/47.

Ministry I.T.P. design and supply of three prototypes provided that last prototype became one of production aircraft.

6/Aircraft 3571/CB10 C – 1949. Cancelled order above for three prototypes and provided for supply of two prototypes of cost not exceeding £2 675 000.

1. BOAC Contract.
   28 July 1949 . . . . 25 aircraft of which the first six were to be powered by Bristol Centaurus engines.

Contract deliveries to commence April 1954 and to continue at a rate of one per month through January 1955, two in February 1955 and thereafter alternate months one and two until balance delivered with the last in October 1955.

2. Supplemental Agreement.
   29 December 1950.

Provided for all aircraft to be "Proteus" powered, restricted ordering of materials to first 15 aircraft and subject to BOAC excercise of rights to cancel or ammend quantity of last ten. Cancellation increased price from £483 000 to £567 000 and amendment of number would be a figure between these two. Delivery delayed by one month on first aircraft.

3. Third Agreement.
   10 August 1955.

Provided for reduction of order from 25 to 23 aircraft of which 15 to be series 100 version and eight series 300 version. Delivery of the first series 100 aircraft in September 1955 thereafter one per month through February 1956, two in March and July 1956, one in April, June and August 1956 making a total of 15. The series 300 version deliveries would commence July 1956 with one per month through October and two each in November and December 1956.

4. Fourth Agreement.
   10 August 1955.

Provided for supply of ten 300LR with delivery October 1956 (1), November and December 1956 (2), January 1957 (1), February 1957 (2), March and April 1957 (2), at £845 000 each.

5. Fifth Agreement.
   25 March 1957.

Provides for the releasing by BOAC of the first 300 series aircraft to the Ministry of Supply and the increase of the 300LR ordered from 10 to 11. It also provided for the Bristol Aeroplane Company to sell the other seven 300 series aircraft of the BOAC order and for BOAC to buy instead seven 300LR aircraft priced at £945 000. Delivery dates for these nine Long Range aircraft were at the rate of one per month commencing January 1958. Delivery of the replacement for the Ministry of Supply aircraft to be later decided.

On June 27, 1957 the 18 Britannia 312s were quoted for delivery on the following dates. (Actual dates in brackets)

G-AOVA	8.57.	**********	G-AOVJ	2.58.	(19.3.58.)
G-AOVB	7.57	(10.9.57.)	G-AOVK	3.58.	(4.4.58.)
G-AOVC	9.57.	(15.11.57.)	G-AOVL	3.58.	(21.4.58.)
G-AOVD	10.57.	(4.12.57.)	G-AOVM	4.58.	(13.5.58.)
G-AOVE	11.57.	(21.12.57.)	G-AOVN	5.58.	(27.5.58.)

G-AOVF	11.57.	(2.1.58.)	G-AOVO	6.58.	(15.7.58.)
G-AOVG	12.57.	(31.1.58.)	G-AOVP	6.58.	(31.7.58.)
G-AOVH	1.58.	(11.2.58.)	G-AOVR	8.58.	(27.8.58.)
G-AOVI	1.58.	(26.2.58.)	G-AOVS	8.58.	(22.9.58.)
			G-AOVT	?	(31.12.58.)

N.B. Because G-AOVA was the prototype aircraft, it was not accepted by BOAC due to the flying hours that had been flown during her test flight programmes. To make up the order of 18 variant 312s it was replaced by G-AOVT.

Bristol Britannia
Key for tables

C = Converted.
D = Delivered.
F = Freighter configuration.
L = Leased.
NN = New name.
NR = New registration.
(NTU) = Not taken up.
P = Purchased.
R = Returned.
RR = Re-registered.
SL = Sub-leased.
T = Transferred.
F = Financed.

Within the details for each aircraft in the relevent tables following their individual histories, the above letters will help identify various happenings for each aircraft.

It is also noted that certain leasing houses backed the purchase of some Britannias and although found within the individual histories and tables it should be borne in mind that they were not the aircraft's operator.

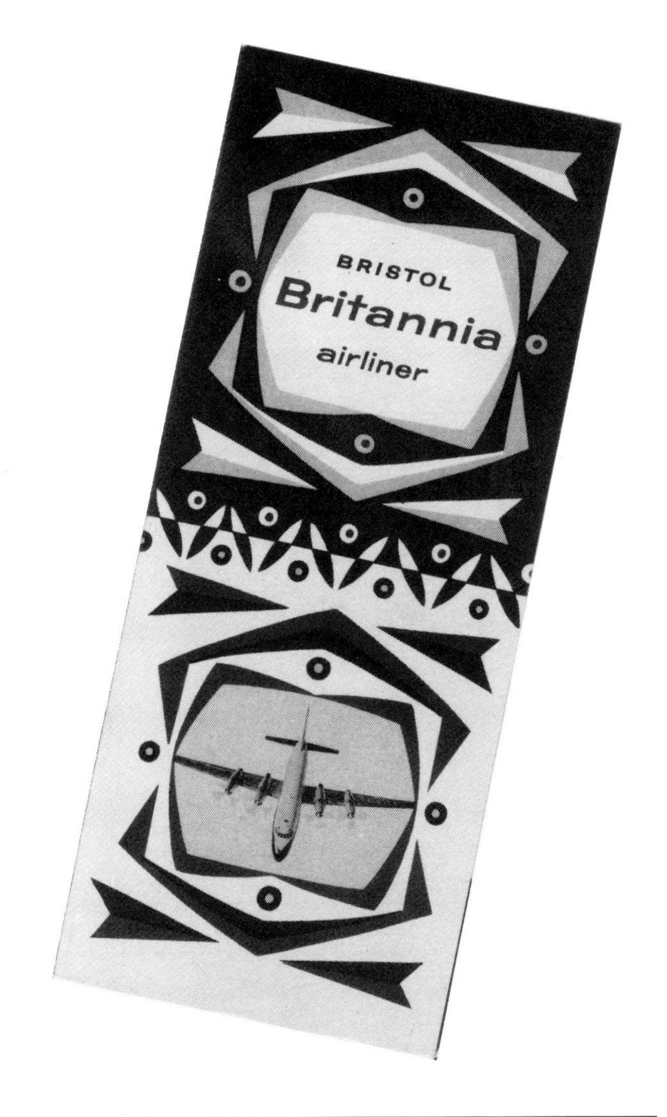

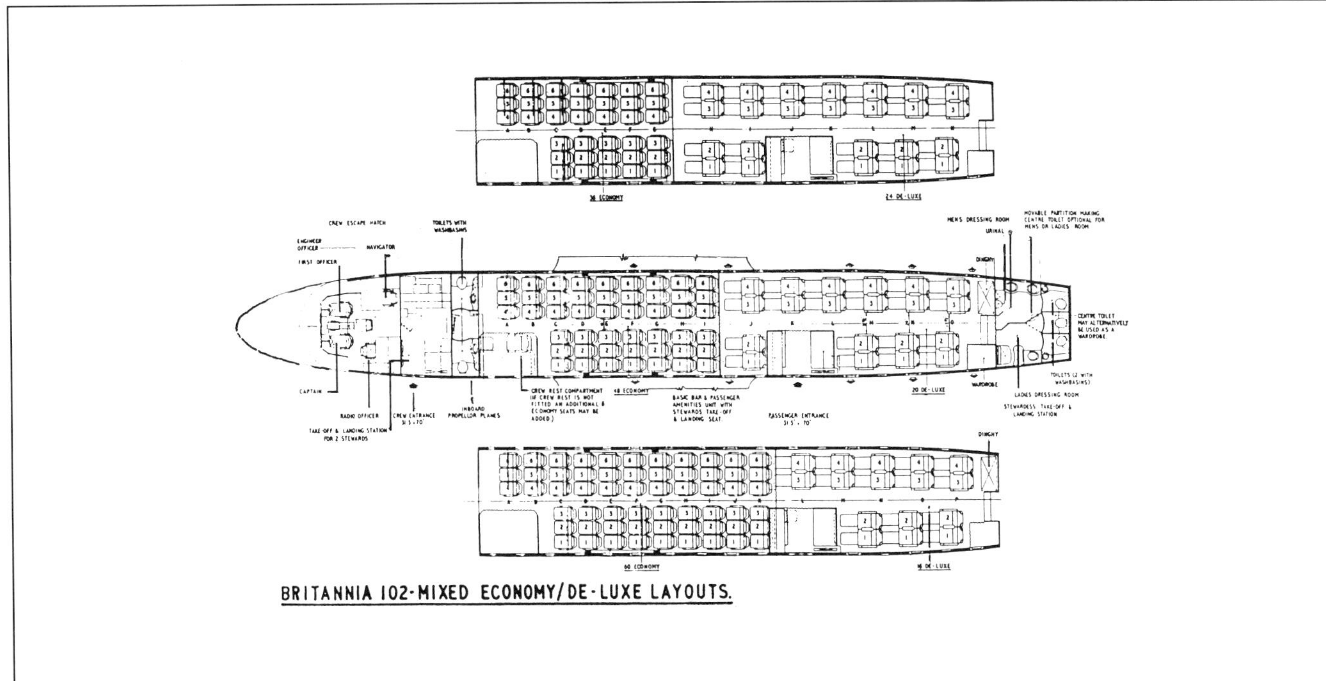

BRITANNIA 102-MIXED ECONOMY/DE-LUXE LAYOUTS.

PART THREE

Bristol Britannia Series 100 Specifications

VARIANTS: 101 (PROTOTYPES)
102 (production aircraft for BOAC)

POWERPLANT G-ALBO: Four Bristol B.Pt.2 Proteus 625 turbo-props developing 2800ehp later uprated to 3200ehp driving 16ft de Havilland four-bladed hollow steel propellers. Other powerplants fitted to the first prototype, G-ALBO consisted of: one Bristol Proteus 755 (4120ehp), two Bristol Proteus 705 (3900ehp), one Bristol Orion (5500ehp) and a Bristol Proteus 765 (4400ehp).

POWERPLANT SECOND PROTOTYPE & EARLY PRODUCTION ONLY: Four Bristol B.Pt.3 Proteus 705 turbo-props developing 3870ehp driving 16ft de Havilland four-bladed propellers.

POWERPLANT PRODUCTION AIRCRAFT: Four Bristol B.Pt.3 Proteus 705 turbo-props uprated to 3900ehp driving 16ft de Havilland four-bladed hollow steel propellers.

Note: Some variant 102 Britannias were later fitted with the four-bladed round-tipped Duralumin propellers.

DIMENSIONS:

Wingspan	140ft 0in.	
(G-ALBO prior to tip modifications).		
Wingspan	142ft 3.5in.	
Overall length	114ft 0in.	
Height	36ft 8in.	
Wing area	2075sq. ft.	

PAYLOAD & PERFORMANCE: Still air range, maximum payload (25 000lb) over 3450 statute miles at a cruising speed of 362mph.

Still air range, maximum fuel (including reserves) 4580 statute miles at a cruising speed of 328mph with 13 736lb payload.

CREW: 7.

PASSENGER ACCOMMODATION: First class, 61. Mixed, 22 first class and 54 tourist class. Tourist, 90/98.

CARGO ACCOMMODATION: 665cu.ft.

FUEL CAPACITY: 6690 imperial gallons.

WEIGHTS: Empty 88 000lb. All up weight (G-ALBO) 130 000lb. (Increased to G-ALRX's. All up weight (G-ALRX) 140 000lb. weight later). All up weight (102 variants including fuel) 155 000lb.

Total built: 17 (plus two ground test fuselages).

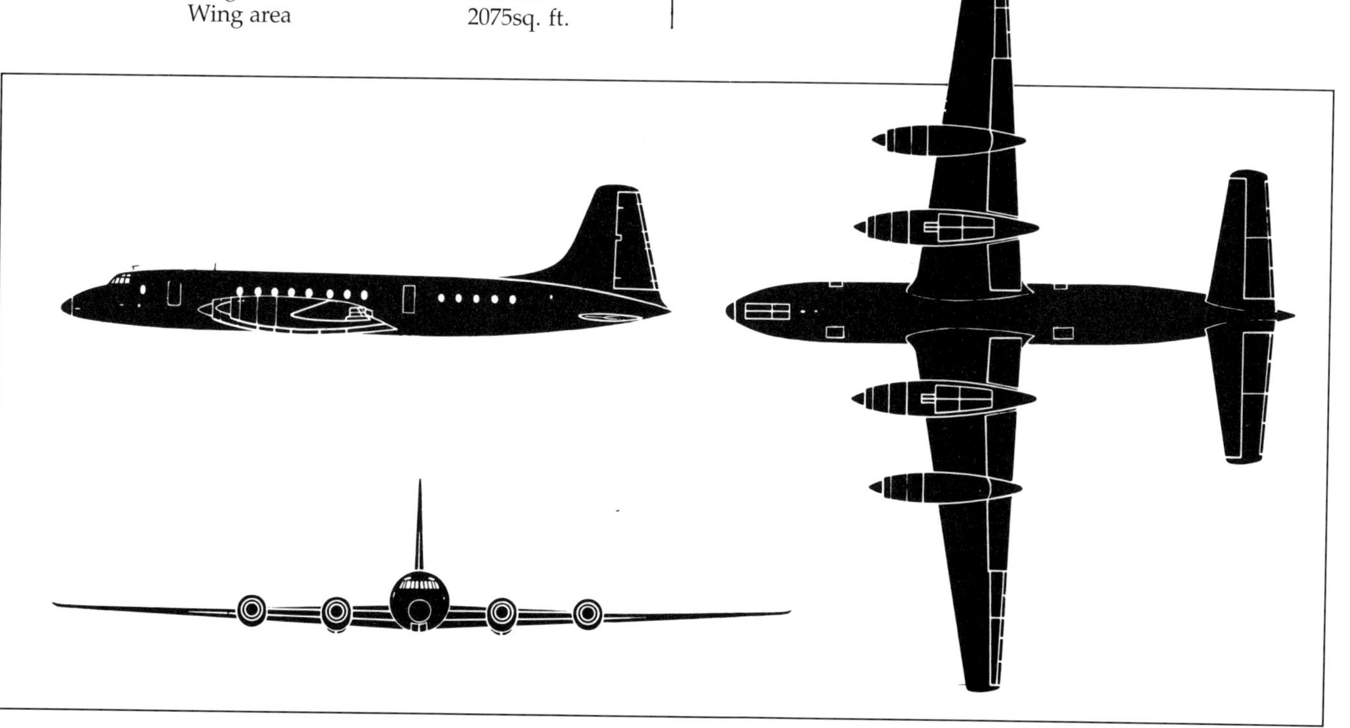

G–ALBO

SERIES 100	VARIANT 101
Constructors No. 12873	Production No. 001
Built at Filton	First flight 16.8.52
C of A: 22.9.52	

The first flight of the Bristol Britannia as G-ALBO takes to the air on her maiden flight from Filton on 16 August 1952. (Bristol Aeroplane Co Ltd/British Aerospace)

Built to Ministry of Supply specification 2/47, the Royal Air Force serial VX-442 was allocated in 1948 but not worn. In 1950 the serial WB-470 was allocated and again not worn.

Registered G-ALBO to the Bristol Aeroplane Company Ltd. on 11 June 1948, this aircraft was retained by the manufacturers for development flying. Originally powered by four Bristol Proteus 625 (B.Pt.2) turbo-props, developing 2800ehp, which were later uprated to 3200ehp. On 11 March 1955 G-ALBO flew with a Bristol Proteus 705 (B.Pt.3) engine fitted to the number two nacelle.

After a spell in the hanger at Filton, being brought up to the standard of G-ALRX following her loss, G-ALBO recommenced flight testing in May 1954. It was during these flights that G-ALBO was almost lost, due to a flap torque tube shearing, whilst carrying out stalling tests. The pilot, Walter Gibb, had selected 'flaps down' and as he selected 'flaps up' the tube sheared and only one side of flaps retracted. He was then left with the aeroplane starting to roll to the point where it nearly flew on its back, causing excessive G's. While still struggling to keep the aeroplane flying, Walter Gibb selected 'flaps down' hoping this would help to level the aircraft out, which it did, although G-ALBO had by now lost a lot of height.

Once G-ALBO landed safely back at Filton, she was found to be suffering from stress wrinkles and was overhauled. G-ALBO had in fact suffered in excess of three G's during those hair-raising moments.

In September 1954, G-ALBO went to Idris, North Africa for preliminary tropical trials and in March 1956, was fitted with two Bristol Proteus 755 engines in both of the outboard nacelles. With this engine configuration G-ALBO was flown on 17 March 1956. On 31 August 1956 a Bristol Orion (BE.25) was fitted to the port outer nacelle and in October 1957 a Bristol Proteus 765 was fitted to the port inner nacelle, replacing the B.P 705. and G-ALBO was reflown on 1 November 1957.

G-ALBO's last experimental flight was on 31 March 1960 and after this flight which numbered 692, she had 1794 hours of test flying to her credit. On 30 October 1960 G-ALBO was flown to RAF St Athan, for use as a ground instructional airframe. The Maintenance Command serial 7708M was allocated.

Following her withdrawal from use, she was broken up and burnt on 12 June 1968, although the forward fuselage was removed to RAF Brize Norton for use within the Air Movements School to aid in the training of loadmasters. G-ALBO's remains were placed on the airfield dump in March 1978.

G–ALRX

SERIES 100	VARIANT 101
Constructors No. 12874	Production No. 002
Built at Filton	First flight 23.12.53
C of A: not allocated	

G-ALRX a variant 101 and the second prototype, seen at Filton while taxiing. Note the revised wingtips and engine exhausts. (Bristol Aeroplane Co Ltd/British Aerospace)

Built as the second prototype for the Ministry of Supply which had placed an order for three prototypes on 2 February 1948. This order was ammended on 5 July 1948 when the three prototypes were cancelled and two series 100 prototypes were ordered.

Originally allocated the Royal Air Force serial VX-447 in 1948, but this was not worn, and in 1950 the serial WB-473 was allocated and again not worn. However this aircraft was built to resemble the production variant which were to be the 102 ordered by BOAC on 28 July 1948. The registration G-ALRX was allocated on 25 June 1951.

In January 1954, G-ALRX commenced her series of flight trials for a certificate of airworthiness from Filton. Disaster struck on the morning of 4 February 1954, when under the command of Captain Bill Pegg, who at the time was Bristol's chief test pilot, G-ALRX suffered an oil fed engine fire the result of a failure in the reduction gear of number three engine, at 11.55am. A decision to force land G-ALRX was quickly made and the area chosen was the frozen foreshore of the River Severn.

A wheels-up landing was made near Littleton Wharf, between Oldbury-Upon-Severn and Littleton-Upon-Severn. G-ALRX slid through the frozen mud on the foreshore of the Severn and as she was about to stop she turned her back on the banks of the river as if to ignore the rescue attempts which followed. All 13 persons aboard who included Dr.A.E. Russell, Bristol's chief designer, and their sales manager, Mr. Farnes, scrambled out safely thanks to a superb piece of flying by Bill Pegg and Mr. G. Malouin (KLM) who was flying in the co-pilot's position, although the radio operator suffered minor cuts and bruises. G-ALRX was engaged on this flight with two representatives from KLM and nine of their flight test crew.

G-ALRX was swamped by the incoming tide and totally wrecked by saltwater, despite the valiant rescue attempts by the Army, 501 squadron R.Aux.A.F., local haulage firms and emergency services who all inadvertenly played a role in her eventual downfall, because of the stresses and strains needed to move her up the bank of the river.

The number three engine was removed and sent for examination and all other possible salvageable parts, were also removed. The remainder of G-ALRX was then cut up for removal back to Filton where the forward fuselage was refurbished and used as an instructional airframe.

It is of interest to note that the forward section of G-ALRX is still in existence today (May 1992) at A&AEE Boscombe Down, Wiltshire. In the colours of the RAF Britannias, it has been given the name 'Sirius II', probably something to do with XL-638!

Employed today in the Aeromedical and Safety School, it is used with the addition of an inflatable emergency slide to help reduce the fears of people who dislike exiting an aircraft in a hurry!

G-ALRX's total flying time was a mere 51 hours and 10 minutes accumulated over 24 test flights. It is hoped that once Sirius II is no longer required by the MOD that she will be preserved as the oldest Britannia, as well as the second prototype!

G-ALRX as she is in 1992 at Boscombe Down. (© Crown Copyright 1992/MOD reproduced with the permission of the Controller of HMSO)

G–ANBA

SERIES 100	VARIANT 102
Constructors No. 12902	Production No. 007
Built at Filton	First flight 5.9.54
C of A: 2.3.55	

G-ANBA the first production variant 102 for BOAC. Note the missing eye-level windows above the cockpit windscreens. (Bristol Aeroplane Co Ltd/British Aerospace)

Ordered by BOAC and first registered G-ANBA on 7 January 1954. G-ANBA was the first of the 15 variant 102 Britannias destined for BOAC service. Although 17 series 100 were manufactured only 15 went into commercial service, the other two aircraft being the prototypes G-ALBO and G-ALRX which were the variant 101.

This aircraft embarked on tropical trials carried out between Johannesburg and Khartoum which concluded in March 1955. It was during these trials that G-ANBA amassed a total of 652 test flight hours. G-ANBA was employed as a C of A

Following her use as a flight development aircraft for C of A trials – G-ANBA is seen at Belfast undergoing overhaul and modifications to full production standard. (Short Bros. Belfast)

development aircraft by the manufacturers between September and December 1955 after the loss of the second prototype G-ALRX. On 13 January 1956, G-ANBA was flown to the Short's factory at Belfast, for overhaul and modification work to bring her up to full production standard. She flew again from Belfast on 16 May 1957. The following day G-ANBA arrived at Weston Airways of Weston-Super-Mare to receive the finishing touches.

Officially on BOAC's charge from 12 August 1957, G-ANBA returned to Filton for internal fitments and was finally delivered to BOAC at London (Heathrow) Airport ten days later, entering service on 14 September 1957 as BA 704/83.

G-ANBA was leased to Nigeria Airways on 13 April 1959, returning to BOAC in 1960. Malayan Airways leased her on 19 December 1961 and on both occasions the main BOAC livery was worn with title stickers and adjusted tail logos.

Returning to BOAC on 17 January 1962 G-ANBA flew her last service on 14 October 1962 as BA BCH/1095 between Pisa and London. Withdrawn from service and flown to Marshall's of Cambridge for storage on 21 November 1962.

Purchase by the South American airline Paraense Transportes Aeroes S.A. did not take place and she was transferred to London (Heathrow) Airport for storage until purchased by Britannia Airways of Luton, known previously as Euravia, on 26 March 1965.

Operated by Britannia Airways until withdrawn from service and stored at their Luton base from November 1969. Finally broken up and scrapped in June 1970 after flying a total of 22 514 hours and 7158 landings.

G–ANBB

SERIES 100	VARIANT 102
Constructors No. 12903	Production No. 013
Built at Filton	First flight 18.1.55
C of A: 8.6.55	

G-ANBB a variant 102 in the first livery adopted by Britannia Airways who in fact changed their name from Euravia following introduction of the type. (David Cox, Britannia Airways)

Ordered by BOAC on 28 July 1949 as part of a 25 strong order, which was amended in December 1950 with the cancellation of ten aircraft. Registered G-ANBB on 1 January 1954 to the Bristol Aeroplane Company Ltd and retained initially by the manufacturers for use on C of A flight testing, totalling 277 flying hours.

On 25 July 1955 G-ANBB was flown to the Short's factory at Belfast, for overhaul and to be brought up to full production standard. She left Belfast on 6 December 1956 for Filton and left Filton on 14 January 1957 to fly to Weston Airways at Weston-Super-Mare for finishing work to be carried out.

Four months later G-ANBB returned to Filton on 31 May 1957 to be fitted with internal furnishings and, following checking, BOAC took charge of G-ANBB on 10 June 1957, delivery at London (Heathrow) Airport followed eight days later. The date on service was 16 July 1957 flying as BA 934/1.

Nigeria Airways leased this aircraft in June 1959 and she was returned during the early part of 1960. In 1961 G-ANBB was leased to Cathay Pacific Airways from 12 January until 31 January when she was returned. G-ANBB operated her last flight for BOAC on 14 November 1964 on a service between Accra to London (Heathrow) Airport.

Withdrawn from service by BOAC G-ANBB, like all other variant 102s of their fleet, was flown to Marshall's of Cambridge for storage in November 1962.

Retreived from storage, G-ANBB was leased by Britannia Airways on 18 November 1964 and, painted in their first livery, operated out of Luton Airport.

Tragically, G-ANBB was lost on 1 September 1966 at 00.47 local time while approaching Ljublijana Airport, Yugoslavia. With only 2.8kms to touchdown she hit trees on high ground and crashed. Of the seven crew on board only one stewardess survived, and 91 of the 110 passengers were killed.

G–ANBC

SERIES 100	VARIANT 102
Constructors No. 12904	Production No. 003
Built at Filton	First flight 26.6.55
C of A: 27.8.55	

G-ANBC in BOAC's early white livery. (Bristol Aeroplane Co Ltd/British Aerospace)

Registered G-ANBC to the Bristol Aeroplane Company Ltd on 7 January 1954 as part of the 15 strong variant 102 order placed by BOAC in December 1950. Originally employed on C of A flight trials between July and November 1955, G-ANBC also carried out tests on the storm warning radar and other operational installations. These tests were completed during December, 1955

On 9 September 1955 G-ANBC operated the first route proving flight from London (Heathrow) to Johannesburg. She was the first Britannia 102 delivered to BOAC, delivery taking place at London (Heathrow) Airport on 30 December 1955. She went on service with BOAC on 12 February 1957 as BA 115/486.

A rather accident-prone aircraft, G-ANBC was damaged in a landing accident on 8 September 1958. While landing on a wet greasy runway at Rangoon she overshot causing the nose wheel to collapse which damaged the underside of the forward fuselage. No one was injured. Temporary repairs commenced on 17 December 1958 while spares were awaited from Filton, arriving on board Britannia 252, G-APPE. G-ANBC finally left Rangoon for Filton on 28 March 1959, flying back unpressurised with the undercarriage in the landing position, and arriving back at Filton on 1 April 1959. She was repaired using a new nose section from the test airframe (12875) and reflown on 15 August 1959.

Re-delivery to BOAC was on 20 August 1959 and on 22 August 1959 G-ANBC entered service on BOAC's London to Sydney route. G-ANBC was leased to Ghana Airways in early 1960 and returned to BOAC later that year.

The second landing accident, proved to be G-ANBC's last. While landing at Khartoum Airport on 11 November 1960 G-ANBC suffered a hydraulic systems failure and had to land wheels-up and, thankfully, once more no injuries were sustained among those on board. Damaged beyond repair, she was removed from the British register in February 1961, and used for spares. Her remains were donated to the use of the Sudanese Fire Brigade for training.

G–ANBD

SERIES 100	VARIANT 102
Constructors No. 12905	Production No. 004
Built at Filton	First flight 14.11.55
C of A: 30.12.55	

Registered G-ANBD to the Bristol Aeroplane Company on 7 January 1954 this Britannia was part of the 15 variant 102s ordered by BOAC. Delivery took place at London (Heathrow) Airport on 30 December 1955, alongside G-ANBC, as the first of the series.

Although initially used for route proving flights and crew training excercises, G-ANBD flew the route proving flight to Tokyo from London on 19 June 1957.

G-ANBD continued in BOAC's service until withdrawn and flown to Cambridge for storage with Marshall's in November 1962.

BKS Air Transport Ltd leased G-ANBD from 16 November 1965, from BOAC. Britannia Airways, while waiting for the delivery of their first Boeing 737's, sub-leased G-ANBD on 27 April 1968, wearing BKS livery and Britannia Airways titles on the upper fuselage. Once the sub-lease had ceased, G-ANBD was returned to BKS on 10 October 1968.

BKS Air Transport Ltd finally withdrew G-ANBD from service and stored her at Southend Airport, Essex in January 1970. She was broken up in May 1970 and scrapped following a 20 180 hours flying career involving 8279 landings.

G-ANBD in the livery of BKS Air Transport Ltd. (Aviation Photo News)

G–ANBE

SERIES 100
Constructors No. 12906
Built at Filton
C of A: 2.3.56

VARIANT 102
Production No. 005
First flight 17.1.56

G-ANBE cruising in BOAC's livery. The upturned wingtips clearly seen. (Bristol Aeroplane Co Ltd/British Aerospace)

Registered G-ANBE on 18 January 1956. Ordered by BOAC and officially taken on charge 2 March 1956, although not delivered to London (Heathrow) Airport until 7 March 1956. On 23 April 1956 while flying between Livingstone, in Northern Rhodesia, and Nairoboi in Kenya, G-ANBE encountered the first of the 'icing problems' by which the Britannia Proteus powerplants were to be dogged.

On 30 January 1957 G-ANBE flew a record transatlantic flight from Prestwick Airport to Winnipeg, a distance of 3800 statute miles in 11 hours, 11 minutes at a speed of 366 miles per hour.

BOAC leased G-ANBE to Nigerian Airways in April 1958; Ghana Airways during 1960 and Malayan Airways February to March 1963, returning to BOAC on 3 April 1963.

Withdrawn from service by BOAC and flown to Marshall's of Cambridge for storage in April 1963. G-ANBE was leased by Britannia Airways on 1 February 1966 and purchased on 16 March 1970.

G-ANBE's last flight for Britannia Airways was on 6 December 1970. Withdrawn from service she was stored at Luton Airport from December 1970. Scrapped during July 1972 following a career of 21 761 flying hours and 7638 landings.

G-ANBE at Cambridge in open storage following her retirement from BOAC service. (Aviation Photo News)

G–ANBF

SERIES 100
Constructors No. 12907
Built at Filton
C of A: 13.3.56

VARIANT 102
Production No. 006
First flight 23.2.56

G-ANBF at Hong Kong's Kai Tak airport in the lease livery of Malayan Airways. (Aviation Photo News)

Registered G-ANBF on 18 January 1956. Ordered by BOAC and delivered to London (Heathrow) Airport on 14 March 1956 and following modifications between 28 March 1956 and 5 February 1957, G-ANBF went on service with BOAC as BA 115/484 on 2 February 1957.

Like most other series 102 Britannias in BOAC service G-ANBF was leased out, first to Malayan Airways on 10 October 1961 returning to BOAC on 14 November 1961, then to Nigeria Airways from November 1961 until 20 November 1962 and finally back to Malayan Airways on 22 November 1962 until 12th December when she returned to BOAC. G-ANBF's last flight with BOAC was on 17 December 1962 as BA BRH/BCH 1097 between Singapore and London.

Withdrawn from service by BOAC, G-ANBF was flown to Marshall's of Cambridge on 26 January 1963 for storage and eventual resale or lease.

Britannia Airways leased G-ANBF from 12th February 1965. Painted in full house livery G-ANBF was later purchased by them. Her last flight for Britannia Airways was on 26 October 1969 and it was at Luton Airport that G-ANBF was stored from October 1969 until broken up and scrapped during May 1970, following 23 836 flying hours and 7523 landings.

G-ANBF at Luton Airport in the livery of Britannia Airways. (David Cox, Britannia Airways)

G–ANBG

SERIES 100	VARIANT 102
Constructors No. 12908	Production No. 007
Built at Filton	First flight 29.3.56
C of A: 30.4.56	

Registered G-ANBG to the Bristol Aeroplane Company Ltd on 18 January 1956, this aircraft was one of 15 variant 102s ordered by BOAC in December 1950. Previously BOAC had ordered 25 such aircraft on 28 July 1949, but amended their order to 15 variant 102s in December 1950. Delivered to BOAC at London (Heathrow) Airport on 8 May 1956, entering service on 15 March 1957 as BA 121/7 following modifications at Filton.

During service with BOAC, G-ANBG was used on route proving flights to Sydney, Australia and also Hong Kong on 2 February 1957.

G-ANBG was fitted out with a VIP layout and furnishings for a demonstration flight to Australia in 1957. The Australian Prime Minister the Rt. Hon. R.G. Menzies and Dame Pattie Menzies sampled the Britannia on a flight between Sydney and Canberra, accompanied by Phillip Hood, BOAC's Regional Representitive for the South West Pacific, and the Governor-General, General Sir William Slim.

Problems were experienced with G-ANBG, and because of the connotation 'No Bloody Good' that was read into her registration it was decided to re-register with an out of sequence registration, G-APLL. This was applied from 19 March 1958 and she first flew under the new registration on 21 March.

Nigeria Airlines leased G-APLL during 1959 and although still wearing BOAC's livery she also wore Nigerian fin markings and fuselage titles of the stick on type. British United Airways chartered this aircraft, and applied 'On charter to BUA' on her rear upper fuselage. Following her return to BOAC, G-APLL suffered damage during a landing at Barcelona on 4 November 1961 when just after touchdown she swung off the runway but immediately rejoined it and taxied in normally. Damage was confined to the starboard inboard flap and No.3 propellor and was caused when she struck fence posts at the edge of the runway.

G-APLL was leased out to Malayan Airways on 10 May 1962 until 6 June when she was returned. Another lease period to Malayan Airways commenced on 3 July 1962 until 1 August when once more she returned to BOAC and later operated her last flight for BOAC on 11 November 1962 between Accra and London as BA 288/059.

G-APLL was withdrawn from service by BOAC and mothballed at Marshall's of Cambridge from November 1962 and remained there until sold to BKS Air Transport Ltd, on 16 November 1965. G-APLL flew her last service for BKS on 21 February 1969 which involved a flight from London (Heathrow) Airport back to BKS's base at Newcastle.

Withdrawn from use, G-APLL was stored at Newcastle Airport in February 1969 and during September that year was broken up and scrapped, following a flying career of 20 159 hours and 7772 landings.

G-ANBG still in the hanger at Filton, wearing that 'superstitious' registration. (Peter R March)

G–ANBH

SERIES 100
Constructors No. 12909
Built at Filton
C of A: 25.5.56

VARIANT 102
Production No. 008
First flight 9.5.56

G-ANBH at London (Heathrow) wearing Nigeria Airways stickers. (Aviation Photo News)

Registered G-ANBH on 18 January 1956. Ordered by BOAC but retained by the manufacturers between May and September 1956 to establish the cause of the engine icing problems (see engine icing tests section). On completion of these tests, G-ANBH was flown to Shorts at Belfast for overhaul and modification, arriving at Weston Airways, Weston-Super-Mare for further modifications on 14 February 1957. Flown to London (Heathrow) Airport and accepted by BOAC on 24 July 1957.

Leased by Nigeria Airways in 1958, she returned to BOAC the same year and was withdrawn from service by BOAC. Flown to Marshall's of Cambridge for storage on 14 November 1962. Leased to BKS Air Transport Ltd on 10 March 1965 and flown to Southend. She was later purchased by them on 30 September 1965. G-ANBH operated her last service with BKS Air Transport Ltd, on 25 October 1968 when she flew from Newcastle to London (Heathrow) Airport.

Withdrawn from service in October 1968, by BKS, G-ANBH was stored at Southend Airport. Finally broken up and scrapped during September 1969, following a career of 21 148 flying hours and 7637 landings.

G-ANBH at Heathrow Airport. (Aviation Photo News)

G–ANBI

SERIES 100
Constructors No. 12910
Built at Filton
C of A: 28.6.56

VARIANT 102
Production No. 009
First flight 24.5.56

G-ANBI in the livery of BOAC at London (Heathrow) Airport. (Bristol Aeroplane Co Ltd/ British Aerospace)

Ordered by BOAC and delivered to London (Heathrow) Airport, on 29 June 1956 following modifications. While in service with BOAC, G-ANBI flew the first scheduled Britannia service from London (Heathrow) to Johannesburg on 1 February 1957 as BA 121/1.

Leased to Ghana Airways for a short time from April 1960, she returned to BOAC the same year; Malayan Airways leased her on 12th April 1962 until 9 May 1962, when she returned to BOAC.

G-ANBI operated her last flight for BOAC on 21 October 1962 as BA 164/121 between Nairobi and London. Withdrawn from service by BOAC and stored at Marshall's of Cambridge from 7 January 1963 until leased to Britannia Airways on 3 February 1966. G-ANBI was later purchased on 29 April 1966.

G-ANBI's last flight for Britannia Airways was 27 September 1969 after which she was withdrawn from service and scrapped in February 1970 at Luton Airport, following a career of 21 521 flying hours and 6146 landings.

G–ANBJ

SERIES 100
Constructors No. 12911
Built at Filton
C of A: 10.8.56

VARIANT 102
Production No. 011
First flight 5.8.56

Ordered by BOAC, G-ANBJ was initially used on a sales tour of North America and Canada by Bristol's from 12 August 1956. The aircraft covered approximately 24 000 miles during this mammoth tour which followed an impressive trans-Atlantic flight from London (Heathrow) to New York. As the

G-ANBJ outside BOAC's maintenance headquarters at London (Heathrow) minus titles. (Aviation Photo News)

tenth variant 102 Britannia, it was heralded as 'The world's largest, fastest, quietest jet-prop airliner', by the British press and the American public were urged to visit New York's Idlewild Airport to see for themselves this extraordinary aircraft. The initial flight between London and Montreal, Canada was covered in 10 hours and 44 minutes, which actually cut the normal flying time by 6 hours.

During the tour strong interest was shown by Capital Airlines, who ordered five series 300 but because of financial difficulties withdrew from their option. Northeast (USA) placed an order for five Britannia 300 series but again they too withdrew because of financial difficulties. The tour lasted 18 days and G-ANBJ returned on 30 August 1956.

September 1956 saw G-ANBJ employed by Bristol's at Filton for research into the engine icing problem lasting until December 1956, although offically on charge to BOAC from 23 November 1956. In early 1957 G-ANBJ was sent to Sydenham for modification to full production standard and who finally delivered to BOAC at London (Heathrow) Airport on 21 February 1957. G-ANBJ went on service with BOAC on 4 March 1957 as BA 708/1.

During service with BOAC, G-ANBJ was leased to Malayan Airways on 8 February until 7 March 1962. Leased again to Malayan Airways on 5 June 1962 until 4 July 1962. G-ANBJ operated her last service for BOAC on 1 October 1962 as BA 168/039 on a flight between Mauritius and London. Withdrawn from service G-ANBJ was flown to Marshall's of Cambridge for storage on 7 November 1962. She was to be purchased by Paraense Transportes Aeroes S.A. but was never taken up. Stored at London (Heathrow) from September 1963.

With the addition of a rear starboard door G-ANBJ was leased to Euravia in November 1964 and when Britannia Airways purchased her on 5 May 1965 she was painted in their new livery. Withdrawn from use by Britannia Airways and stored at Luton Airport and later scrapped during March 1971, following a career of 23 852 flying hours and 7798 landings.

G–ANBK

SERIES 100	VARIANT 102
Constructors No. 12912	Production No. 012
Built at Filton	First flight 14.9.56
C of A: 12.2.57	

G-ANBK in the original BKS livery. (Military Aircraft Photographs)

Stored at Filton from September 1956, Ordered by BOAC and delivered to London (Heathrow) Airport on 12 February 1957, taken on charge from 28 November 1956. On service from 2 March 1957, G-ANBK was operated during the flight as BA 704/55, following modifications at Filton.

Leased from BOAC by Nigerian Airways during 1961, and returned to BOAC in late 1961. Withdrawn from BOAC service following her last flight with them on 15 October 1962 as BA 132/014 on a flight from Salisbury to London. G-ANBK was flown to Marshall's of Cambridge for storage in November 1962.

On 17 March 1964 G-ANBK was leased to Airways Holidays Limited under a hire/purchase agreement and was flown by BKS Air Transport Limited on their behalf, delivery taking place on 11 April 1964. Withdrawn from use and stored during re-organisation from October 1969. BKS changed its name to Northeast Airlines (U.K.) and the new markings were applied on 1 November 1970, finally being purchased by them in April 1970.

On 31 December 1971 G-ANBK operated the last service by a Britannia aircraft for Northeast Airlines arriving at Newcastle after leaving London (Heathrow) Airport on what was also the last ever flight by a Bristol Britannia 102 variant.

Withdrawn from service G-ANBK was stored at Newcastle (Woolsington) in December 1971 and scrapped during July 1972, after a flying career of 25 008 hours and 10 827 landings.

G-ANBK in a hybrid livery incorporating BKS and British Air Services, seen at Newcastle in front of one of Dan Air's DC3. (Military Aircraft Photographs)

G–ANBL

SERIES 100	VARIANT 102
Constructors No. 12913	Production No. 014
Built at Filton	First flight 24.2.57
C of A: 1.3.57	

G-ANBL is seen in the lease markings of Southern Cross International who operated her from mid May to mid June 1970. (Andy Anderson)

Ordered by BOAC G-ANBL was first delivered to them at London (Heathrow) Airport on 2 March 1957, although officially she was on their books from 11 December 1956. During service with BOAC, G-ANBL was leased to Cathay Pacific Airways who operated her in BOAC's livery and registration but wearing Cathay Pacific's titles. Delivery to Cathay Pacific took place on 12 December 1960 and G-ANBL was operated under lease until 31 January 1961 when she was returned to BOAC.

BOAC withdrew G-ANBL from service in 1962, and in the November of that year she was ferried to Marshall's of Cambridge for storage, lease or sale. A purchase by the South American airline Paraense Transportes Aeroes S.A. did not materialise and G-ANBL was stored at London (Heathrow) Airport from September 1963.

In November 1964, Euravia Airways (later Britannia Airways) leased G-ANBL, although she never operated in Eurâvia markings and was painted in Britannia Airway's first livery following the airline's name change. Delivery to Britannia Airways took place on 26 June 1965. While in service with Britannia Airways, this aircraft was leased to the Australian airline Southern Cross International, and, wearing a similar livery to Britannia's, she was delivered on 20 May 1970, and operated until returning to Britannia Airways in mid-June the same year.

Britannia Airways purchased G-ANBL on 29 July 1970 and not long after she was withdrawn from service at Luton Airport and stored in December 1970. Finally G-ANBL was broken up and scrapped from July 1972, following 23 588 flying hours and 7790 landings.

G–ANBM

SERIES 100	VARIANT 102
Constructors No. 12914	Production No. 015
Built at Filton	First flight 6.3.57
C of A: 11.2.57	

G-ANBM in the livery of Sir Freddie Laker's airline Laker Airways. (Aviation Photo News)

Ordered by BOAC, G-ANBM was officially taken on charge on 19 December 1956 with delivery taking place at London (Heathrow) Airport on 11 March 1957. G-ANBM went into service on 16 March 1957 as BA 115/495 following modification work carried out at Cambridge.

Nigeria Airways leased G-ANBM for a short time during the period of October 1959 until early 1960 when she was returned to BOAC and again was operated like other BOAC

Britannias in the main livery of the owning company, with slight variations to the tail logos and stick on titles.

Another Far Eastern country to operate this particular aircraft was Malaya, and it was their airline, Malayan Airways, which next, took up a lease on G-ANBM. Delivery to Malayan Airways was on 15 November 1961 until 18 December the same year when she was returned to BOAC. Another lease period followed, when Malayan Airways again took delivery on 18 January 1962 until 7 February 1962. Returned to BOAC once again, Malayan Airways took out another lease on this aircraft from 25 September 1962 for a period of a month when BOAC had her returned to them on 24 October 1962.

BOAC withdrew G-ANBM from service in 1962, following her last service on 24 October when she returned to London (Heathrow) Airport operating as BA 991/027 on a flight between Hong Kong and London. She was placed at Cambridge for storage on 19 December 1962.

Laker Airways, took G-ANBM from Cambridge on lease and in their rather smart livery operated her from 8 April 1966. During service with Laker, G-ANBM was sub-leased to Air France on 29 July 1966 until 25 September when she was returned to Laker Airways.

Another sub-lease period followed when Treffield International operated G-ANBM from 29 April 1967 until 11 June the same year. During this period she was painted in Treffield's livery sporting a very large Union Jack on the tail fin.

Purchased by National Aero leasing on 19 January 1969 G-ANBM was re-registered as PK-ICA and sold to Indonesian Angkasa Civil Air Transport of which delivery took place on 11 February 1969.

Operated alongside G-ANBN, which was re-registered PK-ICB, this aircraft was finally withdrawn from use at Jakarta, Indonesia in June 1970 and broken up for scrap in December 1971.

G–ANBN

SERIES 100	VARIANT 102
Constructors No. 12915	Production No. 016
Built at Filton	First flight 11.4.57
C of A: 3.5.57	

Ordered by BOAC, G-ANBN was delivered to them at London (Heathrow) Airport on 4 May 1957 as one of fifteen variant 102 Britannia aircraft and entered service on 31 May as BA 121/18.

G-ANBN was chartered for the first ever Royal flight to be operated by the Bristol Britannia, when she was used to convey Her Majesty the Queen Mother to South Africa on 1 June 1957.

G-ANBN was chartered by many airlines such as East African Airways Corporation, during 1958, returning to BOAC the same year. Nigeria Airways leased her on 1 October 1960 returning to BOAC in 1961, Malayan Airways operated G-ANBN on lease from BOAC from 8 March until 11 April 1962. Malayan Airways leased G-ANBN once more, from 28 August until 26 September 1962 after which she returned to BOAC. The final lease period for Malayan Airways was between 23 October and 21 November 1962 when she also flew her last service as 991/028 on a flight from Hong Kong to London after which G-ANBN was returned to BOAC and withdrawn from service.

Flown to Marshall's of Cambridge on 16 January 1963, G-ANBN was stored and mothballed until Laker Airways leased her from 21 April 1966. Laker then sub-leased G-ANBN to Air Carriers of Zambia on 16 November 1967 until 23 January 1968. Monarch Airlines of Luton Airport, leased G-ANBN during 1968 from Laker Airways. Another Luton based airline, Britannia Airways operated her on lease from Laker Airways, from 16 April to Laker on 17 October 1968.

Purchased by National Aero Leasing on 21 January 1969 she was re-registered PK-ICB for Indonesia Angkasa Civil Air Transport, with delivery taking place on 11 February 1969. PK-ICB was subsequently stored at Jakarta, Indonesia from June 1970 and broken up for scrap in December 1971.

PK-ICB ex G-ANBN in Indonesian Angkasa Civil Air Transport livery. (Peter J Bish)

G-ANBN at London (Heathrow) wearing the lease markings for East African Airways Corporation. (Aviation Photo News)

G–ANBO

SERIES 100	VARIANT 102
Constructors No. 12916	Production No. 017
Built at Filton	First flight 17.5.57
C of A: 31.5.57	

Ordered by BOAC, G-ANBO was the last variant 102 built and her delivery to BOAC at London (Heathrow) Airport took place on 31 May 1957. On 18 June 1957 she commenced operations with BOAC as BA 115/522. BOAC leased G-ANBO to Cathay Pacific Airways from on 12 December 1960 to 11 January 1961. During the lease period, only Cathay Pacific Airways titles were worn in place of the BOAC titling and the speedbird emblem was removed from the tail fin.

Malayan Airways operated G-ANBO on lease from 1 September until 18 October 1961, and following a brief return to BOAC was leased to East African Airways Corporation during late 1961. Once returned to BOAC she was again leased by Malayan Airways from 31 July 1962 for a month until 29 August 1962. G-ANBO was withdrawn from service by BOAC following her last flight on 14 October 1962, operating as BA 164/120 between Nairobi and London.

G-ANBO was ferried to Marshall's of Cambridge on 10 December 1962 for storage. G-ANBO remained mothballed at Cambridge until interest was shown by Euravia Airways who leased her on 4 January 1965 and, with the addition of an extra starboard rear emergency door, Britannia Airways as they became known, purchased G-ANBO on 16 March 1970.

G-ANBO operated her last flight for Britannia Airways on 15 October 1970 and following her landing at Luton Airport was withdrawn from service. G-ANBO was later broken up for scrap during May 1971. She had completed 24 517 hours flying and 7506 landings.

G-ANBO outside the hangar at London with a new top coat and the BOAC livery removed. (Aviation Photo News)

G-ANBO the last of the variant 102 Britannias built, in Cathay Pacific Airways livery albeit lease markings. (Aviation Photo News)

PART FOUR

Bristol Britannia Series 250 Specifications

VARIANTS: 252 (Britannia C Mk2 in RAF service).
253 (Britannia C Mk1 in RAF service).
Built to Ministry of Supply specification C.176P.

Note: Once withdrawn from RAF service and the aircraft had been civilianised, they were designated as 252F and 253F respectively.

POWERPLANT: Four Bristol Proteus 765 turbo-props developing 4400ehp (initially in RAF variant 252), driving four-blade Duralumin round-tipped propellers.

POWERPLANT: Four Bristol Proteus 255 turbo-props (military version of Proteus 765), driving four-blade Duralumin round-tipped propellers, developing approximately 4400ehp but with additional water injection to offset reductions in engine performance under certain conditions e.g. high altitude.

DIMENSIONS:	Wingspan	142ft. 3.5in.
	Overall length	124ft. 3in.
	Height	37ft. 6in.
	Wing area	2075sq. ft.

PAYLOAD & PERFORMANCE: Variant 252, Still air range, maximum payload (33 100lb) over 4268 statute miles at 355 mph.

Still air range, maximum fuel (including reserves) 5334 statute miles at a cruising speed of 355mph with 21 724lb payload.

Variant 253, Still air range, maximum payload (37 400lb) over 4268 statute miles at 360mph.

Still air range, maximum fuel (including reserves) over 5334 statute miles at a cruising speed of 357mph with 26 024lb payload.

PASSENGER ACCOMMODATION: Up to 139 passengers. 53 stretchers, 6 medical attendants and 2 iron lungs. Air Ambulance role.

FUEL CAPACITY: 8580 imperial gallons. (Avtur, Avcat, or Avtag.)

WEIGHTS: Variant 252. Empty 94 900lb. All up weight (including fuel) 185 000lb.
Variant 253. Empty 90 600lb. All up weight (including fuel) 185 000lb.

CARGO SPACE: 5850 cu. ft. (252)
6120 cu. ft. (253)

Total Built: Variant 252. 3
Variant 253. 20

Total 23 series 250

Note: The Variant 252 was basically a mixed freight/passenger aircraft. It differs from the Series 310 in having a forward freight loading door measuring 74.5in. by 93in. and a strengthened forward fuselage floor. The Variant 253 is also fitted with the same door and is essentially a cargo transport, built to RAF requirements but can also be used for troop carrying and Medi-vac.

The Bristol Britannia in RAF service

The Bristol Britannia in RAF service was operated by two squadrons, numbers 99 and 511. These squadrons previously operated Handley Page Hastings transport aircraft and prior to these the Avro York.

Based at RAF Lyneham, Wilts, the Britannia was accepted by both squadrons and were operated by each until central servicing of the aircraft had been established. Following central servicing arrangements the Britannias were pooled, in a similar way to a civilian airline being operated jointly by crews of both squadrons. Pooling of the Britannia squadrons commenced in September 1960, at RAF Lyneham and the system remained until the Britannia fleet was moved to RAF Brize Norton, Oxon, in January 1970.

Once the fleet had left RAF Lyneham, the base was then used to house the RAF Hercules transport aircraft, becoming the Hercules' main base.

RAF Brize Norton had already been accommodating a Britannia derivative in the shape of the Short Belfast, formally known as the Bristol 195. The aircraft was originally ordered to the amount of 12 aircraft but reduced to 10. Operated by 53 Squadron, the Belfast operated alongside the VC10 transport fleet of 10 Squadron, also based at Brize Norton.

The central servicing system was retained for the Britannias at RAF Brize Norton and the pooling of both squadrons continued. Following the reduction in the need for a strategic airlift capability, the Britannia fleet was disbanded in the mid 1970s and together with the Comet and Belfast squadrons were removed from the RAF fleet.

The Britannias were stored at both RAF Kemble and St Athan, and later either sold or leased to civilian operators, who obtained these aircraft in new paint schemes albeit RAF livery, and extremely low flying hours. In fact they were a good buy for many companies who intended using these aircraft for freight operations and for spares.

In the following histories each aircraft tells its own story, whether they flew in civilian service or were just broken up for spares. Either way following their de-mobbing, the ex-RAF Britannias were the mainstay of the type which brought aircraft nearer to its 40th anniversary.

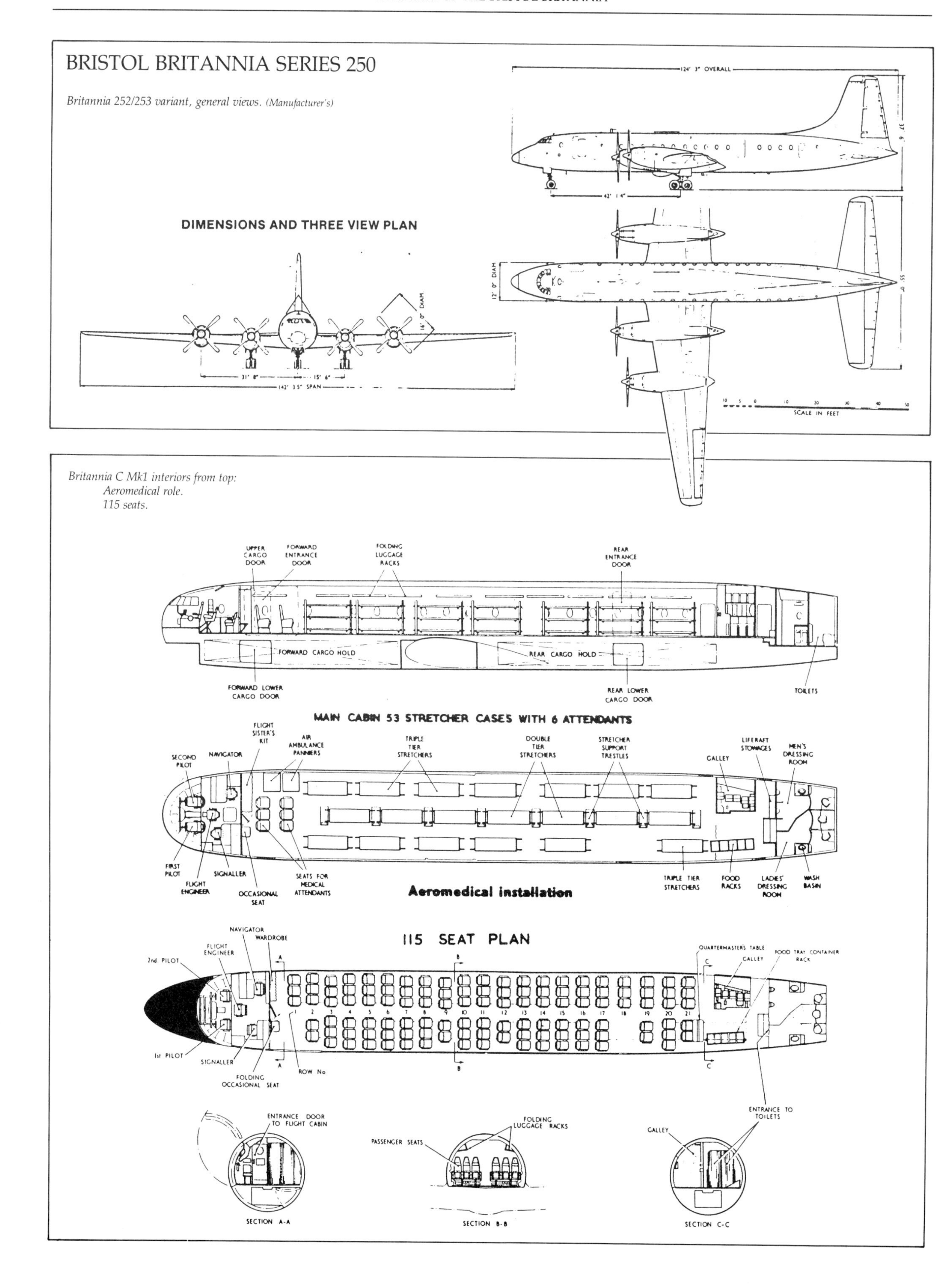

BRISTOL BRITANNIA SERIES 250

Britannia 252/253 variant, general views. (Manufacturer's)

Britannia C Mk1 interiors from top:
Aeromedical role.
115 seats.

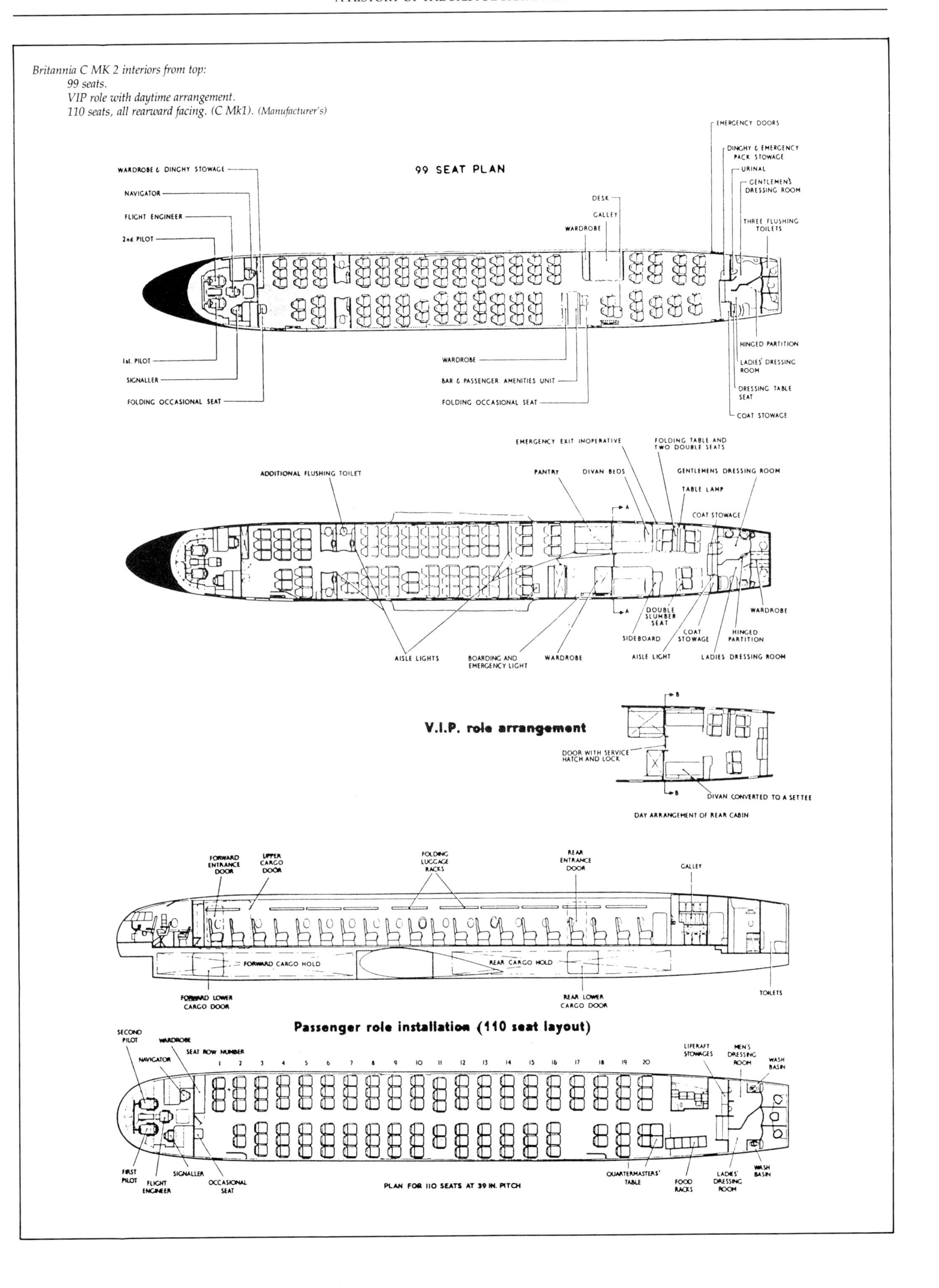

Britannia C MK 2 interiors from top:
99 seats.
VIP role with daytime arrangement.
110 seats, all rearward facing. (C Mk1). (*Manufacturer's*)

G–APPE

SERIES 250
Constructors No. 13450
Built at Belfast
C of A: 10.11.58

VARIANT 252/Cmk2
Production No. 001
First flight 13.10.58

G-APPE the first variant 252 seen at London (Heathrow). (Aviation Photo News)

Built to contract 11804 for the Ministry of Supply, dated February 1955. Officially on Ministry of Supply charge from 9 November 1958 and delivered via Filton on 12th November 1958.

G-APPE carried spare parts for G-ANBC to Rangoon in record time on 13th March 1959, operating in civil markings. Royal Air Force Transport Command colours were applied in late March 1959, serialled XN-392 she was named 'Acrux'. Evaluated by A&AEE Boscombe Down until 24 May 1959, she was damaged by salt spray at Belfast, causing her return to Filton for repairs to underside of fuselage and wings. Delivered to RAFTC No.99 Squadron at RAF Lyneham on 27 October 1959 she was operated within Nos. 99 and 511 Squadrons' Britannia pool at RAF Lyneham from 29 March 1961. Withdrawn from service and stored at Baginton, Coventry from December 1975, XN-392 had flown 12 652 hours and made 10 380 landings whilst in service with the RAF by the end of December 1975.

Purchased by Aer Turas Teorante on 18 December 1975 she was broken up and scrapped during April and May 1976 after operation by City Airways fell through.

XN-392 a variant C Mk.2 of Royal Air Force Air Support Command, at RAF Lyneham. (Aviation Photo News)

G–APPF

SERIES 250
Constructors No. 13451
Built at Belfast
C of A: 14.1.59

VARIANT 252/Cmk2
Production No. 002
First flight 7.12.58

9Q-CPX at London (Heathrow) Airport in the markings of Domaine de Katale. (Aviation Photo News)

Built to contract 11804 for the Ministry of Supply, dated February 1955. Registered G-APPF. Later painted in Royal Air Force Transport Command colours and serialled XN-398, she was named 'Altair'. Officially handed over on 19 March 1959 to No. 99 Squadron RAF. Used within the Britannia pool at RAF Lyneham from 17 May 1961.

Withdrawn from RAF service and ferried to RAF St Athan on 25 April 1975 for storage and eventual re-sale. Purchased by Euroworld and flown to Stansted Airport on 11 September 1975 for overhaul by Aviation Traders Engineering limited.

Purchased in February 1977 by Zaire Aero Service, and registered 9Q-CPX she was operated by Domaine de Katale in November 1977 before being returned to Zaire Aero Service. Again to Domaine de Katale and finally back to Katale Aero Transport before being withdrawn from service and stored. Whilst owned by Katale Aero Transport, the VIP area was retained at the rear of the aircraft and used by Katale's owner Herbert Van Orerburg. At the end of March 1981, 9Q-CPX had flown 14 211.31 hours and made 10 482 landings. Now No longer in service, January 1991, and later scrapped, in Goma, Zaire.

G–APPG

SERIES 250
Constructors No. 13452
Built at Belfast
C of A: 26.3.59

VARIANT 252/Cmk2
Production No. 003
First flight 3.3.59

Built to Contract 11804 to provide the Ministry of Supply with 3 Britannia Aircraft, dated February 1955. G-APPG's first

XN-404 the last Britannia 252, outside BOAC's maintenance headquarters in Transport Command livery. (Aviation Photo News)

flight was on 2 March 1959 in civil markings. Operated by A&AEE Boscombe Down for evaluation purposes from 8 April 1959. Early April 1959 she was painted in Royal Air Force Transport Command markings, serialled XN-404. Allocated to No. 99 Squadron on 6 April 1959, she was named 'Canopus'. In RAF service the series 252 was known as the C Mk2. She was pooled at RAF Lyneham on 27 February 1961.

Withdrawn from RAF use on 17 July 1975, XN-404 was ferried to RAF St Athan for storage and re-sale. Purchased by Shackleton Aviation on 17 December 1975 she was flown to Hurn Airport the same day. Air Faisal were to purchase XN-404 after its delivery to Luton Airport, but this never took took place. XN-404 totalled 13 865 flyings hours and had carried out 9862 landings.

During November 1976, XN-404 was broken up and scrapped on behalf of Air Faisal.

XL–635

SERIES 250	VARIANT 253/Cmk1
Constructors No. 13397	Production No. 001
Built at Belfast	First flight 29.12.59

XL-635 in an interesting artists impression, wearing a variation of the RAFTC livery that was not borne. (Bristol Aeroplane Co Ltd/British Aerospace)

Built to contract 12829. Suffering from corrosion of the underside and wings caused by salt spray whilst at Queens Island, Belfast, XL-635 was not delivered until a protective covering was developed to seal the damaged skinning. She was retained at Belfast until January 1960, although spending some time at A&AEE Boscombe Down for pre-service trials. Finally delivered to Royal Air Force Transport Command No. 99 Squadron on 30 January 1960, she was named 'Bellatrix' and operated with the Britannia pool at RAF Lyneham from 22 December 1960. In January 1970 the two Britannia squadrons were transferred to RAF Brize Norton, Oxfordshire, and all the Royal Air Force's Britannia aircraft were operated from there, within 99 and 511 Squadrons.

She was withdrawn from service and ferried to RAF St Athan for storage and re-sale on 9 June 1975. Purchased by Young Cargo on 5 September 1975, XL-635 was flown to Stansted Airport and registered OO-YCA on 11th September 1975. She was painted in full livery and flown to Gosselies, Belgium in October 1975, returning to Stansted in 1977.

Withdrawn from use, her engines used for spares, OO-YCA was finally broken up and scrapped in July 1977 after a career of 20 268.20 flying hours and 6859 landings.

OO-YCA in Young Air Cargo livery, minus powerplant. (Aircraft Photographic)

XL–636

SERIES 250	VARIANT 253/Cmk1
Constructors No. 13398	Production No. 002
Built at Belfast	First flight 23.4.59

XL-636 in the final livery worn in RAF service, next to one of No.10 Squadron's VC 10 aircraft at RAF Brize Norton. (Aviation Photo News)

Built to contract 12829 and delivered to Royal Air Force Transport Command on 4 June 1959, allocated to No. 99 Squadron, serialled XL-636 she was named 'Argo'. She operated within the Britannia pool at RAF Lyneham from 2 November 1960 and was withdrawn from service and flown to RAF Kemble for storage on 22 December 1975.

Registered OO-YCE from 23 February 1976, she was purchased by Young Air Cargo on 6 May 1976 and flown to Stansted Airport the same day. On 13 May 1976 OO-YCE was flown to Brussels and after short service with Young Cargo, OO-YCE was withdrawn from use and stored at Ostend, Belgium in December 1977 with 17 958 flying hours and 7918 landings to her credit.

Broken up and scrapped at Ostend, Belgium during August 1978.

XL-637

SERIES 250	VARIANT 253/Cmk1
Constructors No. 13399	Production No. 003
Built at Belfast	First flight 12.5.59

XL-637 in open storage at RAF Kemble. (Military Aircraft Photographs)

Built to contract 12829, and delivered to Royal Air Force Transport Command on 26 June 1959, she was serialled XL-637 and named 'Vega'. She was taken on charge by No. 99 Squadron from 28 June 1959 and operated within the Britannia pool at RAF Lyneham from 9 September 1960.

Once withdrawn from RAF service, XL-637 was flown to RAF Kemble for storage on 30 December 1975. By the end of December 1975, she had flown 18 673.45 hours and made 8243 landings. She was purchased by Captain J.de Bry on 8 March 1976, and on 7 May 1976 XL-637 was re-positioned at Southend for conversion to a variant 253F for civilian use by Aviation Traders Limited for operation by Young Air Cargo.

Purchased by Young Air Cargo and operated as OO-YCH until leased to Liberia World Airways in August 1977 she was allocated the registration EL-LWH.

OO-YCH was returned to Young Air Cargo in September 1977 and flown to Manston, Kent. Withdrawn from service on 2 December 1978. Purchased by Domaine de Katale on 27 April 1979, she was registered 9Q-CKG and flown to Ostend, Belgium. After flying to Goma, Kivu in Zaire, 9Q-CKG was re-registered 9Q-CBT and stored. Reportedly withdrawn from use and broken up. Now confirmed in early 1992.

XL-638

SERIES 250	VARIANT 253/Cmk1
Constructors No. 13400	Production No. 004
Built at Belfast	First flight 22.6.59

XL-638 the only Britannia lost during RAF service, still sporting black propeller blades. (Peter R March)

Ordered by the Royal Air Force in November 1955 and built to contract 12829, this aircraft was delivered to 99 squadron Royal Air Force Transport Command on 5 August 1959 and once taken on charge on 7 August was serialled XL-638, named 'Sirius', designated a C Mk1. Following the pooling of 99 and 511 Squadrons Britannia fleet at RAF Lyneham, Wiltshire, XL-638 was operated within the pool from 30 June 1960.

XL-638 disgraced herself on 12 October 1967 when she overran the runway whilst landing at RAF Khormaksar, Aden. Unfortunately she was damaged beyond repair and written off. Thankfully no lives were lost and the Bristol Britannia in RAF service kept her unblemished record... apart from this little episode!

Because of her close proximity to the runway following her accident, it was decided to remove the tail section by an extreme measure – it was blown off! XL-638 had flown 9371.30 hours and made 3700 landings.

XL-639

SERIES 250	VARIANT 253/Cmk1
Constructors No. 13448	Production No. 005
Built at Belfast	First flight 28.8.59

Built to contract 12829, her maiden flight was from Belfast on 28 August 1959 and she was delivered to No.99 Squadron Royal Air Force Transport Command on 8 October 1959.

EI-BDC parked on the apron at Luton Airport next to 9G-ACE, ex XM-520. (Aircraft Photographic)

Serialled XL-639 she was named 'Atria'. During her service and like all other RAF Britannia's, XL-639 wore the titles Royal Air Force Transport Command, Royal Air Force Air Support Command and finally Royal Air Force, on the upper part of her fuselage. She operated within the Britannia pool at RAF Lyneham from 12 October 1960.

Withdrawn from service on 23 October 1974 she was stored at RAF Kemble. After purchase by the Guinness Peat Aviation Company on 10 February 1976, her RAF markings were painted out. She was withdrawn from service after a few months at Stansted Airport, Essex in May 1976. The Irish registration EI-BDC was applied at Stansted Airport. EI-BDC never saw active service for Guinness Peat and was sold to Airline Engineering of Luton on 10 February 1977.

She was leased by Aer Turas and operated without titles from 18 June 1977. Sub-leased to Cyprus Airways on 19 June 1977 returning to Aer Turas on 5 July 1977, and back to Airline Engineering in September 1977. Cyprus Airways leased EI-BDC from 17 September 1977 returning her to Airline Engineering on 8 October 1977. She went back to Cyprus Airways in October 1977 returning on 7 November 1977.

Purchased by Eurafric on 20 January 1978 she was operated by them until purchased by Redcoat Air Cargo on 4 June 1978. Painted in full livery and registered G-BRAC, she was named 'Christian'. Working with G-AOVS, these two Britannias were seen regularly in the BBC Television series 'Buccaneer'. During the series the livery remained the same except for a title change to 'Redair'. At the end of June 1978, G-BRAC had made a total of 7617 landings and flew 19 016.08 hours.

On a return flight from Boston to Shannon on 16 February 1980, G-BRAC was lost on take-off in severe icing conditions, near Billerica, Mass, killing six of the seven people on board.

G-BRAC ex XL-639 in flight in the livery of Redcoat Air Cargo Ltd, who tragically lost her on 16 February 1980. (Military Aircraft Photographs)

XL–640

SERIES 250	VARIANT 253/Cmk1
Constructors No. 13449	Production No. 006
Built at Belfast	First flight 8.10.59

EI-BCI 'Rhino One' at Luton Airport, a variant 253F. (Flightlines International)

Built to contract 12829 her first flight was from Belfast on 8 October 1959 and delivered to No. 511 Squadron Royal Air Force Transport Command on 30 October 1959. Serialled XL-640 and named 'Antares', this aircraft, along with all twenty series 253 Britannias was designated a C.Mk1 whilst in RAF service. She operated within the Britannia pool at RAF Lyneham from 16 January 1961.

Withdrawn from service she was stored at RAF Kemble from 3 September 1975 with 17 359 hours and 7669 landings to her credit by the end of September 1975. She was purchased by Monarch Airlines of Luton on 13 January 1976 and stored at Coventry. She was later ferried to Luton Airport in September 1976 after purchase by Aer Turas fell through. Painted in the markings of Eurafric carrying a Rhino on the tail logo, she was known by the chaps at Airline Engineering as 'Rhino One'. Never operated by Eurafric, she exited the paintshop on 2 March 1977 registered EI-BCI for Aer Turas on 4 April 1977 and was leased by them from 31 March 1978. She returned to Eurafric on 10 April 1978. She was leased again by Aer Turas from 25 May 1978 until 6 September 1978 when she returned once again to Eurafric.

After a long spell at Luton Airport, Redcoat Air Cargo leased EI-BCI, repainted her in their livery (not very different

G-BHAU in a lovely night shot with Readcoat Air Cargo Ltd. (Peter J Bish)

from Eurafric), registered G-BHAU and called her 'Amy'. She was accepted by them on 13 August 1979. In service with Redcoat Air Cargo Ltd by the end of March 1981 G-BHAU's flying hours had increased to 20 563.05 and her landings 8469. Purchased by Swordvale Aviation Limited on 2 December 1981 she was operated by Redcoat between Forli, Italy and Nigeria carrying cattle.

Purchased by Katale Aero Transport in April 1982 and registered 9Q-CHU she was later withdrawn from service and stored at Kinshasa, Zaire and broken up for scrap in 1986.

XL-657

SERIES 250	VARIANT 253/Cmk1
Constructors No. 13454	Production No. 007
Built at Belfast	First flight 23.11.59

Ordered by the Royal Air Force in December 1956, and built to contract 12829 this aircraft was delivered to No. 511 Squadron Royal Air Force Transport Command, serialled XL-657 named 'Rigel'. Delivery to the Royal Air Force took place on 23 December 1959, she was transferred to the Britannia pool at RAF Lyneham, Wiltshire on 24 February 1961 and was operated by both 99 and 511 Squadrons Royal Air Force.

Following the disbandment of the Britannia fleets due to government cut backs, XL-657 was withdrawn from service on 13 August 1975 and flown to RAF St Athan for storage. The total of her flying hours with the RAF was 18 781, and XL-657 had carried out 8437 landings.

Purchased by Monarch Airlines of Luton on 31 December 1975 she was flown to their base at Luton Airport and following an overhaul and minor repaint was then flown on to Kigali Airport, Rwanda on 10 March 1976 following

XL-657 named 'RIGEL' on the ramp at RAF Lyneham, Wilts. (Military Aircraft Photographs)

purchase by Center Air Afrique. The registration 9U-BAD was allocated on 5 March.

Barely a year later 9U-BAD was impounded for the non-payment of overdue debts and withdrawn from service at Charleroi, Belgium on 25 February 1977. 9U-BAD was later broken up and scrapped.

9U-BAD ex XL-657 with Centre Air Afrique. (Flightlines International)

XL-658

SERIES 250
Constructors No. 13455
Built at Belfast

VARIANT 253/Cmk1
Production No. 008
First flight 3.12.59

EI-BBY in the livery of the Intercontinental Meat Company Ltd. (Flightlines International)

Built to contract 12829, and delivered to RAF Transport Command on 4 February 1960. She was allocated to No. 511 Squadron, serialled XL-658, and named 'Adhara'. She was used within the Britannia pool at RAF Lyneham. Withdrawn from use by the RAF, XL-658 was stored at RAF Kemble in January 1975 until purchased by Airline Engineering of Luton on 26 May 1976.

Registered EI-BBY on 18 June 1976 and delivered to the Intercontinental Meat Company, in the markings of Interconair at Hurn, on 10 August 1976, named 'Deirdre'. Her career was short lived. Whilst approaching Shannon Airport on 30 September 1977, en-route to collect livestock, EI-BBY crash-landed and caught fire. Everyone aboard escaped without injury and a month later in October 1977, EI-BBY was broken up and scrapped following a career which totalled 20 205.49 flying hours and 8547 landings.

EI-BBY following her downfall at Shannon. (Andy Anderson)

XL-659

SERIES 250
Constructors No. 13456
Built at Belfast

VARIANT 253/Cmk1
Production No. 009
First flight 1.2.60

XL-659 in the original Transport Command livery following her acceptance and is still sporting black propellers. (Aviation Photo News)

Built to contract 12829, she was delivered to No. 511 Squadron RAF Transport Command on 4 March 1960, and named 'Polaris', serialled XL-659. Operated within the Britannia pool at RAF Lyneham, between 99 and 511 Squadrons, later at RAF Brize Norton until withdrawn from service and ferried to RAF St Athan on 14 May 1975. A total of 19 051.40 hours were flown and 8054 landings made during her service with the RAF.

Purchased by Young Air Cargo, XL-659 was flown to Stansted Airport on 5 September 1975, and registered OO-YCB two weeks later. In the colours of Young Cargo wearing a revised red cheatline with all RAF insignia removed, she first appeared outside the hanger on 12 January 1976. March 1976 saw OO-YCB wearing 'In Co-operation with Liberia World Airlines' stickers.

Flown to Ostend, Belgium in late August 1976, OO-YCB was used as a source of spares for Young's fleet of Britannias. OO-YCB was scrapped at Ostend, in December 1977 following a career of 19 600.49 hours and 8245 landings in total.

OO-YCB was one of 9 Britannia aircraft owned by the Belgian airline, Young Air Cargo. (Aviation Photo News)

XL–660

SERIES 250	VARIANT 253/Cmk1
Constructors No. 13457	Production No. 010
Built at Belfast	First flight 4.3.60

XL-660 in the markings of Trans Gulf Air Cargo, seen at Luton. (Ron "Ginge" Giblin)

Built to contract 12829, for six aircraft, later increased to ten. She was delivered to No. 511 Squadron Royal Air Force Transport Command on 23 April 1960, serialled XL-660 named 'Alphard'. She transferred to No.99 Squadron on 1 May 1960 and pooled in September of the same year at RAF Lyneham.

Withdrawn from RAF service in January 1976, XL-660 was stored at RAF Kemble with 19 158.15 hours and 8495 landings to her credit until purchased by Air Faisal on 14 May 1976 and previously flown to Luton Airport on 11 May 1976. (It is of interest to note that this aircraft carried the titles 'Air Faisel' but then it was changed to 'Air Faisal' – could this have been a spelling mistake or a change of name?). Painted in the markings of Transgulf Air Cargo during May 1976 but never flown in these markings. The markings were removed on 6 February 1977. Registered G-BEMZ on 11 February 1977 for U.M. Patel, who were trading as Air Faisal, and named 'Al Medina', joining XM-490 (G-BDLZ) on flights between Bombay and Dubai, after delivery to Baghdad in late February.

G-BEMZ was impounded by H.M. Customs and Excise in August 1979 for suspected drug smuggling. With an expired Certificate of Airworthiness she was sold by H. M. Customs and Excise to T. F. Richter and Company Ltd, on 13 September 1979, trading as Gaylan Air Cargo.

She was financed by Black Arrow Leasing Ltd on 14 February 1980 and leased to Gaylan Air Cargo on 4 September 1980 registered A6-HMS, and re-registered G-BEMZ on 3 April 1980. At the end of March 1981, this aircraft had flown 21 480.37 hours and made 9058 landings. Redcoat Air Cargo leased G-BEMZ and operated her on behalf of Dantana from 22 September 1981 for the Forli and Kano cattle flights until she was purchased by Swordvale Aviation Limited on 2 December 1981. Sold to Katale Aero Transport in November 1982, she was registered 9Q-CGP and named 'Mandefu'. After being withdrawn from use she was reportedly broken up. Confirmed in early 1992.

A6-HMS in the livery of Gaylan Air Cargo. (Aviation Photo News)

G-BEMZ with Air Faisal, a variant 253F, seen at London (Heathrow). (Aviation Photo News)

9Q-CGP following purchase by Katale Aero Transport. (Aviation Photo News)

XM–489

SERIES 250	VARIANT 253/Cmk1
Constructors No. 13434	Production No. 011
Built at Belfast	First flight 7.4.60

XM-489 lowering her undercarriage. (Peter R March)

Built to contract 14293 and ordered by the Royal Air Force, this aircraft was delivered to Royal Air Force Transport Command, allocated to No. 511 Squadron, serialled as XM-489 named 'Denebola'. Delivery took place on 4 May 1960 at RAF Lyneham. Like the other Britannia aircraft within RAF service this one operated out of the Britannia Pool at RAF Lyneham from September 1960.

Following XM-489's withdrawal from service in September 1975, she was ferried to RAF Kemble where she remained in open storage until sold to the Belgian firm, Young Air Cargo on 10 February 1976. During service with the RAF she had flown 19 243 hours and carried out 8316 landings by the end of September 1975.

This aircraft had a very short civilian life. After being allocated the registration OO-YCC, and re-positioned to the Belgian company's base at Gosselies, OO-YCC was not operated by Young Air Cargo, instead used primarily as a source of spares for their other airworthy Britannia aircraft. OO-YCC was finally broken up for scrap during 1978.

XM-489 at RAF Kemble wearing the young Air Cargo registration OO-YCC. 'Who pinched the wheels?' (Military Aircraft Photographs)

XM–490

SERIES 250	VARIANT 253/Cmk1
Constructors No. 13435	Production No. 012
Built at Belfast	First flight 16.5.60

XN-490 gleaming in the sunshine at RAF Lyneham. (Andy Anderson)

Built to contract 14293 and delivered to Royal Air Force Transport Command at RAF Lyneham on 8 June 1960, allocated to No. 511 Squadron, she was serialled XM-490 and named 'Alderbaran'. This aircraft was transferred to the Britannia pool on 7 November 1960.

Withdrawn from RAF service in August 1975, XM-490 was ferried to RAF St Athan on 13 August 1975 for storage with a total of 18 673 hours and 8637 landings to her credit.

Purchased by Euroworld on 29 October 1975, she was flown to Luton Airport the next day before flying on to Stansted Airport the following day. Allocated the registration G-BDLZ when purchased on 17 November 1975 by U.M. Patel and M.I. Raj, G-BDLZ was operated in their company name of Air Faisal. The livery was applied 'around the old' RAF livery and she was named 'Al Mubarak'. She was operated together with G-BEMZ (ex-XL-660) between Bombay and Dubai.

Leased to Air Works, India in December 1976, G-BDLZ was returned to Air Faisal in early September, 1977. Both of Air Faisal's Britannias were immobilized due to drug smuggling allegations in early August 1978 and by the end of August 1978, G-BDLZ had flown a total of 22 306.48 hours and carried out 9437 landings.

G-BDLZ was withdrawn from use at Luton in May 1979 and broken up during September 1979.

XM–491

SERIES 250	VARIANT 253/Cmk1
Constructors No. 13436	Production No. 013
Built at Belfast	First flight 16.6.60

XM-491 on approach to RAF Lyneham. (Andy Anderson)

Built to contract 14293 and delivered to No. 511 Squadron Royal Air Force Transport Command on 6 July 1960, she was named 'Procyon' and serialled XM-491. She operated within the Britannia pool at RAF Lyneham from 15 May 1961.

XM-491 was withdrawn from service by the RAF, XM-491 was ferried to RAF St Athan on 9 June 1975 for storage following a flying career of 18 077.30 hours and 7717 landings.

Purchased on 8 September 1975 by Aer Turas of Ireland and delivered to Luton Airport, she was given the registration EI-BBH, and named 'City of Cork'. She entered service with them on 28 October 1975. EI-BBH was leased by Cyprus Airways on 9 September 1976 and returned on 12 April 1978; by the end of that month, she had accumulated a total of 22 330.04 hours and 9038 landings. Leased by Gemini Air Transport from 23 March 1979 until 23 May 1979 when she was returned to Aer Turas.

G-BDLZ at Luton Airport in Air Faisal livery, but without a tail logo. (Andy Anderson)

EI-BBH ex-XM-491 owned by Aer Turas and leased to Cyprus Airways, seen at Luton Airport about to unload freight. (Tony Furlong)

EI-BBH was purchased by Katale Aero Transport from November 1981, and registered 9Q-CMO in the name of Transair Cargo (a subsidery of Katale). No longer in service and possibly broken up. Confirmed in early 1992.

XM–496

SERIES 250	VARIANT 253/Cmk1
Constructors No. 13508	Production No. 014
Built at Belfast	First flight 24.8.60
C of A: 20.5.76	

G-BDUP as a variant 253F with Afrek Ltd. (Flightlines International)

Built as part of contract 15527, and delivered to the Royal Air Force Transport Command at RAF Lyneham on 17 September 1960, serialled XM-496 and named 'Regulus'. She was taken on RAFTC charge from 19 September 1960 and used within the Britannia pool from her acceptance.

XM-496 was withdrawn from RAF use on 27 October 1975 and stored at RAF Kemble with 18 413.45 hours and 8122 landings to her credit. XM-496 was purchased by Monarch Airline's Airline Engineering on 6 January 1976. Converted at Luton by Airline Engineering to 253F configuration and registered G-BDUP on 31 March 1976, and two weeks later she was painted in the livery of Afrek Ltd, who purchased her on 21 May 1976 and was delivered to them in Athens on 6 June 1976 with a private C of A. Later withdrawn from use and stored in Athens, Greece.

Purchased by Monarch Aircraft Engineering Ltd on 30 July 1984 and ferried to Luton for overhaul, then sold to the Cuban Airline, AeroCaribbean, in August 1984. She was painted in their full livery, and registered CU-T120. CU-T120 operated her last flight on 21 March 1990 (thereby ending all Cuban Britannia operations). While flying between Peru and Havana, No. 4 engine was shut down, an emergency declared, and a landing at Guayaquil, Ecuador made. The following day a three-engined ferry was organised and on arrival at Havana, Cuba she was grounded due to lack of spares and has never flown since. Currently still in existence, early 1992.

XM–497

SERIES 250	VARIANT 253/Cmk1
Constructors No. 13509	Production No. 015
Built at Belfast	First flight 17.11.60

XM-497 in the early Transport Command livery and as yet un-named. (Bristol Aeroplane Co Ltd/British Aerospace)

Built to contract 15527, this aircraft was delivered to RAF Transport Command on 2 December 1960 at the Britannia pool at RAF Lyneham, and operated jointly by 99 and 511 Squadrons. Serialled XM-497 she was named 'Schedar'.

The last Britannia to be built at Belfast, XM-497 was also the 'last' Britannia built, excluding the Canadian derivatives. Once withdrawn from RAF service, XM-497 was flown to RAF Kemble on 9 December 1975 for storage following a flying career of 18 177.30 hours and 7215 landings.

Purchased by Young Air Cargo on 23 April 1976, and registered OO-YCF on 5 May 1976. She was transferred to Stansted Airport, Essex on 7 May 1977. Following the removal of the RAF insignia, the titles Young Cargo were applied above the cabin windows and the cheatline was repainted red, minus the flash by the nose section, but on the tail fin the number 497 and fin insignia remained.

Remaining at Stansted, '497', (OO-YCF was not applied) was used for spares, and broken up in July 1977. The remains were used by the Airport Fire Brigade at the BAA Fire School until totally burnt out in May 1981.

XM-497 remained at Stansted Airport as a source of spares and did not take up the registration OO-YCF that was allocated. (Flightlines International)

XM–498

SERIES 250	VARIANT 253/Cmk1
Constructors No. 13510	Production No. 001
Built at Filton	First flight 30.9.59

EL-LWG one of two Britannia 253F's operated by Liberia World Airways. (Military Aircraft Photographs)

Built as part of contract 15527, she was delivered to No.99 Squadron Royal Air Force Transport Command at RAF Lyneham on 19 October 1959. Serialled XM-498 and named 'Hadar', she was operated within 99 and 511 Squadrons' pool from 7 July 1961.

Withdrawn from use by the Royal Air Force on 30 December 1975 and stored at RAF Kemble with a total of 18 205.45 hours and 7980 landings in RAF service. Flown to Stansted Airport in early April 1976 she was repainted in the colours of Young Air Cargo and registered OO-YCG, before being delivered to Brussels the second week of May 1976. OO-YCG flew back to Stansted Airport, and was repainted in the livery of Liberian World Airlines for lease, and was registered EL-LWG on 11 July 1976. Withdrawn from use OO-YCG was stored at Manston, Kent in September 1978.

Purchased for and painted in the livery of Domaine de Katale, she wore the titles Katale Aero Transport, and left Manston for Zaire on 8 May 1979 and was re-registered 9Q-CDT in July 1980.

Withdrawn from use 9Q-CDT was stored at Kinshasa, Zaire and sold to Business Cash Flow Aviation as a source of spares for 9Q-CHY July 1988. Confirmed scrapped in early 1992.

9Q-CDT ex EL-LWG with crude tail section livery deletion. (Aviation Photo News)

9Q-CDT undergoing a repaint. (Flightlines International)

XM–517

SERIES 250	VARIANT 253/Cmk1
Constructors No. 13511	Production No. 002
Built at Filton	First flight 24.11.59

9Q-CAJ or is it G-BEPX? at Luton Airport. (Military Aircraft Photographs)

Built to contract number 15527, and wheeled out of the production hanger on 20 November 1959. Delivered to No. 511 Squadron Royal Air Force Transport Command where she was accepted on 2 December 1959, serialled XM-517 and

With the rear fuselage removed, as well as the outer wing and engines, G-BEPX was marked up Rolls Royce (Proteus) Test. (Andy Anderson)

named 'Avoir'. During XM-517's service she carried the livery of the Royal Air Force Transport Command, Royal Air Force Air Support Command and finally Royal Air Force. She operated within the Britannia pool at RAF Lyneham from 20 February 1961.

XM-517 was repainted by Marshall's of Cambridge during October and November 1972 and flown to RAF St Athan in April 1975 after the disbanding of 99 and 511 Squadrons. By the end of August 1975, she had flown 18 897.35 hours and landed 8962 times. Sold to Monarch Airlines, she was re-registered 9Q-CAJ and marked in the titles of AMAZ (Agence et Messageries Aeriennes du Zaire), and delivered to this company in August 1976 in Brussels. Returned to Luton she was registered G-BEPX for Airline Engineering Limited who purchased her on 14 April 1977.

August 1977 saw the removal of the wings from out-board of the inner nacelles, and the rear fuselage. The title 'Rolls Royce Proteus Test' was applied and the remainder was used as a Proteus ground running test rig. In this form she was actually 'taxied' which according to one of the test crew 'felt really weird'.

G-BEPX was finally scrapped at Luton Airport during April 1980 with a total of 19 203.50 hours and 9066 landings to her credit.

XM–518

SERIES 250	VARIANT 253/Cmk1
Constructors No. 13512	Production No. 003
Built at Filton	First flight 18.12.59

XM-518 in open storage at RAF Kemble with OO-YCD marked up for Young Air Cargo. (Military Aircraft Photographs)

Built to contract 15527, and wheeled out of the production hangar on 17 December 1959 she was allocated to No. 511 Squadron, RAF Transport Command. Delivery took place on 30 December 1959. XM-518 was named 'Spica', and operated with 99 and 511 Squadrons Britannia pool at RAF Lyneham from 23 November 1960.

Withdrawn from service by the RAF on 24 November 1975 with a total of 19 641.25 flying hours to her credit and 8114 landings, she was ferried to RAF Kemble for storage and eventual re-sale.

Registered OO-YCD on 23 February 1976 she was purchased by the Belgian cargo airline Young Cargo on 4 March 1976 and ferried to their base at Gosselies, Belgium the next day. OO-YCD was then used as a source of spares for Young Cargo's other Britannias. OO-YCD was broken up at Gosselies, Belgium during 1978.

XM-519

SERIES 250	VARIANT 253/Cmk1
Constructors No. 13513	Production No. 004
Built at Filton	First flight 28.1.60
C of A: 2.7.76	

G-BDUR minus No.2 spinner. (Flightlines International)

Built as part of contract 15527, and wheeled out of the production hangar on 25 January 1960, she was allocated to No. 511 Squadron on 8 February 1960 named 'Capella'. XM-519 went to 99 and 511 Squadrons pool on 28 November 1960 at RAF Lyneham.

Withdrawn from use by the RAF this aircraft was repainted by Marshall's of Cambridge and stored at RAF Kemble from November 1975 with 18 815.45 hours and 8637 landings logged. Sold to Airline Engineering of Luton on 13 February 1976 and registered G-BDUR on 31 March 1976 and Afrek took delivery on 2 July 1976. Withdrawn from use and stored at Athens, Greece prior to being purchased by Monarch Aircraft Engineering Ltd once more, on 30 July 1984 and ferried to Luton for overhaul.

Purchased by the Cuban Airline, AeroCaribbean, in August 1984, she was re-registered CU-T121. This aircraft is now in open storage at Havana, Cuba and due to the lack of spares is no longer operating, although still in existence early 1992.

CU-T121 in service with the Cuban airline Aerocaribbean. (Flightlines International)

XM-520

SERIES 250	VARIANT 253/Cmk1
Constructors No. 13514	Production No. 005
Built at Filton	First flight 9.3.60

XM-520 in open storage at RAF St. Athan. (Military Aircraft Photographs)

XM-520 was the last Britannia to be built at Filton, and the seventh aircraft of contract 15527. Wheeled out of the production hangar on 8 January 1960 and delivered to No. 511 Squadron Royal Air Force Transport Command on 19 March 1960 she was named 'Arcturas'. XM-520 joined 99 and 511 Squadrons' Britannia pool on 22 March 1961 at RAF Lyneham.

Withdrawn from use by the RAF, XM-520 was stored at RAF St Athan, awaiting sale or lease from 14 May 1975. At the end of her RAF service she had 18 790.15 hours and 8446 landings logged. XM-520 was sold to Gemini Air Transport on 16 September 1975. The title Geminair was worn along with the new registration 9G-ACE, retaining most of the RAF colour scheme. Redcoat Air Cargo Ltd operated 9G-ACE for one year from May 1976 on a dry lease and management contract until 6 May 1977. At the end of March 1981 9G-ACE had logged 25 646.37 hours and 9866 landings. She was registered 9Q-CUM, when purchased by Lukum Air Services in September 1981.

Withdrawn from service and stored at Kinshasa, Zaire, she was sold to Katale Aero Transport for spares and broken up at Kinshasa in July 1986.

9G-ACE was the last Britannia built at Filton and is seen in the livery of Gemini Air Transport. (Ghana). (Peter J Bish)

PART FIVE

Bristol Britannia Series 300 Specifications

VARIANTS: 301 (PROTOTYPE)
303 (Aeronaves de Mexico SA)

POWERPLANT: Four Bristol Proteus 755 turbo-props developing 4120ehp driving 16ft de Havilland four-blade hollow steel propellers. Later round-tipped Duralumin propeller blades were fitted.

POWERPLANT PRODUCTION AIRCRAFT: Four Bristol Proteus 765 turbo-props developing 4450ehp driving 16ft de Havilland four bladed hollow steel propellers, which were later supplemented for the newer round tipped Duralumin propeller blades. These were less liable to stone damage when operating in reverse pitch and were more efficient.

DIMENSIONS:		
	Wingspan	142ft 3.5in.
	Overall length	124ft 3in.
	Height	37ft 6in.
	Wing area	2075sq. ft.

PAYLOAD & PERFORMANCE: Still air range, maximum payload (29 500lb) over 3496 statute miles at a cruising speed of 357mph. Still air range, maximum fuel (including reserves) 4441 statute miles at a cruising speed of 357mph with 19 244 lb payload.

CREW: 4–7.

PASSENGER ACCOMMODATION: First class, 73. Tourist, 93/101. Maximum coach, 139.

CARGO ACCOMMODATION: 910cu.ft.

FUEL CAPACITY: 6690 imperial gallons.

WEIGHTS: Empty 92 500lb (manufacturers). Empty 98 000lb (operators). All up weight (including fuel) 185 000lb.

Total built: 3.

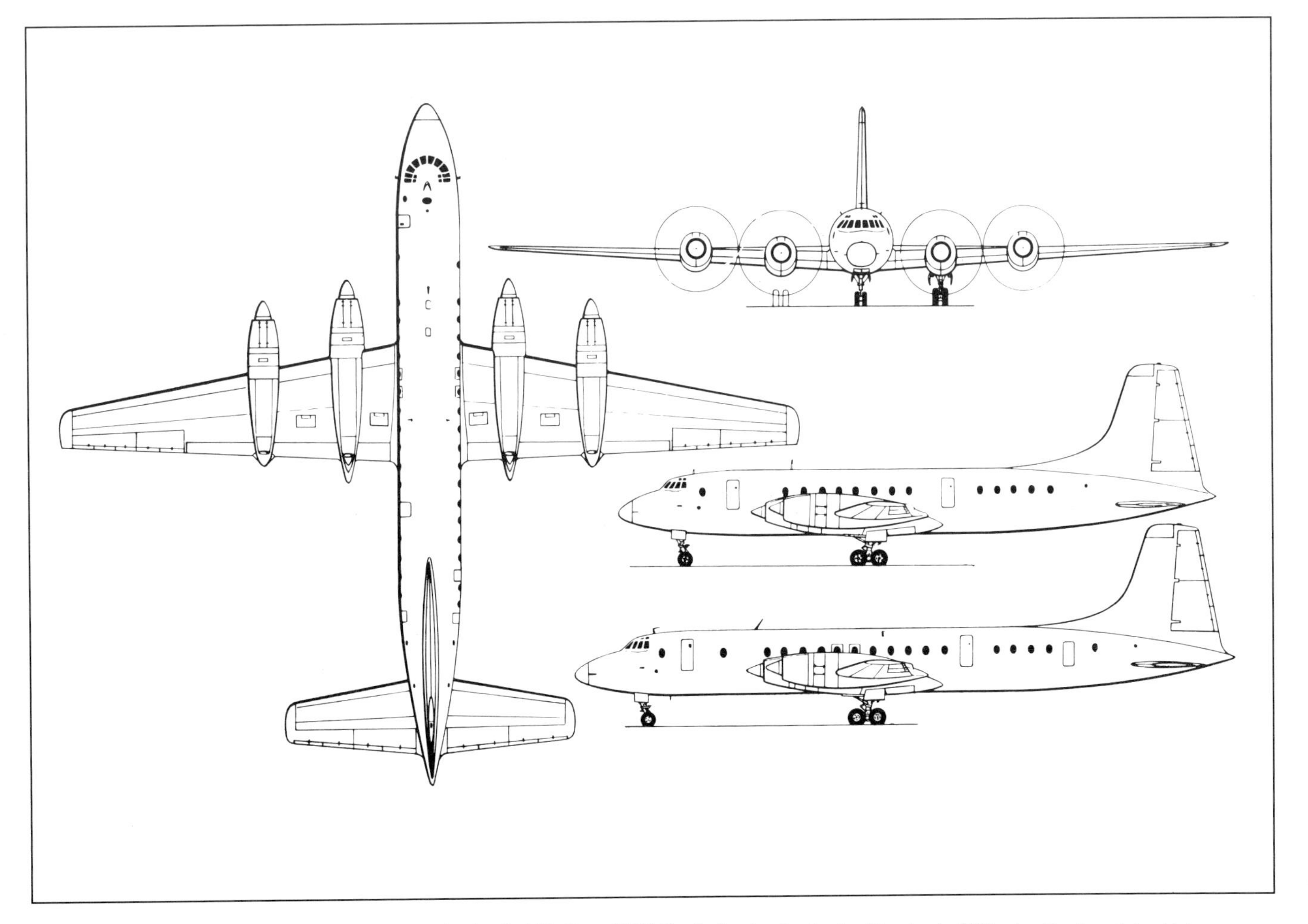

Britannia 100 and 300 series comparative views, showing the 114ft 0in. and 124ft 3in. fuselage lengths. Front and top view is of 300 series. (Greenborough Associates)

BRISTOL BRITANNIA 312
Cutaway Drawing Key

1 Radome
2 Weather radar scanner
3 Radar tracking mechanism
4 Radar receiver and transmitter
5 ILS aerial
6 Nosewheel bay bulkhead
7 Nosecone construction
8 Forward pressure dome
9 Control column linkages
10 Rudder pedals
11 Nose undercarriage wheel bay
12 Hydraulic retraction jack
13 Nosewheel leg strut
14 Twin nosewheels
15 Steering linkage
16 Nosewheel leg doors
17 Pitot tube
18 Cockpit floor level
19 Nosewheel steering control
20 Control column handwheel
21 Instrument panel
22 Instrument panel shroud
23 Windscreen panels
24 Overhead switch panel
25 Cockpit eyebrow windows
26 Co-pilot's seat
27 Pilot's seat
28 Navigator's station
29 Aerial mast
30 Cockpit roof escape hatch
31 Periscope sextant mounting
32 Radio racks
33 Radio operator's station
34 Cabin air system vent valve
35 Forward underfloor cargo hold
36 Air system ducting
37 Escape 'chute stowage
38 Cabin attendant's folding seat
39 Crew entry door
40 Forward galley
41 Wardrobe compartment
42 Entry door, open position
43 Cabin bulkhead
44 Forward passenger cabin
45 Six-abreast tourist-class seating; maximum seating capacity 133 passengers in all tourist-class layout
46 Forward toilets, port and starboard
47 Underfloor freight hold
48 Floor beam construction
49 Cabin wall trim panels
50 DF loop aerials
51 Radio aerial mast
52 Starboard inner engine nacelle
53 Air cooled transformer rectifier
54 Inner wing fuel cells; total fuel system capacity 8,486 Imp gal (38 576 l)
55 Starboard outer engine nacelle
56 Detachable engine cowling panels
57 Annular engine air intake
58 Propeller spinner
59 De Havilland hydromatic variable pitch, reversible four-bladed propellers
60 Propeller blade root de-icing boots
61 Hot-air leading-edge de-icing
62 Outer wing integral fuel tank
63 Starboard navigation light
64 Wing tip fairing
65 Aileron balance
66 Starboard two-segment aileron
67 Aileron servo tabs
68 Tab control linkage
69 Flap guide rails
70 Flap screw jack
71 Starboard double-slotted fla down position
72 Life raft stowage
73 Jet exhaust nozzle
74 Fuselage centre section construction
75 Wing spar attachment fusela main frames
76 Wing centre section carry-through
77 Central flap drive motor
78 Emergency exit hatch, port ar starboard
79 Cabin floor panelling
80 Cabin air vents
81 Removable cabin divider
82 Overhead luggage racks
83 Passenger service units
84 Tourist class seating
85 Emergency exit hatch, port ar starboard
86 Four-abreast first-class seating; 93-passenger capacity in mixed-class layou
87 Curtained window panel
88 Rear bar/galley units
89 Fuselage frame and stringer construction
90 Aft cabin seating
91 Starboard emergency exit doo
92 Fin root fillet
93 Starboard tailplane
94 Starboard elevator
95 Fin electric mat leading-edge de-icing
96 Fin construction
97 Fin tip fairing
98 Anti-collision light
99 Rudder construction
100 Rudder servo tabs

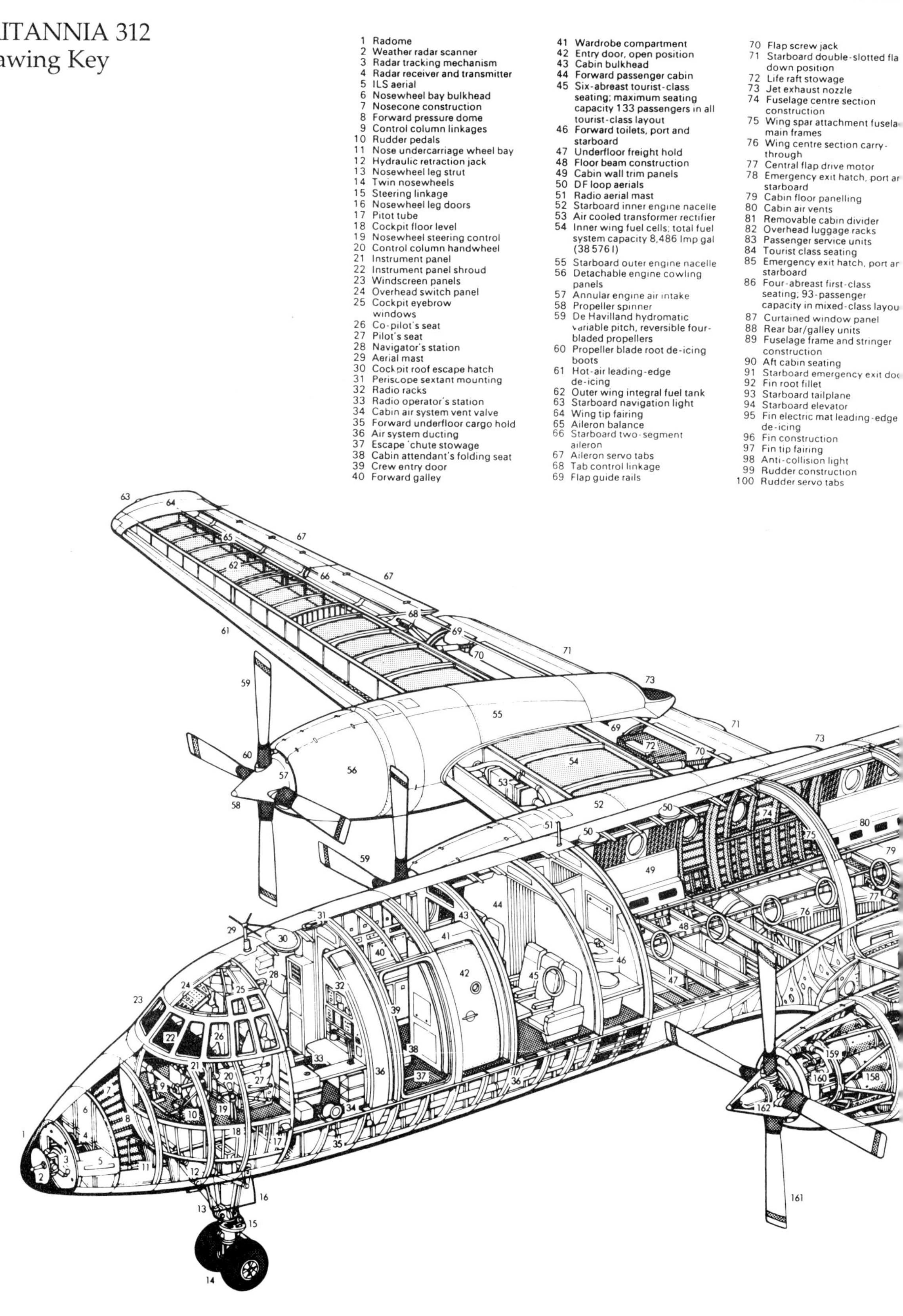

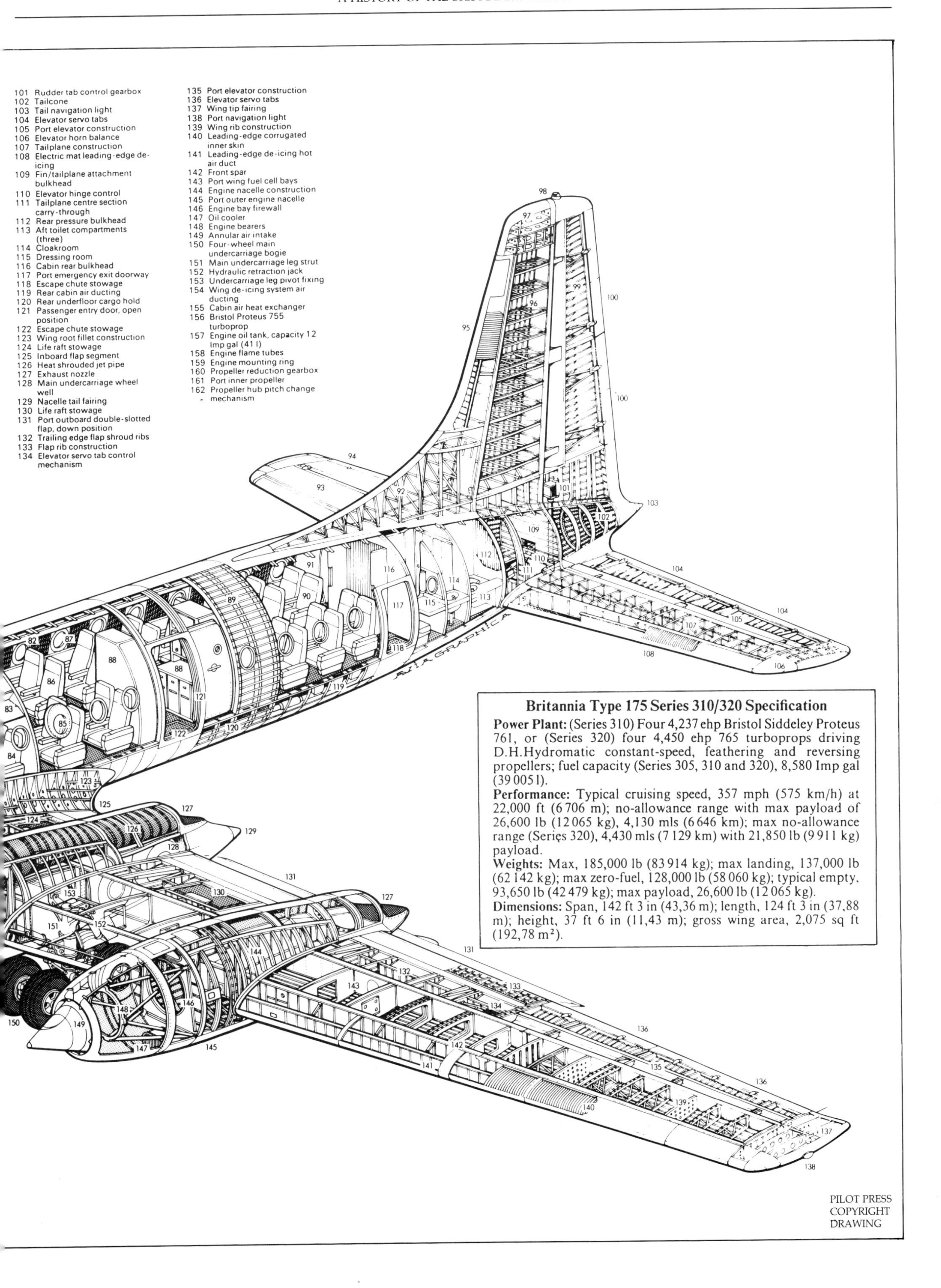

Britannia Type 175 Series 310/320 Specification

Power Plant: (Series 310) Four 4,237 ehp Bristol Siddeley Proteus 761, or (Series 320) four 4,450 ehp 765 turboprops driving D.H.Hydromatic constant-speed, feathering and reversing propellers; fuel capacity (Series 305, 310 and 320), 8,580 Imp gal (39 005 l).

Performance: Typical cruising speed, 357 mph (575 km/h) at 22,000 ft (6 706 m); no-allowance range with max payload of 26,600 lb (12 065 kg), 4,130 mls (6 646 km); max no-allowance range (Series 320), 4,430 mls (7 129 km) with 21,850 lb (9 911 kg) payload.

Weights: Max, 185,000 lb (83 914 kg); max landing, 137,000 lb (62 142 kg); max zero-fuel, 128,000 lb (58 060 kg); typical empty, 93,650 lb (42 479 kg); max payload, 26,600 lb (12 065 kg).

Dimensions: Span, 142 ft 3 in (43,36 m); length, 124 ft 3 in (37,88 m); height, 37 ft 6 in (11,43 m); gross wing area, 2,075 sq ft (192,78 m²).

BRISTOL BRITANNIA SERIES 300

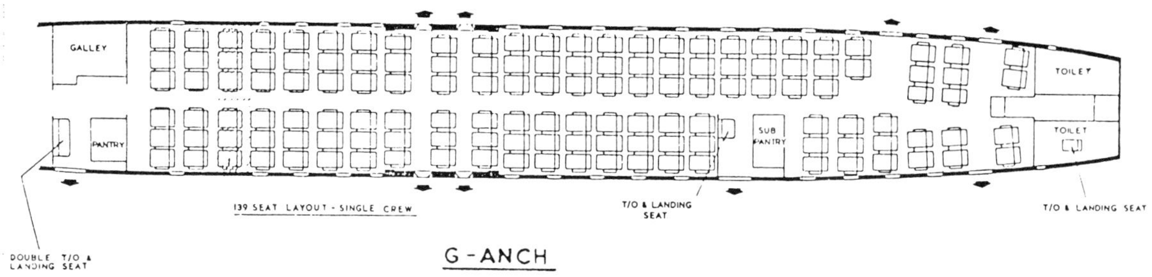

GALLEY
PANTRY
SUB PANTRY
TOILET
TOILET
139 SEAT LAYOUT - SINGLE CREW
T/O & LANDING SEAT
T/O & LANDING SEAT
DOUBLE T/O & LANDING SEAT

G-ANCH

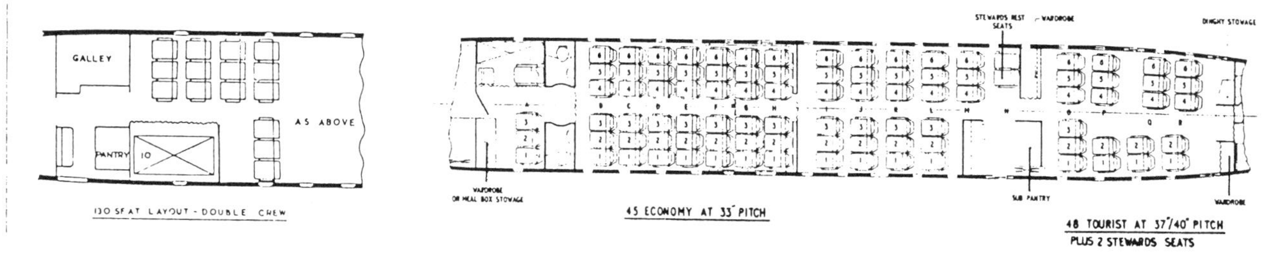

GALLEY
AS ABOVE
PANTRY
130 SEAT LAYOUT - DOUBLE CREW

45 ECONOMY AT 33" PITCH
48 TOURIST AT 37"/40" PITCH
PLUS 2 STEWARDS SEATS

54 ECONOMY AT 34" PITCH
36 TOURIST AT 37"/40" PITCH
PLUS 2 STEWARDS SEATS

66 ECONOMY AT 34" PITCH
PLUS 2 STEWARDS SEATS
30 TOURIST AT 37"/40" PITCH

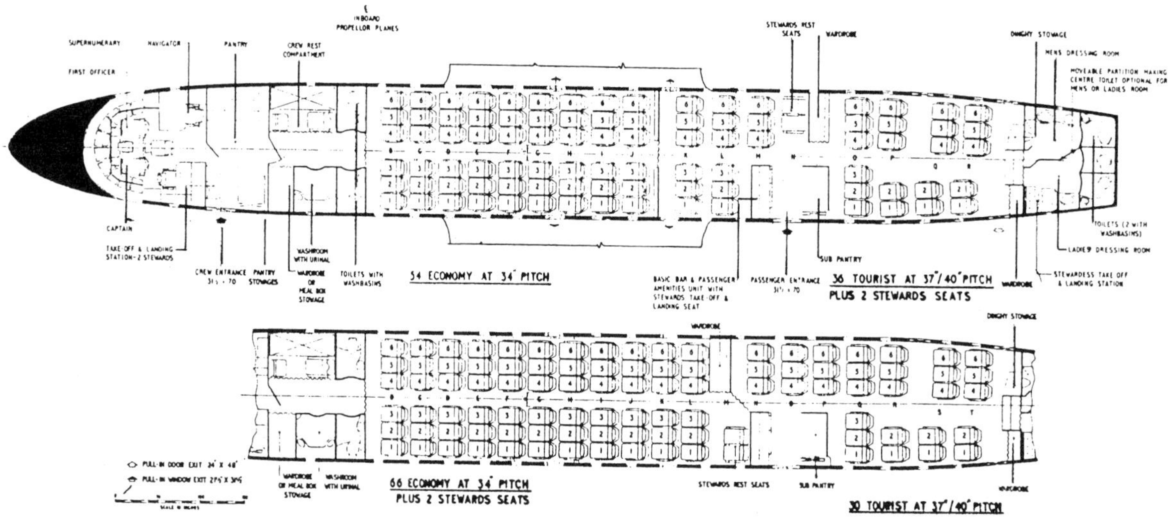

BRITANNIA 312- MIXED ECONOMY/TOURIST LAYOUTS

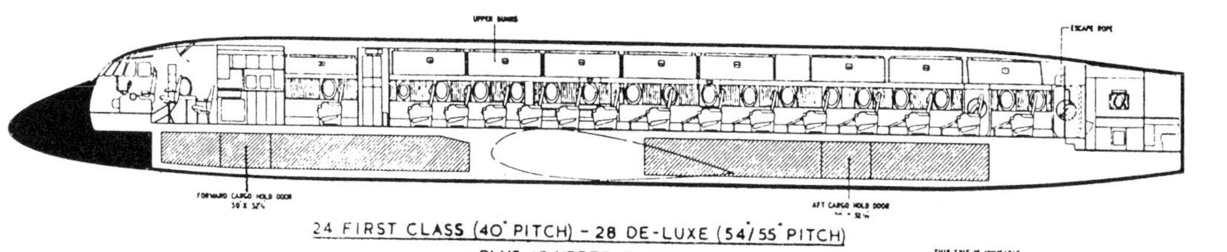

24 FIRST CLASS (40" PITCH) - 28 DE-LUXE (54"/55" PITCH)
PLUS 15 UPPER BUNKS

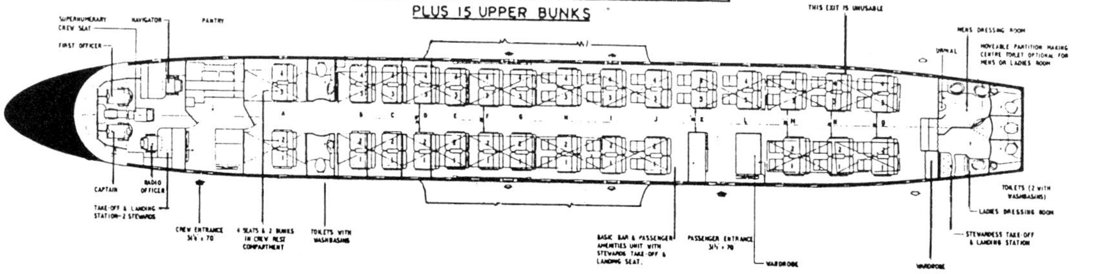

BRITANNIA 312 - 52 SEAT FIRST CLASS/ DE-LUXE LAYOUT

G–ANCA

SERIES 300
Constructors No. 12917
Built at Filton
C of A: 19.11.56

VARIANT 301
Production No. 001
First flight 31.7.56

G-ANCA the first series 300 in the basic markings of Capital Airlines of America. (Jim Oughton/Bristol Aeroplane Co Ltd)

This Britannia was built in answer to a Ministry of Supply contract, that required a prototype 'stretched' Britannia. On 11 March 1955 under the ownership of the Bristol Aeroplane Company Ltd the registration G-ANCA was allocated. G-ANCA was employed by the Bristol Aeroplane Company, initially on the Flight Development Programme for the C of A flight testing relating to the new 300 and 310 series Britannias.

Initially powered by the Proteus 755 engine, she was to have been powered by the Bristol Orion (BE 25) powerplant, but this did not transpire.

Painted at Filton in the colours of Capital Airlines, prior to first flight, she was flown to the USA for a sales tour. Once back in the United Kingdom G-ANCA wore a slightly revised livery and was marked Bristol Britannia 301 on her upper fuselage.

G-ANCA was tragically lost while on a local test flight near Filton. It was on 6 November 1957 at 10.07am, when G-ANCA took off from the runway at Filton for a routine test flight. One hour and fifty minutes later, while turning for the final leg of her landing run, she crashed hitting the ground, at Downend near Bristol. All 15 people on board, were killed. A fault within the autopilot was thought to have caused the crash.

In all 268 test flights carried out by G-ANCA, a total of 721 flight test hours were accumulated.

G-ANCA landing at Filton, with 'Bristol Britannia 301' on her upper fuselage, she was the prototype series 300. (Bristol Aeroplane Co Ltd/British Aerospace)

G–ANCB

SERIES 300
Constructors No. 12918
Built at Belfast
C of A: 30.10.57

VARIANT 302
Production No. 019
First flight 21.6.57

XA-MEC in an artists impression of Aeronaves De Mexico livery. (Bristol Aeroplane Co Ltd/British Aerospace)

Originally ordered by BOAC, this aircraft was the first production aircraft of the series 300. The registration G-ANCB was allocated on 20 January 1956 and when not required by BOAC, G-ANCB was released for resale in December 1956.

The G-class registration G-18-1 was allocated in June 1957, and the aircraft was flown in this registration from Belfast to Weston Airways of Weston-Super-Mare on 21 June 1957 for modification work to be carried out. She was flown on to Filton for the fitment of internal furnishings and final checks, on 10 October 1957.

Aeronaves De Mexico S.A., purchased this Britannia on 31 May 1957 and while at Filton she was repainted in their livery registered XA-MEC, and named 'Ciudad de Mexico'. Delivery to Aeronaves de Mexico took place from Filton to Mexico City on 1 November 1957 and during her service with this airline, she was renamed twice, firstly as 'Tenochtitlan' then 'Acapulco'.

Between the months of November and December 1957, XA-MEC was employed on route proving flights between Mexico City and New York. On one of these flights, XA-MEC flew a record distance of 2092 statute miles in 5 hours and 8 minutes at an average speed of 401 miles per hour, this flight took place on 1 January 1958.

On 9 July 1965 XA-MEC was damaged beyond repair in an accident at Tijuana, Mexico when the undercarriage collapsed during landing, causing extensive damage. The aircraft was subsequently written off.

G–ANCC

SERIES 300
Constructors No. 12919
Built at Belfast
C of A: 20.11.57

VARIANT 302
Production No. 021
First flight 24.7.57

XA-MED at Filton. (Bristol Aeroplane Co Ltd)

Originally ordered by BOAC, but cancelled, the aircraft was offered for resale in December 1956. The Bristol Aircraft Limited had the registration G-ANCC allocated to her on 8 January 1957 but she was first flown on 24 July 1957 wearing the G-class registration G-18-2 for her flight from Belfast to Weston Airways of Weston-Super-Mare for modification work. Like G-ANCB, this aircraft was then flown to Filton for the fitting of internal furnishings and final checking on 20 November 1957.

Although purchased by Aeronaves De Mexico on 31 May 1957, G-ANCC remained at Filton to be painted in Aeronaves livery, and registered XA-MED.

XA-MED left Filton on 15 December 1957 for the transfer to Mexico City, arriving two days later. In service with Aeronaves De Mexico she carried the name 'Ciudad De Nueva York', later 'Mexico City' and 'TzinTzunTzan'. She returned to the United Kingdom in 1966, following purchase by Transglobe Airways on 12 May 1966, XA-MED was re-registered G-ANCC and painted in full Transglobe livery. She continued in Transglobe's service for two years until sold to International Aviation Services (IAS) in 1968 and was to have been used as a spares source for the other Britannias which were used on the African Safari Airways contract during 1968. This did not transpire and she was flown to Biggin Hill on 16 March 1970 for open storage and broken up for scrap during August, 1970.

PART SIX

Bristol Britannia Series 305 Specifications

VARIANTS: 306 (conv' 307).
307 (British United Airways).
308 (Transcontinental S.A.).
309 (Ghana Airways).

POWERPLANT: Four Bristol Proteus 755 turbo-props developing 4120ehp (Basic version).

POWERPLANT: Four Bristol Proteus 765 turbo-props developing 4450ehp (Air Charter-British United Airways).

Driving the four-bladed Duralumin propellers.

DIMENSIONS:	Wingspan	142ft 3.5in.
	Overall length	124ft 3in.
	Height	37ft 6in.
	Wing area	2075sq. ft.

PAYLOAD & PERFORMANCE: Still air range, maximum payload (33 100lb) over 4268 statute miles at a cruising speed of 357mph.

Still air range, maximum fuel (including reserves) 5334 statute miles at a cruising speed of 345mph with 21 724lb payload.

CREW: 4–7.

PASSENGER ACCOMMODATION: First class, 82. Mixed – first class, 12, Tourist 69. Standard tourist, 110. Maximum coach, 139.

CARGO ACCOMMODATION: 845cu.ft.

FUEL CAPACITY: 8580 imperial gallons.

WEIGHTS: Empty 90 500lb (manufacturers). Empty 94 900lb (operators). All up weight (including fuel) 165 000lb (built with a thinner fuselage covering and lighter stressed alighting gear).

Total Built: 5.

Note: Two variant 308 aircraft were sold to British Eagle International Airlines in 1964 and were converted to 308F standard with the addition of a forward freight door of 72in. by 88in. (two spare RAF variant 252 freight doors were used) which increased their freight capacity to 5850 cu.ft. Two variant 307 and five variant 312 Britannias were also converted to freighter configuration although the doors used were larger in size.

Bristol Siddeley Proteus Mark 765. (Rolls Royce plc)

G–ANCD

SERIES 300	VARIANT 305
Constructors No. 12920	Production No. 023
Built at Belfast	First flight 1.6.57
C of A: 25.3.58	

G-ANCD a variant 305 for Northeast Airlines (USA) seen at Filton and never delivered as the order was later cancelled. (Bristol Aeroplane Co Ltd/British Aerospace)

Originally ordered by BOAC but not taken up and released for resale, this aircraft was then ordered by Capital Airlines but once again the option was not taken up. Northeast Airlines of the United States ordered this, plus four other variant 305 aircraft, in December 1956 but due to financial problems the order was withdrawn and cancelled in June 1958.

Laid down as a variant 302, she was re-designated a 305 following her first flight from Belfast to Filton on 1 June 1957 and for the flight the registration G-18-3 was allocated. The registration G-ANCD was allocated to this aircraft on 3 January 1958 while she was still in the ownership of the Bristol Aeroplane Company. To comply with strict U.S. Certification Regulations, over 150 modifications were carried out and once the U.S. registration N6595C was allocated, was only worn on the aircraft while in the hanger at Filton.

Painted in the full livery of Northeast Airlines, with the fleet number of 795 under the flightdeck windows, registered as G-ANCD on 29 January 1958 and flown from Filton to London (Heathrow). Due to the cancellation of Northeast Airlines order, G-ANCD was available for resale.

Re-painted in the livery of Compania Cubana De Aviacion on 28 May 1958 and still wearing the British registration G-ANCD was first flown on 4 June 1958 and during the latter part of that month embarked on a sales tour of Spain, Portugal and South America.

Re-registered 4X-AGE and painted in the livery of El-Al, the Israeli airline, on 8 July 1958 she was leased to them from 17 July via Filton as a variant 306 while they were awaiting the arrival of their fourth variant 313. 4X-AGE returned to the Bristol Aircraft Ltd on 6 March 1959.

Re-registered as G-ANCD on 20 March 1959 to the Bristol Aircraft Ltd she was leased to Air Charter Ltd on 24 March 1959 and designated a variant 307 from June 1959. Delivery from Filton on 24 March saw G-ANCD modified to almost full 320 specification, powered by the Bristol Proteus 765 engines.

On 1 July 1960 G-ANCD was operated within the British United Airways fleet, although from 23 August 1960 she was owned by Air Charter Ltd. Lloyd International Airlines leased this aircraft from 17 February 1969 and she was converted to a variant 307F at Stansted Airport, the work carried out by Aviation Traders Limited. During service with Lloyd International G-ANCD was sub-leased to East African Airways in February 1969, with the appropriate stickers applied.

G-ANCD a variant 307 in Air Charter of London livery. (Aviation Photo News)

G-ANCD in British United's smartest livery. (Aviation Photo News)

5Y-AYR ex G-ANCD a variant 307F, showing the addition of the large freight door, at Luton Airport. (Aviation Photo News)

5Y-AYR in All Cargo Airlines livery. (Aviation Photo News)

Financed by Aivex Holdings Ltd and Shackleton Aviation on 27 July 1973, G-ANCD was leased to International Aviation Services on 22 September 1973 for a three year contract following an overhaul by Britannia Airways at Luton Airport. Registered 5Y-AYR for African Cargo Airways, she was leased by them from 13 May 1975 until purchased by Westwings Aviation Services on 1 February 1977 following the demise of African Cargo although the flight crews were retained. Black Arrow Finance leased 5Y-AYR from May 1977 and Transgulf Air Cargo leased her from November 1977. Air Faisal Ltd sub-chartered 5Y-AYR during the early part of 1978 and All Cargo Airlines leased her from December that year but although painted in their livery was not operated and after 3 months was repossessed by Westwings Aviation as no payment had been received.

At the end of July 1978 this aircraft had totalled 42 150.58 hours and carried out 9149 landings. Finally she was operated by Gaylan Air Cargo from August 1979 until withdrawn from use and stored at Hurn Airport, Bournemouth from October 1982. 5Y-AYR ended her days at Hurn Airport when she was gradually broken up and scrapped. (The starboard forward overwing emergency hatch is now part of the author's Bristol Britannia collection, purchased for a mere £5.00, during her scrapping.)

G–ANCE

SERIES 300	VARIANT 305
Constructors No. 12921	Production No. 002
Built at Belfast	First flight 3.9.58
C of A: 12.9.58	

Destined for BOAC, the option on this aircraft was cancelled and the aircraft was offered for resale. Capital Airlines were to have purchased this, plus the next four aircraft built, but this was also cancelled. Northeast Airlines, an American airline placed an order for five variant 305 Britannias to which the registration N6596C was allocated with fleet number 796 and again due to monetary problems Northeast had to pull out of the deal in June 1958.

This aircraft was British registered G-ANCE to Bristol Aircraft Limited on 3 January 1958, converted to a variant 307 and flown as such on 3 September 1958 from Belfast to Filton. Purchased by Air Charter Limited of London, in August 1958,

G-ANCE in British United livery. (Military Aircraft Photographs)

G-ANCE remained at Filton from 5 September 1958 for checking, furnishing and crew training until taken on charge by Air Charter Ltd on 9 September 1958.

Delivery to Air Charter Ltd, took place at Southend Airport on 17 September 1958 and on 1 October 1958 G-ANCE operated their first charter flight to Christmas Island. On 1 July 1960 Air Charter merged into British United Airways and G-ANCE was painted in the livery of BUA. Modifications were made to bring her up to full 320 series standard prior to delivery to BUA.

In June 1966, G-ANCE was again modified, this time to a variant 307F which included the addition of a large freight door on the portside of the forward fuselage, the work being carried out by Aviation Traders Limited. Lloyd International Airlines leased G-ANCE from BUA on 26 February 1969 and operated her for nearly four years until she was stored at Stansted Airport after the collapse of Lloyd. She was rescued by Monarch Airlines, who purchased her on 22 June 1973.

IAS Cargo Airlines leased G-ANCE from Monarch from 20 January 1974 until 31 January. In 1974 G-ANCE was re-registered with the Irish registration of EI-BAA for Aer Turas Teorante. This cargo carrier, leased/purchased her from 6 May 1974 with the name 'City of Dublin' and used her for carrying livestock, racehorses etc. During Aer Turas' lease, EI-BAA was operated for the Pauling Construction Company in Saudia Arabia between 11 November 1974 and 17 January 1975, when she was returned to Aer Turas.

At the end of August 1978, EI-BAA had flown 42 703.59 hours and made 11 150 landings. EI-BAA's last flight was to end at Dublin Airport, her namesake, and it was here that she was gradually stripped down for spares and finally scrapped during May 1981.

EI-BAA as a variant 307F with Aer Turas of Ireland. (Aviation Photo News)

G–ANCF

SERIES 300	VARIANT 305
Constructors No. 12922	Production No. 003
Built at Belfast	First flight 19.11.58
C of A: 1.1.64	

G-ANCF being attended to at an RAF airfield and is seen in British Eagle livery (once preserved she will again be seen in this livery). (Andy Anderson)

Originally ordered by BOAC, the order was cancelled and this aircraft was made available for resale. The American airline, Capital Airlines showed interest but they too pulled out of the purchase. Another American airline, Northeast Airlines, ordered this plus another four variant 305, but due to problems in obtaining the neccessary credit in June 1958, they too cancelled their order. The registration N6597C was allocated with the fleet number '797', later cancelled.

Registered as G-ANCF to the Bristol Aircraft Ltd on 3 January 1958, this Britannia flew her first flight as G-18-4 while at Belfast on 19 November 1958. Following the first flight, G-18-4 was stored at Belfast until 20 October 1959 when she was re-designated a variant 308 after being purchased by the South American airline Transcontinental S.A. on 24 August 1959.

G-18-4 flew from Belfast to Filton on 24 October 1959 wearing the registration G-14-1 for the ferry flight and after arrival, was painted in full Transcontinental livery and allocated the registration LV-PPJ. While at Filton work was carried out on the internal furnishing of the aircraft as well as being modified to almost full 320 series standard. Prior to delivery, LV-PPJ was engaged on crew training at Filton before finally flying on to London (Heathrow) Airport on 16 December 1959 for the delivery flight to Argentina. Once in service with Transcontinental S.A., the registration LV-GJB was allocated during 1960.

Withdrawn from service by Transcontinental, LV-GJB was stored at Buenos Aires-Ezeiza, Argentina from November 1961. Transcontinental S.A. went into liquidation in 1961 and LV-GJB was sold to British Eagle International Airlines on 16 January 1964 and re-registered with the British registration G-ANCF on 2 March 1964.

British Eagle converted G-ANCF to a 308F configuration during July 1964, which involved the fitting of a large freight door on the port side front fuselage and strengthened wooden floor. This was to enable G-ANCF and her sister ship G-ANCG to fly to Woomera, Australia on contract work for the Weapons Research Establishment.

G-ANCF was named 'New Frontier' while in service with British Eagle but the name 'Resolution' was applied in later service. Following the collapse of British Eagle International Airlines, G-ANCF was flown to Luton Airport after being sold to Monarch Airlines on 6 December 1968.

G-ANCF later owned by Invicta International Airlines, seen at Newcastle (Woolsington) Airport. (Aircraft Photographic)

IAS Cargo Airlines leased G-ANCF from Monarch on 31 December 1973 until 23 January 1974 when she returned to Monarch Airlines.

G-ANCF continued flying to Woomera, Australia and also worked in conjunction with Trans Australia Airlines carrying flood relief supplies to Darwin following the disastrous cyclone of February 1974. The last flight that G-ANCF operated for Monarch, was in December 1975, when she flew from Adelaide via Singapore, Karachi, and Ankara, finally arriving at Luton Airport on 18 December.

African Cargo Airways leased, G-ANCF on 1 February 1976 following overhaul, she was registered 5Y-AZP, and delivered from Luton to Athens on 9 February 1976. Invicta International Airlines sub leased 5Y-AZP for the period 14 June 1976 to 7 January 1977 and purchased her on 7 January 1977, she was re-registered G-ANCF on 10 January continuing in service until withdrawn from use and stored at Manston, Kent.

When Invicta International ceased operating, G-ANCF was being overhauled in the hangar at Manston Airport, but was instead stripped of all useful items and towed to the airfield fire ground.

G-ANCF was rescued from the fire ground dump by Proteus Aero Services and stored awaiting the outcome of her future. After being dismantled the fuselage was stored at Brooklands Museum on 5 April 1988 with the wing centre section being transported to RAF Quedgeley. G-ANCF is in the process of restoration, rebuilding and repainting for display at the new Bristol Aero Collection at Filton. The livery of British Eagle will be applied and the name 'New Frontier'. G-ANCF is now owned by the Britannia Aircraft Preservation Trust. (See page 158.)

At the end of March 1981, G-ANCF had totalled 37 569.51 hours flying and had made 8389 landings.

G–ANCG

SERIES 300	VARIANT 305
Constructors No. 12923	Production No. 004
Built at Belfast	First flight 20.11.59

LV-GJC a variant 308 in Transcontinental S.A. livery. (Aviation Photo News)

Ordered originally by BOAC the order was later cancelled and she was offered for resale, an option by Capital Airlines was not taken up and the aircraft was released again for sale. Allocated the registration N6598C and the fleet number '798' for Northeast Airlines of the United States, but they too cancelled their order in June 1958 following monetary problems, associated with the necessary credit.

Following three cancelled orders, this aircraft remained at Belfast, British registered G-ANCG she was allocated to the Bristol Aircraft Ltd on 3 January 1958. Work on converting G-ANCG to a variant 308 commenced after her arrival at Filton on 21 November 1959. For the ferry flight she was registered G-14-2, and was then modified to nearly full 320 standard, emerging as a variant 308, and ordered by Transcontinental S.A.

Painted in their full livery after crew training was complete, LV-PPL as she was then registered, was delivered via London (Heathrow) Airport to Argentina on 17 December 1959 and, once in service, was re-registered LV-GJC. After the collapse of Transcontinental S.A., LV-GJC was withdrawn from use and stored at Idlewilde Airport, New York in October 1961.

Purchased by British Eagle International Airlines on 23 February 1964, she was re-registered G-ANCG on 6 April 1964, and converted to a variant 308F for use on the charter contract to Woomera, Australia in company with G-ANCF. Named 'Enterprise' later 'Trojan'.

G-ANCG was damaged beyond repair while landing with her wheels up on a foamed runway at Manston Airport, Kent on 20 April 1967 at 15.18 hrs GMT. No injuries were received by the occupants who were five flight crew, four cabin crew, two supernumary crew and 54 passengers. The fuselage was later transported to Southend Airport were it was seen near the main runway with the freight door having been removed, possibly for a spare.

G-ANCG on finals after another British Eagle flight, and still a variant 308. (Andy Anderson)

G-ANCH

SERIES 300	VARIANT 309
Constructors No. 12924	Production No. 001
Built at Belfast	First flight 19.2.60

Registered G-ANCH on 3 January 1958, originally destined for BOAC and Capital Airlines (USA), but not taken up. Allocated the registration N6599C for Northeast Airlines, fleet numbered 799, part of a consignment of five Britannias, later cancelled as Northeast Airlines (USA) could not raise the necessary credit. Construction of this aircraft was completed in June 1958 and N6599C was stored at Belfast until December 1959.

9G-AAG a variant 309 outside BOAC's maintenance headquarters, in the attractive livery of Ghana Airways. (Aviation Photo News)

Leased by Ghana Airways in the Spring of 1960, registered 9G-AAG, and taken on charge by Ghana Airways as a variant 309 (although laid down as a 302 variant) on 27 July 1960, she remained at Filton for crew training until mid-September 1960. Marked up as G-41 before being re-registered G-ANCH with Bristol Aircraft Limited on 1 June 1965 and leased to British United Airways on 4 June 1965 returning to Bristol Aircraft Limited on 7 October 1965. Leased to Ghana Airways on 7 October 1965 and Transglobe Airways on 30 September 1967. British Eagle International Airlines were to take delivery of G-ANCH on 13 February 1968 but this did not take place and G-ANCH returned to Ghana Airways in March 1968. She was leased to Monarch Airlines on 25 September 1968 until returned to Ghana Airways on 4 May 1972. She operated on the Hadj between Accra and Jeddah for Ghana Airways each year.

She was withdrawn from service and stored at Lydd, Kent in May 1972, until purchased by IAS Cargo Airlines in December 1972 registered G-ANCH and ferried from Lydd to Biggin Hill with the undercarriage locked down. At the end of April 1974, G-ANCH had flown 18 474.59 hours and made 5062 landings.

9G-AAG outside the BUA hanger wearing the ferry registration G-41 and minus the rudder livery. (Andy Anderson)

She was finally withdrawn from service and scrapped at Biggin Hill, Kent in August 1983.

PART SEVEN

Bristol Britannia Series 310 Specifications

VARIANTS: 311 (Prototype, later a 312 and finally a 319)
312 (BOAC)
313 (El Al)
314 (Canadian Pacific Airlines)
317 (British United Airways)
318 (Cubana)

POWERPLANT: Four Bristol Proteus 755 turbo-props developing 4120ehp (Basic version) driving 16ft de Havilland four-blade hollow steel propellers.

POWERPLANT: Four Bristol Proteus 761 turbo-props developing 4175ehp driving 16ft de Havilland four-blade hollow steel propellers. (Fitted to BOAC, El-Al, and Canadian Pacific Airlines Britannias).

POWERPLANT: Four Bristol Proteus 765 turbo-props developing 4400ehp driving 16ft de Havilland four-blade hollow steel propellers.

Note: The propeller blades were supplemented to the Duralumin four-bladed round-tipped type which were less liable to be damaged by the stones thrown up when the engines were running with the props in reverse pitch.

DIMENSIONS:

Wingspan	142ft 3.5in.
Overall length	124ft 3in.
Height	37ft 6in.
Wing area	2075sq. ft.

PAYLOAD & PERFORMANCE: Still air range, maximum payload (34 900lb) (variant 312) over 4268 statute miles at a cruising speed of 357mph.

Still air range, maximum fuel (including reserves) 5310 statute miles at a cruising speed of 357mph with 23 524lb payload.

CREW: 4–7.

PASSENGER ACCOMMODATION: First class, 82. Mixed, 12 first class and 69 tourist class. Maximum coach, 139.

CARGO ACCOMMODATION: 900cu.ft.

FUEL CAPACITY: 8580 imperial gallons.

WEIGHTS: Empty 82 537lb (manufacturers).
93 100lb (operators).
All up weight (including fuel) 185 000lb.

Total built: 35

The last airworthy Britannia seen in a fine air to air shot while with A. & A.E.E. Boscombe Down. (Steve Piercey Collection)

G–AOVA

SERIES 310	VARIANT 311
Constructors No. 13207	Production No. 018
Built at Filton	First flight 31.12.56
C of A: 25.1.57	

G-AOVA the prototype of the 310 series. (Bristol Aeroplane Co Ltd/British Aerospace)

Registered G-AMYK to the Bristol Aeroplane Company Ltd on 25 February 1952 and originally planned as a Series 200, this aircraft was not completed as such and the registration was withdrawn on 11 March 1955.

As a 300LR variant, the registration G-AOFA was allocated to this aircraft on 21 November 1955 while she was still owned by the manufacturers but this too was withdrawn on 1 January 1956. The registration G-AOVA was allocated to the Bristol Aeroplane Company Ltd on 21 November 1955.

G-AOVA was not only the prototype to the 310 series but because she was later upgraded to a variant 312 she became the first of the production variants, being finally rebuilt to full 320 specifications and sold as the sole 319 variant.

As the variant 311, G-AOVA remained with the manufacturers as a flight development aircraft, being used on certification flight tests and later winterisation tests, which were carried out from 29 January to 10 March 1957 in Canada.

G-AOVA, although not purchased by BOAC as part of their 18 strong order of 312 variant Britannias, was leased by them on 15 July 1957 as a variant 312 for use on route-proving flights. Two flights carried out in record time were, a non-stop transatlantic crossing from New York to Rome, a distance of 4700 statute miles in 12 hours 20 minutes on 9 March 1957. On another flight, this time between London and Vancouver, Canada, G-AOVA covered a greater distance of 5100 statute miles in 14 hours and 40 minutes on 29 June 1957.

Tropical trials were carried out with G-AOVA in the Far East during August 1957, then between 26 November and 14 December 1957 and in the early part of 1958, finishing in December that year. Re-designated a variant 312 from September 1957 until March 1958 and later reverting back to a variant 311 in April 1958, flying very little after this period.

Hunting Clan Air Transport Ltd leased G-AOVA in January 1959. She returned to Bristol Aircraft Ltd for conversion to 319 variant during the end of the year. G-AOVA was completed to almost full 320 series standard at the beginning of 1960.

G-AOVA designated a variant 312 from September 1957 until March 1958. (Peter R March)

G-AOVA taking off at London (Heathrow) during the turbo-prop era. (Aviation Photo News)

Following release by BOAC, the Bristol Aircraft Ltd sold this aircraft to Ghana Airways in September 1960 as the sole variant 319. Delivery took place at Filton on 9 November 1960 with the aircraft repainted in Ghana's livery and registered 9G-AAH, named 'Osagyefo', which translated means 'Wise-one'.

Re-registered G-AOVA and purchased by Vickers Armstrong (Aircraft) Ltd in 1963 she was returned to Bristol Aircraft Services Ltd on 31 December that year, and withdrawn from use and stored at Filton.

British Eagle International Airlines leased G-AOVA for one month commencing on 1 January 1964 and following her return to Filton she was leased to British United Airways from 12 February until 19 April 1964, returning to Bristol Aircraft Services on the same day. G-AOVA was again leased to British Eagle on 25 April 1964 named 'Justice'. On 29 December 1964 G-AOVA was purchased by British Eagle.

Following the demise of British Eagle, G-AOVA was purchased by CCT Aircraft Leasing Ltd on 25 March 1969. On the same day G-AOVA was leased to Caledonian Airways and named 'County of Fife', operating until her return to CCT Aircraft Leasing Ltd in November 1969. Lloyd International Airways leased G-AOVA from 13 December 1969, but on the same day sub-leased her to Caledonian Airways, returning her to CCT Aircraft Leasing Ltd in February 1970.

Withdrawn from use and stored at Baginton Airport, Coventry, from October 1970 and later following purchase by Airline Engineering in June 1971 she was broken up for spares from October 1971, before being scrapped.

G–AOVB

SERIES 310	VARIANT 312
Constructors No. 13230	Production No. 022
Built at Filton	First flight 5.7.57
C of A: 30.8.57	

G-AOVB taxiing in at London (Heathrow) Airport in the lease markings of BWIA and is only dated by the cars of the era. (Military Aircraft Photographs)

Ordered by BOAC, but initially used by the manufacturers for development and certification test flights between May and September 1957, and carried out routine proving flights between September and December 1957. Between 27 March and 7 May 1957, G-AOVB was at Cambridge for modification prior to delivery to BOAC on 10 September 1957.

During her first route proving flight between London and New York on 28 September 1957, G-AOVB had to land at Miami on 30 September 1957 with two damaged engines caused by the compressor blades rubbing against the casings. One of the proving flights was made in a record time when the distance between London and New York of 3444 statute miles was flown in 10 hours and 19 minutes. G-AOVB eventually went into service with BOAC on 22 May 1958 as BA 581/120.

On 5 November 1958 G-AOVB was marked up in the temporary lease markings of East African Airways Corporation. On 3 December 1958 G-AOVB struck a hangar door at New York, no injuries occurred but the aircraft was under repair for almost a month until 10 January 1959. G-AOVB was leased to BWIA during 1960 and also returned the same year.

G-AOVB left London (Heathrow) Airport on 20 July 1963 at 15.30 hours bound for Boston, USA as RCH 3471. At 02.56 hours she touched down at Boston. G-AOVB later departed Boston and landed at Kin at 00.20 on 22 July. It was then found that because of loose gravel on the runway at Boston, she had damaged all four propellers and departure from Kin was delayed until 19.30 hours on 26 July 1963. BOAC subsequently instigated court proceedings against Boston Corporation. G-AOVB operated her last flight for BOAC on 21 September 1963 between New York and London as BA 552/234.

G-AOVB was leased to British Eagle International Airlines on 15 October 1963 on a hire-purchase agreement over five years with the option of purchase when required. She was painted in their full livery and named 'Resolution', later 'Endeavour'. While with British Eagle she was converted to freighter (312F) configuration. She returned to BOAC

LV-JNL with A.E.R. Argentina. (Aviation Photo News)

in November 1968, only to be sold to AER Argentina on 9 October 1969, registered LV-PNJ. Once in service the registration was changed to LV-JNL in February 1970.

The aircraft was written off on 12 July 1970 near Ezeiza, Argentina while landing in fog.

G–AOVC

SERIES 310	VARIANT 312
Constructors No. 13231	Production No. 029
Built at Filton	First flight 22.10.57
C of A: 15.11.57	

G-AOVC with Donaldson International Airlines under tow at Gatwick Airport. (Military Aircraft Photographs)

Registered G-AOFC to the Bristol Aeroplane Company, but not taken up. Ordered by BOAC she was delivered to London (Heathrow) Airport on 15 November 1957. On 19 December 1957 G-AOVC flew BOAC's inaugural service between London, New York and back to London as BA 501/1. The aircraft took off from London (Heathrow) Airport at 10.35 hours G.M.T. and flew a track of London, Prestwick, the southern tip of Greenland, Gander, Boston and finally New York. G-AOVC diverted some 350 miles from the direct course in order to avoid headwinds of 146mph. But the aircraft instead met headwinds of 100mph and in all the average headwind for the whole flight was 45mph. The altitudes flown by G-AOVC were up to a maximum of 31 000 feet and the average true airspeed was 350mph, of which the average ground speed was 305mph.

The total distance of this outward bound flight was 3750 statute miles. G-AOVC landed at Idlewild International Airport, New York, at 23.10 hours G.M.T. on 19 December 1957. On 21 December 1957 G-AOVC took off from Idlewild International Airport, New York, at 23.12 hours G.M.T. on a track from New York, Gander, south of Ireland, Bristol and finally landing at London (Heathrow) Airport. During the return flight a tail wind of 55mph was experienced and the aircraft flew at altitudes of up to 24 000 feet. G-AOVC's average true airspeed was 350mph with the average ground speed being 405mph. The total distance flown on this flight was 3515 statute miles and at 08.00 hours G.M.T. the aircraft landed at London (Heathrow) Airport on 22 December 1957.

Between 30 April 1958 and 31 May 1958 G-AOVC was at Marshall's of Cambridge for modification. On the evening of 10 November 1961 while being positioned into No. 17 hangar at New York, the top of the tail fin struck a roof girder causing slight damage although no casualties. Another incident was on 20 September 1963 when the fuselage skin in the vicinity of the rear door was punctured by a catering truck while loading at London (Heathrow) Airport. The aircraft was operating as BA RCH/3984. On 9 April 1964 G-AOVC operated her last flight for BOAC, as BA RCH/RRH 3449, between Detroit and London via Prestwick.

Leased to British Eagle on 14 May 1964 under a supplementary agreement and delivered the following day, named 'Sovereign'. Due to the demise of British Eagle, G-AOVC was purchased by Donaldson International Airways on 20 May 1969 and named 'Mikado'.

Withdrawn from service on 28 September 1970 and scrapped during 1973 at Stansted Airport. Used by the D.T.I. Fire Training School at Stansted Airport.

G–AOVD

SERIES 310	VARIANT 312
Constructors No. 13235	Production No. 030
Built at Filton	First flight 13.11.57
C of A: 3.12.57	

Initially registered as G-AOFD to the Bristol Aeroplane Company Ltd on 21 November 1955 as a 300LR variant but cancelled on 1 January 1956 as not built to this specification, but instead built as a 312 variant.

Ordered by BOAC in December 1956 she was wheeled from Filton's production hangar on 9 November 1957 as G-AOVD. Taken on BOAC'S charge on 4 December 1957 and delivered to London (Heathrow) Airport on 6 December she entered service on 14 December 1957 as BA 501/9. Between 20 May 1958 and 18 June 1958 G-AOVD was at Cambridge for modification.

G-AOVD had an extremely short career with BOAC, while carrying out a C of A flight from London (Heathrow) Airport on 24 December 1958 she crashed during approach to Hurn Airport killing seven flight observers and two of the five flight crew on board. The aircraft was flying in fog when possibly an altimeter mis-reading caused the tragic accident. G-AOVD crashed and burst into flames at Sopley Farm, Winkton near Christchurch at 11.58/59 GMT. G-AOVD had taken off from London (Heathrow) at 10.09 GMT. and following this tragic accident, the only identifying piece of the aircraft was the tail fin found upside down virtually complete amongst trees.

G-AOVD at London (Heathrow). (Aviation Photo News)

G–AOVE

SERIES 310	VARIANT 312
Constructors No. 13236	Production No. 032
Built at Filton	First flight 8.12.57
C of A: 20.12.57	

G-AOVE outside BOAC's maintenance headquarters. (Aviation Photo News)

Registered to the Bristol Aeroplane Company Ltd as G-AOFE on 21 November 1955 but cancelled due to never being built as a 300LR variant and the registration was withdrawn on 1 January 1956. With the registration G-AOVE allocated, this aircraft was ordered by BOAC in December 1956 and wheeled from the hangar at Filton nearly a year later on 29 November 1957. Delivery to BOAC took place at London (Heathrow) Airport on 21 December 1957 and G-AOVE entered service on 17 January 1958 as BA 501/5.

G-AOVE spent some time at Cambridge for modification between 18 June and 27 July 1958. On 10 February 1959 G-AOVE struck a ground power unit while taxiing at Gander, no injuries were inflicted on the passengers and the aircraft was taken out of service for repair.

G-AOVE was leased to British United Airways after being delivered to Stansted Airport via London (Heathrow) Airport on 27 September 1961 and later repainted in BUA livery from 5 October 1961. A sub-lease to Middle East Airlines commenced on 21 April 1964 and ended on 21 May 1964, during this time G-AOVE was operated in BUA's livery. On 21 May 1964 after returning to BUA, G-AOVE re-located back to BOAC on 5 June 1964.

British Eagle International Airlines Ltd leased this aircraft from BOAC on 6 June 1964 for a period of two months under the terms of an agreement dated 5 June. On 8 October 1964 BOAC received a letter from British Eagle wishing to extend the lease to 5 January 1965 which was agreed. G-AOVE was painted in full livery with the name 'Adventurer' although several name changes followed such as 'Perserverance' then 'Talisman' and finally when purchased by British Eagle on 30 November 1966 the name 'Renown' was allocated.

Following the demise of British Eagle International Airlines, G-AOVE was sold to the Spanish airline Air Spain. The registration EC-WFK was allocated following purchase in November 1966 and immediately changed to EC-BFK for commercial service. The name 'Mediterraneo' was allocated followed by 'Isla Canarias'. Withdrawn from service, EC-BFK was stored at Palma Airport in 1972.

International Aviation Services purchased this aircraft in September 1973 and once all available spares had been removed, she was scrapped during 1974, still at Palma.

G–AOVF

SERIES 310	VARIANT 312
Constructors No. 13237	Production No. 034
Built at Filton	First flight 18.12.57
C of A: 31.12.57	

G-AOVF a variant 312F in IAS Cargo Airlines livery. (Aviation Photo News)

Initially destined for the 300 series long-range variant and registered G-AOFF on 21 November 1955, to the Bristol Aeroplane Company Ltd but was not taken up, registration was cancelled on 1 January 1956, when the aircraft was not built as such. Rolled out of the production hangar at Filton, on 14 December 1957 she was later delivered to BOAC at London (Heathrow) Airport on 2 January 1958. From 4 July to 20 August 1958, G-AOVF was at Cambridge for modification work. G-AOVF entered service as BA 563/132 on 6 September 1958.

On 19 April 1958 G-AOVF was employed on a Royal Tour of the West Indies carrying H.R.H. Princess Margaret. The Princess flew in this aircraft on inter-island flights as well as BOAC's associate airline BWIA. H.R.H. Princess Margaret was the first member of the Royal Family to fly a BOAC long-range Britannia. On 7 May 1958 at 07.15am G-AOVF arrived back at London (Heathrow) Airport following the mammoth 11 000 miles tour of the Caribbean. G-AOVF had left Nassau, Bahamas at 04.00 GMT for the return journey of 4500 miles, refuelling at Gander the same day. The total journey time was 14 hours 15 minutes. On returning to London (Heathrow) Airport H.R.H. Princess Margaret was met by Her Majesty Queen Elizabeth II, and for BOAC, in the unavoidable absence of the Chairman, by Sir George Cribbett, Deputy Chairman, and Mr Basil Smallpiece, Managing Director. In command of G-AOVF throughout the tour was Captain Donald Anderson, Manager of the Britannia 312 flight.

On 13 April 1963 while climbing out of Antigua, an explosion was heard on the starboard side of the aircraft and due to this No. 3 engine was shut down. The aircraft returned to Antigua and after arrival the problem found to have been caused by a tyre exploding. Damage was centered around the undercarriage bay and jet exhaust pipe. All the passengers were transferred to another aircraft and BA 422/112 was terminated for repairs.

G-AOVF suffered another in-flight emergency on 29 May 1963 while operating the BA 645/494 service during the descent into Montreal, Canada. For some reason an oxygen cylinder was ignited and had to be extinguished by a cabin steward. In the process one unfortunate woman had her hair singed and another had her dress slightly burned; the

G-AOVF at Manston Airport, Kent, the base of Invicta International. (Military Aircraft Photographs)

steward burned his thumb but the only damage to the aircraft was caused by the extinguishing agent when it stained two seats. G-AOVF operated her last service with BOAC on 11 January 1964 as BA RCH/3243 on a flight between New York and London.

British Eagle International Airlines, leased G-AOVF from 4 March 1964 on a five year hire-purchase lease agreement with the option to buy. The name 'Friendship' was allocated and she was converted to a variant 312F configuration during 1968 whilst still with British Eagle. Returning to BOAC on 27 November 1968, G-AOVF was then purchased by Monarch Airlines of Luton on 22 January 1970 she was withdrawn from use and put into storage at Luton Airport from the end of January 1970.

Back in operation, G-AOVF was leased by Donaldson International Airlines from 21 April 1970 and allocated the name 'Nike', she was later purchased on 24 July 1972. G-AOVF was again withdrawn from service and stored at Baginton, Coventry Airport, from the end of July 1972.

International Aviation Services (UK) Ltd purchased G-AOVF on 31 October 1972 who in turn leased her to African Safari Airlines on 1 November 1972 later returning to IAS Cargo Airlines on 19 December 1972 named 'African Queen'. Invicta (1976) Ltd leased G-AOVF from April 1976 but after a brief return to IAS Cargo, she returned to Invicta International Airlines who in turn purchased her on 2 November 1978.

Redcoat Air Cargo Airlines, leased G-AOVF on 3 August 1979 and once more she returned to Invicta International and up to 30 September 1980 G-AOVF had notched up 44 025 flying hours, carried out 11 371 landings and covered some 11 006 250 nautical miles which is equivalent to flying around

9Q-CAZ leased from Invicta International by I.A.C. Cargo Airlines. (Aviation Photo News)

the world 688 times. On 6 January 1981, G-AOVF was re-registered 9Q-CAZ and leased to IAC Cargo Airlines until 4 June, when she returned to Invicta International.

Purchased by Merchant Air Ltd on 21 February 1984, and sold to Proteus Aero Services in May 1984, but was not operated, G-AOVF was flown to RAF Cosford on 31 May 1984 for preservation at the Aerospace museum. She can now be seen in the livery of her first owners and pioneers of Britannia Fleets, BOAC whose modern-day airline, British Airways, kindly helped with the repaint in December 1985 (see Preserved Britannia section).

G–AOVG

SERIES 310	VARIANT 312
Constructors No. 13238	Production No. 037
Built at Filton	First flight 10.1.58
C of A: 31.1.58	

G-AOVG is seen outside BOAC's maintenance headquarters wearing BEA emblems on her cheatline for her lease. (Tony Furlong)

Registered G-AOFG on 21 November 1955 to the Bristol Aeroplane Company Ltd as a 300LR version but the registration was cancelled on 1 January 1956 as the aircraft was not built to this specification. Ordered by BOAC in December 1956, registered G-AOVG and now a variant 312, she was flown to Marshall's of Cambridge on 31 January 1958 for the installation of the flight engineer's seat.

During her maiden flight G-AOVG suffered an autopilot emergency and because of the loss of G-ANCA was used for investigations to locate possible causes of her crash. Delivery to BOAC took place on 19 March 1958 at London (Heathrow) Airport.

During April and May of 1961, G-AOVG was leased to British European Airways for their European schedules. During this time she wore the familiar red squares with BEA on her cheatlines, both sides, but BOAC was still kept on her upper fuselage.

After returning to BOAC in May, she remained in service with them until leased out to British Eagle International Airlines on 3 April 1965. Painted in full British Eagle livery and named 'Bounteous' she continued in service until the collapse of the airline when she was repossessed by BOAC on 27 November 1968.

Purchased by Monarch Airlines of Luton Airport on 10 October 1969, G-AOVG was painted in their livery and operated until being withdrawn from service at Luton and scrapped during August 1974. Up to the end of April 1972, G-AOVG had totalled 33 040.09 flying hours and landed 9329 times.

G–AOVH

SERIES 310	VARIANT 312
Constructors No. 12925	Production No. 038
Built at Filton	First flight 29.1.58
C of A: 11.2.58	

G-AOVH seen taxiing at Southend Airport. Under her nose can be seen the remains of G-ANCG following her transfer from Manston. (Aviation Photo News)

Originally destined a variant 305 with the registration G-ANCI but never completed as such. BOAC who had originally ordered this aircraft, amended their order in December 1956 and she was built as a variant 312 for BOAC as part of their 18 strong order. The registration G-ANCI was re-allocated to a de Havilland Heron 1B.

BOAC took G-AOVH, as she was later registered, on charge from 11 February 1958 and with her C of A allocated she was flown to Marshall's of Cambridge for fitting out three days later. BOAC took delivery on 28 March 1958 at London (Heathrow) Airport and she entered service on 17 April 1958 as BA 565/3.

During service with BOAC, this aircraft inaugurated their service to Detroit, USA on 17 April 1958. While at Manchester on 11 May 1963 G-AOVH got her port main undercarriage bogged down in soft ground when taxiing from the runway to the apron causing a delay of 5½ hours to the flight, BA 648/489. G-AOVH also operated BOAC's last scheduled trans-atlantic service by a Britannia on 1 March 1964.

British Eagle International Airlines leased G-AOVH on 6 November 1964 for a two month lease to be extended or terminated on a month-by-month basis under the terms of an agreement dated 5 November 1964. She was painted in their livery with the name 'Crusader' on her nose section and operated by British Eagle until returning to her owners in February 1965.

Caledonian Airways purchased this aircraft on 7 March 1965 and with the purchase being completed by 1 April 1968. They named her 'County of Angus' complementing their colourful livery. Caledonian then leased G-AOVH to Royal Air Maroc on 14 March until she returned again on 5 May 1965.

Monarch Airlines of Luton purchased G-AOVH on 1 April 1968 and after being repainted in their colourful yellow and black livery operated her out of Luton Airport for nearly four years.

Once withdrawn from service in November 1971, she was used as a cabin trainer for cabin crews, minus wings outboard of the inner engine nacelles until finally being broken up and scrapped in June 1972.

G-AOVH in the livery of Monarch Airlines of Luton. (Aviation Photo News)

G–AOVI

SERIES 310	VARIANT 312
Constructors No. 12926	Production No. 040
Built at Filton	First flight 15.2.58
C of A: 25.2.58	

G-AOVI being prepared for lease by BOAC to British United Airways. (Aircraft Photographic)

Ordered by BOAC in January 1956, she was originally destined a variant 305 with the registration G-ANCJ. This aircraft was never built and before being placed on to the jigs the registration was withdrawn and allocated to a de Havilland Heron 1B. Registered as G-AOVI for BOAC who had amended their order and released their option on five 305 variants for resale in December 1956, she was built as a 312 variant for BOAC.

G-AOVI was flown to Marshall's of Cambridge for fitting out on 26 February 1958 prior to delivery to BOAC which followed on 10 April at London (Heathrow) Airport. She entered service on 19 April 1958 as BA 563/78. On 31 August 1961 G-AOVI was damaged by a fork lift truck which caused damage to the starboard elevator horn balance while loading at Boston, USA.

Leased to British United Airways on 22 September 1961 G-AOVI was painted in their livery and operated until returning to BOAC via Stansted Airport at London (Heathrow) Airport on 1 July 1964. Leased again, this time to Caledonian Airways on 18 December 1964 and painted in the livery of this airline, G-AOVI was allocated the name 'County of Argyll' and on 19 January 1965 was purchased from BOAC.

G-AOVI is pictured taxiing during her lease to Royal Air Maroc. (Military Aircraft Photographs)

During ownership by Caledonian Airways, G-AOVI was leased to Royal Air Maroc, in April 1966 and returned during 1966. Two years later she was sold again, this time to Monarch Airlines who purchased her on 14 February 1968 but leased her back to Caledonian Airways three days later until returning to Monarch Airlines on 29 March 1968.

Four years later G-AOVI was withdrawn from use and stored at Luton Airport from January 1972. She was finally broken up and scrapped from April that year.

G–AOVJ

SERIES 310	VARIANT 312
Constructors No. 13418	Production No. 041
Built at Filton	First flight 27.2.58
C of A: 11.3.58	

G-AOVJ in the livery of BOAC at Heathrow. (Aviation Photo News)

Registered G-AOFJ to the Bristol Aeroplane Company Ltd on 21 November 1955 as a 300LR, but the registration was cancelled on 1 January 1956 as she was not built to this specification. Ordered by BOAC in December 1956, designated a variant 312 and allocated the registration G-AOVJ.

G-AOVJ was flown to Marshall's of Cambridge for fitting out on 19 March 1958 and delivered to BOAC at London (Heathrow) Airport on 23 April 1958. On service from 3 May 1958, G-AOVJ operated her first service as BA 563/81. During late 1960, G-AOVJ was fitted out as a VIP aircraft for a royal tour of India which started in the spring of 1961.

During service with BOAC this aircraft was leased out to British West Indian Airways in 1961, still in BOAC livery but wearing the normal stickers that were applied on the fuselage upper surfaces, she returned to BOAC in mid 1961. G-AOVJ suffered a mishap nearly four years later when on 26 May 1964 operating as BA 492/446 on a flight from New York to Bermuda. Just after touching down on the runway, the port main undercarriage collapsed. The same year on 28 November she overran the towing tractor after the tow bar broke. This caused damage to No. 2 engine's propeller and engine cowling.

Leased to Caledonian Airways on 28 April 1965 who painted her in their full livery and allocated the name 'County of Aberdeen'. Just over four years later on 12 November 1969 G-AOVJ was purchased by Caledonian Airways. A year later, she was sold again this time to Donaldson International Airlines, who purchased her in November 1970.

After only a month in their ownership she was withdrawn from use and used as a source of spares at Stansted Airport, finally being relegated to the airfield fire dump for training purposes.

G–AOVK

SERIES 310
Constructors No. 13419
Built at Filton
C of A: 2.4.58

VARIANT 312
Production No. 043
First flight 18.3.58

G-AOVK 'dangling her Dunlops' on finals. (Aviation Photo News)

Ordered by BOAC in December 1956, G-AOVK was flown to Marshall's of Cambridge for fitting out on 8 April 1958. Delivery to BOAC at London (Heathrow) Airport took place on 11 May 1958. G-AOVK went on service on 2 June 1958 as BA 582/122. Operated on BOAC's transatlantic services, G-AOVK was damaged at New York on 25 January 1965 by a Pan American Airways catering truck which struck the starboard tail plane and horn balance. This caused damage to the bottom boom which was holed together with the bottom skin to a depth of 21 inches while the elevator was holed to a depth of 3 inches. G-AOVK's last flight with BOAC was on 29 May 1965.

Leased to British Eagle International Airlines on 31 May 1965. While in service with British Eagle, G-AOVK was allocated the name 'Concord' which was worn on both sides of the nose section. British Eagle purchased G-AOVK on 1 December 1967.

Following the untimely demise of British Eagle, G-AOVK was sold to CCT Aircraft (Leasing) Ltd on 11 April 1969 who in turn sold her to Monarch Airlines, Airline Engineering of Luton Airport, on 24 May 1969.

Withdrawn from use, G-AOVK was finally broken up and scrapped during February 1970 at Luton Airport.

G-AOVK in service with British Eagle. (Aviation Photo News)

G–AOVL

SERIES 310
Constructors No. 13420
Built at Filton
C of A: 18.4.58

VARIANT 312
Production No. 045
First flight 9.4.58

G-AOVL operating under lease to BWIA. Note the interesting ground equipment under the nose – a dining chair. (Aviation Photo News)

Ordered by BOAC and flown to Marshall's of Cambridge on 21 April 1958 for fitting out. Delivered to BOAC at London (Heathrow) Airport on 20 May 1958. Commenced service with BOAC on 16 June 1958 as BA 567/19.

G-AOVL was leased to British West Indian Airways during 1958 and also operated the first BOAC scheduled service to Caracas, Venezuela on 28 October 1958. On 19 January 1963 while at London (Heathrow) Airport, G-AOVL suffered a damaged nose wheel leg during towing to the central area. The aircraft was changed to G-AOVJ but this was delayed due to a bogey jack defect. G-AOVL was again decided upon but not before a delay of 20½ hours. On 25 February 1965 G-AOVL suffered a damaged rudder control.

Withdrawn from service by BOAC following her last service on 28 April 1965 she was leased to British Eagle International Airlines on 30 April 1965, named 'Enterprise', later 'Resolution', and purchased by them on 18 April 1968.

Leased to Monarch Airlines from 17 February 1969 she was purchased on 31 July 1969. Withdrawn from service and scrapped at Luton Airport during July 1971 following use as a cabin staff training airframe.

G–AOVM

SERIES 310
Constructors No. 13421
Built at Filton
C of A: 13.5.58

VARIANT 312
Production No. 048
First flight 29.4.58

XX-367 with A&AEE Boscombe Down. The high visibility propellers are clearly shown to advantage and the name 'Team Spirit' is seen. (Flightlines International)

Ordered by BOAC she was flown to Marshall's of Cambridge for fitting out on 13 May 1958 and delivered to BOAC at London (Heathrow) Airport on 10 June 1958. G-AOVM went into service on 26 June 1958 as BA 581/130. On 27 February 1963 while at Richmond, G-AOVM was taxiing on to the apron after landing when she rolled on to soft ground approximately 15 feet from the hard standing. G-AOVM operating as RCH 3374 was delayed for six hours while waiting for equipment to tow her out. The last service that G-AOVM operated for BOAC was on 26 March 1964 on a flight from Salisbury to London as BA 922/086.

British Eagle International Airlines leased this aircraft on a five year hire-purchase agreement and she was delivered on 29 March 1964. Later named 'Team Spirit', she was purchased by British Eagle and converted to a 312F at Speke, Liverpool in December 1967. G-AOVM operated British Eagle's last flight on 7 November 1968 whilst positioning following the demise of British Eagle International Airlines. G-AOVM was purchased by Air Spain on 6 March 1969 and re-registered EC-BSY, wearing full livery from 1 December 1969. Use by the Australian airline Southern Cross International did not take place and although the livery was applied, it was removed prior to leaving the hangar.

Withdrawn from service and sold to the Ministry of Defence in November 1971 and operated in the markings of Aircraft and Armament Experimental Establishment (A&AEE Boscombe Down), retained name 'Team Spirit', serialled XX-367. Received at Boscombe Down on 3 May 1972. By the end of March 1981 this aircraft had flown 33 100.10 hours and landed 10 203 times.

XX-367 celebrated her 25th Anniversary when she flew back into Filton on 29 April 1983 under the command of Fl.Lt. David Berry and Sqdn Ldr Ken Newman. The flight engineer was Alan Kidson. All were members on the Air Transport Flight 'B' Sqdn. Also on board was Sqdn Ldr Clive Osborne.

Withdrawn from service by the MOD, XX-367 was ferried to Cranfield under the Command of Squadron Leader David Berry for storage until delivery to Katale Aero Transport registered as 9Q-CHY in March 1984, named 'Hubert'. Purchased by Business Cash Flow Aviation and retained name 'Team Spirit'.

Following a revision of BCF's livery, 9Q-CHY was repainted to match their Boeing 707 and a new name was applied to her nose section – 'Mwenye Mikebwe', the grandmother of Dr Mayani. At the end of January 1991, it is reported that 9Q-CHY is still in operation, following a heavy check 2 'Zairean style' overhaul which possibly included the fitting of a new freight floor. This was the one and only Britannia aircraft still operating in 1991.

STOP PRESS

9Q-CHY operated her last flight from Mbuji-Mayi to N'Djili, Kinshasa on Saturday 6 July 1991. Because of serious oil consumption and a very alarming night time approach with engine oil gauges showing absolute minimum allowed, the Britannia was formally grounded by Dr Mayani (owner of BCF) at 11.00am 7 July 1991. This was a tragic day for the Bristol Britannia – although the aircraft is now up for sale. Any takers please contact BCF Aviation, Kinshasa Airport, Zaire.

G–AOVN

SERIES 310	VARIANT 312
Constructors No. 13422	Production No. 013
Built at Filton	First flight 16.5.58
C of A: 23.5.58	

G-AOVN getting airborne and showing the retraction of the main undercarriage. (Aviation Photo News)

Ordered by BOAC, G-AOVN was delivered to them at London (Heathrow) Airport on 4 July 1958 after being fitted out at Marshall's of Cambridge on 27 May 1958. G-AOVN went on service with BOAC on 23 July 1958 as BA 567/40.

On 27 May 1962 while taxiing into position for take-off at London (Heathrow) Airport, both nose wheels sheared at the axle and the aircraft came to a sudden halt, with thankfully no injuries. While at New York, on 26 June 1962 the nose strut inflation adapter was sheared off by the tow bar as it was being disconnected.

Withdrawn from service by BOAC, G-AOVN was leased to British Eagle International Airlines on 2 June 1964, named 'Prospect', and was next to be converted by British Eagle to a 312F but never done. Purchased by Monarch Airlines on 3 June 1969. At the end of April 1972, G-AOVN had flown 33 069.22 hours and made 8916 landings. Leased to African Safari Airways on 28 September 1972, and returned to Monarch on 2 November 1972.

Withdrawn from service by Monarch Airlines and scrapped during February 1974. The nose section was used at Gatwick Airport by Laker Airways for cabin crew training and later by Orion Airways at East Midlands Airport.

G–AOVO

SERIES 310
Constructors No. 13423
Built at Filton
C of A: 11.7.58

VARIANT 312
Production No. 014
First flight 3.7.58

G-AOVO taxiing at London (Heathrow) in BOAC livery. (Andy Anderson)

Ordered by BOAC, and flown to Marshall's of Cambridge for fitting out on 15 July 1958, then delivered to BOAC at London (Heathrow) Airport on 4 September 1958. On service with BOAC on 5 October 1958 flying as BA 567/82. During service with BOAC, G-AOVO was leased to East African Airways Corporation in late 1958 until early 1959 when returned to BOAC.

On 3 July 1961, while under tow at New York, G-AOVO suffered damage due to the tow bar head shear-pin shearing allowing the aircraft to roll backwards and hit the blast fence adjacent to No. 17 hangar. Damage was confined to the port elevator and tail cone, no casualties were caused. The last flight operated by G-AOVO for BOAC was on 23 November 1963 as BA RCH/3198 between Hong Kong and London.

G-AOVO was leased to British Eagle International Airlines on 1 January 1964 under a five year hire-purchase agreement for eventual sale. In service with British Eagle, G-AOVO was painted in full livery and named 'Bonaventure'.

While in service with British Eagle, G-AOVO was tragically lost on approach to Innsbruck on 29 February 1964, when at 14.14 GMT. she crashed into Clungezer mountain in the Austrian Alps, tragically killing three flight crew, five cabin crew and 75 passengers.

G-AOVO in British Eagle service with whom she was tragically lost. (Aviation Photo News)

G–AOVP

SERIES 310
Constructors No. 13424
Built at Filton
C of A: 29.7.58

VARIANT 312
Production No. 015
First flight 22.7.58

G-AOVP a variant 312 with Lloyd International, seen at London (Heathrow). (Aviation Photo News)

G-AOVP following the fitting of the forward freight door and designated a 312F is seen at London (Heathrow) during her sub-lease to East African Airways. (Aviation Photo News)

Ordered by BOAC, G-AOVP was officially taken on charge on 31 July 1958, and flown to Marshall's of Cambridge for fitting out on 19 August 1958, she was delivered to BOAC at London (Heathrow) Airport on 17 September 1958. G-AOVP went into service on 7 February 1959 as BA 162/248A.

While in service with BOAC, G-AOVP was used by Her Majesty the Queen Mother for a royal tour during December 1958.

Leased to British European Airways during April and May 1961 for their European schedules, she returned to BOAC in May 1961. On 2 March 1963 while at Prestwick, the number 2 engine nacelle tail cone was damaged by the air stairs as they were placed into position for disembarking passengers. Operating as BA 646/370, G-AOVP was delayed for one hour. The starboard wing was damaged on 3 August 1964, when during violent storms G-AOVP was blown from her parked position, she was later immobilised. Five days later, G-AOVP operated her last service with BOAC.

Leased to Lloyd International on 15 April 1965 she was operated from Stansted Airport, and converted to 312F in December 1967. Sub-leased by East African Airways during 1968 she was later purchased by Lloyd International on 15 January 1969. By the end of April 1972 G-AOVP had flown 31 392.33 hours and made 8949 landings. Purchased IAS Cargo Airlines on 10 July 1973 and operated until G-AOVP was withdrawn from service and stored at Biggin Hill in August 1974 and later broken up from June 1977. At the end of her career, G-AOVP totalled 36 858.03 hours and 10 132 landings.

G–AOVR

SERIES 310	VARIANT 312
Constructors No. 13429	Production No. 016
Built at Filton	First flight 4.8.58
C of A: 26.8.58	

G-AOVR on finals with No.4 prop feathered. (Aviation Photo News)

Ordered by BOAC and flown to Marshall's of Cambridge on 27 August 1958 for fitting out she was delivered to BOAC at London (Heathrow) Airport on 3 October 1958. On service from 28 November 1958 as BA 549/216.

On 14 April 1963 G-AOVR had to divert to New York after taking off from Niagara, because of grass which had been ingested by Nos. 1 and 4 engines causing rough running. The aircraft was changed at New York and the flight allocated as BA RCH 3500. G-AOVR operated her last flight for BOAC on 26 May 1964.

EC-BFJ at London (Heathrow) Airport in Air Spain livery. (Aviation Photo News)

Sold to British Eagle International Airlines on 22 February 1965, BOAC'S title was relinquished on 17 October 1966. With British Eagle, the name 'Talisman' was allocated.

Purchased by Air Spain on 20 October 1966 and registered EC-WFJ, named 'Atlantico', later 'Isla Canaries', she was re-registered EC-BFJ in October 1966. EC-BFJ had flown a total of 29 716.40 hours and made 8368 landings by the end of April 1972. IAS Cargo Airlines purchased EC-BFJ in April, 1973. Later withdrawn from service she was scrapped during August 1975 at Biggin Hill, Kent. Her cabin fittings were used for the restoration of the cabin interior of G-AOVT at Duxford.

G–AOVS

SERIES 310	VARIANT 312
Constructors No. 13430	Production No. 017
Built at Filton	First flight 5.9.58
C of A: 18.9.58	

G-AOVS seen loading with palletised freight. (Redcoat Air Cargo Ltd)

Ordered by BOAC and taken on charge from 22 September 1958, G-AOVS was flown to Marshall's of Cambridge for fitting out on 24 September 1958. Delivery to BOAC at London (Heathrow) Airport took place on 29 October 1958.

Leased to Lloyd International on 4 July 1965 she returned in July 1965. Sub-leased to British Eagle International Airlines from July to December 1965. She was then purchased and converted to a 312F in June 1966 by Lloyd International Airlines. G-AOVS was leased to El-Al from December 1970 to June 1971 for their freight services, returning to Lloyd International in June 1971.

IAS Cargo Airlines purchased G-AOVS on 18 January 1973 and operated her until she was sold to Aivex Holdings on 28 December 1973, who then leased her back to IAS Cargo Airlines on 28 December 1973 until sold to Westwings Aviation Services Limited on 14 October 1975. But on the same day was leased to IAS, later sub-leased to Invicta (1976) Limited from 1 January 1976 and returned to IAS on 13 June 1976. G-AOVS was withdrawn from service at Luton Airport in January 1977.

G-AOVS as 'G-BRAC' in the BBC TV series 'Buccaneer' wearing REDAIR titles. (Peter J Bish)

Purchased by Aivex Holdings Limited on 21 March 1977 and leased to Redcoat Air Cargo in May 1977, she was named 'Christian'. G-AOVS was then purchased on 4 April 1979. At the end of August 1978, G-AOVS had flown 40 957.30 hours and landed 10 467 times.

G-AOVS received the registration G-BRAC for the BBC Television series 'Buccaneer' after the loss of the real G-BRAC. She was withdrawn from use at Luton Airport in July 1979 with 42 609 hours and 10 889 landings logged in total. The fuselage was transferred to the airport fire ground for non-destructive fire training.

At the end of May 1992, it is reported that the fuselage is still used for non-descructive fire training and is very much in evidence.

Buccaneer cast in front of G-AOVS at Luton. (Peter J Bish)

G–AOVT

SERIES 310	VARIANT 312
Constructors No. 13427	Production No. 018
Built at Filton	First flight 17.12.58
C of A: 30.12.58	

G-AOVT in British Eagle livey, named 'Ajax'. (Peter J Bish)

Destined for BOAC she was wheeled out of the production hangar at Filton on 14 December 1958, fitted with the later series Proteus engines along with other modifications meaning G-AOVT was completed to almost 320 series standard. She was delivered to BOAC at London (Heathrow) Airport on 1 January 1959.

G-AOVT was leased by East African Airways Corporation during 1961, then British European Airways for their European schedules in April and May of 1961, returning to BOAC in May 1961 and finally leased to Nigerian Airways the same year. Operated on lease by British Eagle International Airlines from 13 September 1963, she was named 'Enterprise', later 'Ajax'. Purchased by Monarch Airlines on 8 August 1969. G-AOVT operated its last passenger flight for Monarch on behalf of Northeast Airlines to Lisbon on 13 October 1974 after one of their Trident airliners became unserviceable. She was leased by Invicta International Airlines on 13 December 1974 until 10 March 1975 when she returned to Monarch Airlines.

As she was surplus to requirements, Monarch Airlines donated G-AOVT to the Duxford Aviation Society, Cambridge for public display. Delivery took place on 29 June 1975. G-AOVT had accumulated 35 739 flight hours and carried out 10 834 landings (see Preserved Britannias section).

4X–AGA

SERIES 310
Constructors No. 13232
Built at Filton

VARIANT 313
Production No. 024
First flight 28.7.57

4X-AGA a variant 313, at Filton in the livery of El-Al. (Bristol Aeroplane Co Ltd/British Aerospace)

Ordered by the Israeli airline El-Al, 4X-AGA was flown from Filton on handling and acceptance trials between July and September 1957. Delivery to El-Al took place on 5 September 1957 and she embarked on route-proving flights, returning to Filton on 10 November 1957 for repairs to her rear fuselage, flying back to El-Al on 1 December 1957.

By the end of 1960, this Britannia had flown well over 8000 hours, by far the highest amount of any Britannia in service at that time. British United Airways leased 4X-AGA as G-ASFV from 19 March 1963 operating her on behalf of El-Al during a strike by El-Al's staff and returning to them on 1 April 1963, as 4X-AGA.

Purchased by Globe Air on 3 April 1964, registered HB-ITB. During 1965 HB-ITB was leased to International Air on several operations, but it was in Globe Air's service that HB-ITB crashed and was written off at Nicosia, Cyprus on

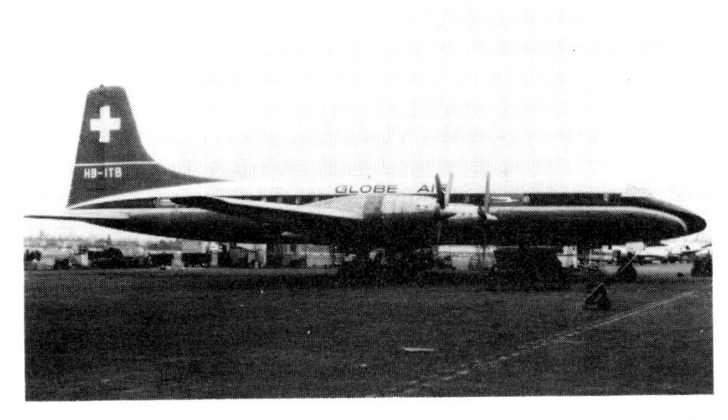

HB-ITB was tragically lost on 19 April 1967, while in service with Globe Air, killing 126 of the 130 on board. (Military Aircraft Photographs)

19 April 1967, after undershooting the runway. Of the 130 persons on board, comprising ten crew and 120 passengers, all but four perished in this tragic accident. Three passengers and one air stewardess survived near the tail section and the largest piece of identifying wreckage was the tail unit, 13 metres long, which was resting on its starboard side 204 metres from the point of impact. To date there still can be found near the runway some of the aircraft's remains.

4X–AGB

SERIES 310
Constructors No. 13233
Built at Filton
C of A: 13.2.62

VARIANT 313
Production No. 025
First flight 2.9.57

4X-AGB in the livery of El-Al. (Aviation Photo News)

Ordered by the Israeli airline El-Al, and delivered to them on 19 October 1957 as 4X-AGB. She flew the first route-proving flight from Tel-Aviv to New York on 25 October 1957. On 22 December 1957, 4X-AGB flew El-Al's first transatlantic service to New York.

Registered G-ARWZ to Bristol Aircraft Services Limited on 13 February 1962 she was delivered to BUA on lease the following day, and returned to EL-AL on 26 March 1965. Purchased by Air Spain in March 1967, she was registered EC-WFL, re-registered EC-BFL and named 'Cantabrico'. By the end of April 1972, EC-BFL had flown 31 461.15 hours and landed 8557 times.

EC-BFL was purchased by IAS Cargo Airlines from September 1973, until being withdrawn from use and used as spares. She was finally broken up in Palma during 1974.

G-ARWZ in BUA livery minus the Union Jack on the tail. (Aviation Photo News)

4X–AGC

SERIES 310	VARIANT 313
Constructors No. 13234	Production No. 027
Built at Filton	First flight 4.10.57
C of A: 12.3.66	

4X-AGC a variant 313 with El-Al. (Aircraft Photographic)

Destined as a series 250 prototype, an all-freight version, she was allocated the registration G-ANGK. Construction never commenced and the registration was cancelled in April 1955 and the construction number re-allocated. Finally completed as a variant 313, registered 4X-AGC she was delivered to El-Al on 28 November 1957.

During service with El-Al, 4X-AGC made a record proving flight from New York to London on 3 December 1957, a distance of 3444 statute miles in 8 hours and 3 minutes. Another record was achieved on 19 December 1957 flying from New York to Tel-Aviv, a distance of 6100 statute miles in 14 hours and 56 minutes, at a block speed of 407mph. This was claimed as a long distance record for a commercial airliner.

Leased by British United Airways as G-ARXA from 12 March 1962, delivery took place on 14 March she returned to

G-ARXA in BUA livery. (Aircraft Photographic)

El-Al on 27 September 1964. Leased to British Eagle on 22 April 1966, registered G-ARXA and painted in full livery, but given no name. With the demise of British Eagle, G-ARXA was purchased by Monarch Airlines. El-Al sub-leased from Monarch on 8 November 1968.

Following her arrival at Luton Airport, she was withdrawn from service by Monarch Airlines and used for spares in November 1970 and later scrapped.

4X–AGD

SERIES 310	VARIANT 313
Constructors No. 13431	Production No. 004
Built at Filton	First flight 21.2.59

HB-ITC a variant 313 with the Swiss airline Globe Air. (Aviation Photo News)

5Y-ALT in African Safari Airways livery dominated by the 'Zebra tail'. (Aviation Photo News)

Ordered by the Israeli airline El-Al. During manufacture 4X-AGD was modified to nearly full series 320 specification. Delivered to El-Al on 7 March 1959 she was operated for them by BUA from 18 March to 8 April 1963 because of a strike by El-Al staff. During that period she flew with the British registration G-ASFU.

Globe Air purchased 4X-AGD on 8 March 1965 re-registered HB-ITC. Purchased by African Safari Airways she was registered 5X-UVH from 26 December 1967, and re-registered 5Y-ALT from 25 May 1970. At the end of April 1970, this Britannia had totalled 29 926.08 flying hours and carried out 9069 landings. Purchased by African Cargo Airways in November 1973, named 'Intrico Pioneer', and later withdrawn from service at Stansted Airport and used for spares in May 1975, the remains being transferred to the Airport Fire Service in June 1975.

CF–CZA

SERIES 310	VARIANT 314
Constructors No. 13393	Production No. 033
Built at Belfast	First flight 11.1.58
C of A: 9.7.65	

Ordered by Canadian Pacific Airlines, and delivered on 9 April 1958, wearing Canadian Pacific's original livery, she was named 'Empress of Buenos Aires', and fleet numbered 421. CF-CZA carried out a record proving return flight between London and Vancouver between 20–24 February 1958, via the north pole. The distance covered was 5100 statute miles in a time of 13 hours and 57 minutes at a block speed of 366mph.

In mid 1959 a new livery was applied and CF-CZA was re-named 'Empress of Hong Kong'. Air Links Ltd purchased CF-CZA in May 1965 and she was operated on behalf of British United Airways. In July 1965 she was registered G-ATGD and painted in the new name of Transglobe Airways and delivered on 9 August 1965.

African Safari Airways purchased G-ATGD on 16 September 1969, firstly registered 5X-UVT and re-registered 5Y-ALP on 26 April 1970. Withdrawn from use and stored at Biggin Hill, Kent in April 1971 and scrapped during December of the same year.

G-ATGD at Gatwick airport in Transglobe Airways livery. (Aviation Photo News)

CF-CZA a variant 314 operated by Canadian Pacific Airlines. (Bristol Aeroplane Co Ltd/ British Aerospace)

CF–CZB

SERIES 310	VARIANT 314
Constructors No. 13394	Production No. 036
Built at Belfast	First flight 14.4.58

CF-CZB in Canadian Pacific's early livery named 'Empress of Vancouver'. (Military Aircraft Photographs)

Ordered by Canadian Pacific Airlines and registered CF-CZB, this Britannia received the fleet number 522. Named 'Empress of Vancouver', and later 'Empress of Lima' she was delivered via Prestwick Airport on 29 April 1958.

Tragically, CF-CZB was written off while attempting an overshoot at Hickham Field, Honolulu, Hawaii on 22 July 1962 and sadly of the 40 people on board, 27 were killed.

CF-CZB renamed 'Empress of Lima' and sporting a replaced leading edge to the tailfin. (Aviation Photo News)

CF–CZC

SERIES 310	VARIANT 314
Constructors No. 13395	Production No. 039
Built at Belfast	First flight 13.5.58
C of A: 12.12.65	

CF-CZC a variant 314 in a fine air to air pose. (Bristol Aeroplane Co Ltd/British Aerospace)

Ordered by Canadian Pacific Airlines as one of six variant 314 Britannia aircraft. CF-CZC was delivered via Prestwick Airport on 20 May 1958 and named 'Empress of Madrid' later 'Empress of Tokyo', fleet numbered 423 later 523. Released by Canadian Pacific Airlines in June 1965 and purchased by Air Links Limited she operated in their new name Transglobe Airways from 30 November 1965 as the British registered G-ATLE. In June 1968, G-ATLE was leased by Trek Airways until the collapse of Transglobe in November 1968.

IAS Cargo Airlines purchased G-ATLE on 30 December 1969 for spares. Withdrawn from use at Gatwick Airport, G-ATLE was laid on her belly near the control tower and used for fire training by the BAA until finally scrapped in 1984.

G-ATLE in Transglobe livery. (Aircraft Photographic)

CF–CZD

SERIES 310	VARIANT 314
Constructors No. 13396	Production No. 004
Built at Belfast	First flight 13.6.58
C of A: 4.2.66	

Ordered by Canadian Pacific Airlines and named 'Empress of Santiago', fleet number 524, CF-CZD was delivered via Prestwick Airport on 27 June 1958. Mid 1959 saw CF-CZD in Canadian Pacific's new livery, re-named 'Empress of Buenos Aires' later 'Empress of Winnipeg'.

CF-CZD in Canadian Pacific's second Britannia livery. (Aviation Photo News)

British registered G-ATNZ was purchased by Caledonian Airways who operated her from 31 January 1966 named 'County of Inverness'. Re-named 'County of Ayr' she was operated by Caledonian/BUA from 17 May 1966. G-ATNZ was taken on lease by IAS Cargo Airlines on 10 March 1971 and purchased on 20 May 1971.

Withdrawn from service and stored at Biggin Hill, Kent in late April, 1971 she was broken up and scrapped during June 1972.

G-ATNZ in Caledonian Airways' smart livery. (Aviation Photo News)

CF–CZW

SERIES 310	VARIANT 314
Constructors No. 13453	Production No. 005
Built at Belfast	First flight 22.7.58
C of A: 5.6.64	

Purchased by Canadian Pacific Airlines, and flown from Belfast to Filton on 24 July 1958 for pre-delivery checks, she was named 'Empress of Edmonton', with fleet number 425, and later named 'Empress of Toronto', registered CF-CZW.

British Eagle International Airlines leased CF-CZW on 20 May 1964 British registered G-ASTF, and named 'Concord'. She returned to Canadian Pacific Airlines on 15 October 1964, and was repainted in their new livery and named 'Empress of Rome'.

Leased to Caledonian Airways registered G-ASTF on 27

CF-CZW a variant 314. (Aviation Photo News)

G-ASTF being scrapped at Gatwick Airport. (Military Aircraft Photographs)

January 1966 she was named 'Flagship Bonnie Scotland', late 'County of Perth'.

Withdrawn from use by Caledonian Airways and storec at Gatwick Airport from November 1969 and scrapped i October 1970.

CF–CZX

SERIES 310	VARIANT 314
Constructors No. 13428	Production No. 006
Built at Filton	First flight 19.6.58
C of A: 6.1.66	

Ordered by Canadian Pacific Airlines, and delivered v Prestwick Airport on 3 July 1958, named 'Empress of San Maria', with fleet number 426, and registered CF-CZ Painted in original CPA livery. Re-named 'Empress Montreal' mid 1959.

Purchased by Caledonian Airways on 28 December 19 named 'County of Midlothian', she was given the Britis registration G-ATMA. On 31 October 1969 she was purc ased again by Canadian Pacific Airlines and registered C CZX and named 'Empress of Canada'. Leased to Africa Safari Airways, registered 5Y-ANS at the end of 196 Purchased by IAS Cargo Airlines from 5 April 1971, th registration changed to G-ATMA in November 1971. Lease

G-ATMA ex 5Y-ANS in African International livery. (Aviation Photo News)

by African International from 9 February 1972 until 18 May 1972, registered firstly 5Y-ANS then G-ATMA.

She was operated again by IAS Cargo Airlines as G-ATMA from 18 May 1972 until being withdrawn from use and stored at Biggin Hill, Kent in June 1973. Scrapped in August 1975.

G–APNA

SERIES 310	VARIANT 317
Constructors No. 13425	Production No. 001
Built at Filton	First flight 10.10.58
C of A: 27.10.58	

Ordered by Clanair Ltd (Hunting Clan). In late 1957 she was officially on Hunting Clan's charge from 11 December 1958, but remained at Filton for crew training until early 1959. G-APNA was painted in the livery of 'The British and Commonwealth Shipping Company (Aviation) Limited' (Hunting Clan's owners), transferring to Hunting Clan Air Transport Limited on 31 May 1960.

G-APNA was leased for periods during 1960-1961 by BOAC, EAAC, and BEA. She was repainted after British United Airways merged in 1960 with Hunting Clan, in the livery of BUA.

Purchased by Donaldson International Airlines on 2 October 1967, and leased to Lloyd International during October 1967. She returned in May 1969. In service with Donaldson G-APNA was named 'Juno'. Withdrawn from service and

G-APNA a variant 317 at London (Heathrow). (Aviation Photo News)

stored at Baginton, Coventry in May 1972. By the end of April 1972 she had flown 33 668.23 hours and landed 7649 times.

IAS Cargo Airlines purchased G-APNA in October 1972, but scrapped her at Baginton in July 1973.

G-APNA partly stripped down prior to scrapping at Coventry (Bagington) Airport. Note the starboard main undercarriage which has sunk into the grass. (Martin Street Photography, Honiton)

G–APNB

SERIES 310	VARIANT 317
Constructors No. 13426	Production No. 002
Built at Filton	First flight 10.11.58
C of A: 21.11.58	

G-APNB the second variant 317, wearing the titles of 'The British and Commonwealth Shipping Company (Aviation) Ltd'. (Aviation Photo News)

Part of an order by Clanair Ltd (Hunting Clan) in December 1956 for two variant 317 Britannia aircraft this one was registered G-APNB and taken on charge from 2 December 1958 but instead remained at Filton in storage until June 1959.

While at Filton G-APNB was painted in the livery of the British and Commonwealth Shipping Company Ltd who were the owners of Hunting Clan Air Transport Ltd. Delivery took place on 30 April 1959.

Previously, on 21 April 1959, G-APNB was transferred to the British and Commonwealth Shipping Company (Aviation) Ltd and the addition of '(Aviation)' was placed on the fuselage titles. G-APNB transferred to Hunting Clan Air Transport Ltd on 31 May 1960 but did not wear these titles.

During periods from 1959 to 1961 G-APNB was chartered for operations by BOAC, East African Airways Corporation and British European Airways. The livery of British United Airways was applied during 1960 following the merger with Hunting Clan. Operations by BUA commenced on 1 July 1960.

G-APNB at London (Heathrow) in crude East African Airways livery. (Aviation Photo News)

Donaldson International Airlines purchased G-APNB from BUA in October 1967 and during the same month she was leased to Lloyd International Airways and operated by them until returned to her owners on 16 January 1969. Once back with Donaldson International the name 'Carillon' was allocated.

Withdrawn from use, G-APNB was stored at Luton Airport from March 1971 until purchased by Airline Engineering Services of Luton Airport on 6 October 1971. Used as a source of spares she was broken up from November and scrapped.

CU–P668

SERIES 310	VARIANT 318
Constructors No. 13432	Production No. 001
Built at Filton	First flight 24.11.58
C of A: 6.4.60	

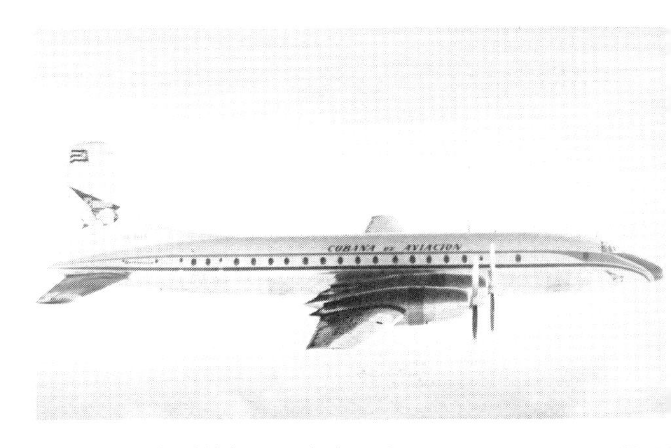

CU-P668 a variant 318 in a superb air to air pose. (Bristol Aeroplane Co Ltd/British Aerospace)

G-APYY was leased to Eagle Airways by Cubana. (Andy Anderson)

Ordered by Cubana de Aviacion, and wheeled out of th production hangar at Filton on 21 November 1958. CU-P66 initially remained at Filton for crew training until 1 December 1958. Delivery to Cubana at Havana, Cuba too place on 18 December 1958, flying from London (Heathrow Airport via the Azores. Registered CU-T668 once in servic with Cubana, she was named 'Libertad'.

CU-T114 owned by another Cuban airline Aerocaribbean, seen at Luton. (Peter J Bish)

Surplus to requirements in early 1960, CU-T668 flew back to Filton in March 1960 for lease to Eagle Airways, commencing 25 March 1960 and taken on charge and British registered G-APYY on 24 March 1960. She was delivered from Filton on 5 April 1960. Eagle Airways changed their name to Cunard Eagle Airways on 1 September 1960 and G-APYY continued in their service until returning to Cubana de Aviacion on 19 September 1961.

She was repainted in Cubana's new livery and re-registered CU-T668, until leased to Ceskoslovenske Aerolinie (CSA) when she was registered OK-MBA from October 1961, and operated until returning to Cubana in May 1964. This Britannia was the first to operate behind the 'Iron Curtain'.

Re-registered CU-T668 she has now been withdrawn from service at Havana, Cuba. By the end of August 1978, CU-T668 had flown 29 356.20 hours and landed 6859 times. The aircraft has now been scrapped.

OK-MBA at London (Heathrow) whilst leased by Ceskoslovenske Aerolinie. (Aircraft Photographic)

CU–P669

SERIES 310	VARIANT 318
Constructors No. 13433	Production No. 002
Built at Filton	First flight 19.1.59

Ordered by Cubana de Aviacion, she was wheeled out of Filton's production hangar on 16 January 1959. Delivery took place on 6 February 1959 at Havana, Cuba. Once in airline

CU-T669 in Cubana's second livery worn by the Britannia. (Military Aircraft Photographs)

service the registration CU-P669 was changed to CU-T669 during February 1959. CU-T669 continued in service with Cubana was often seen at Luton Airport for servicing until May 1984.

At the end of February 1981, CU-T669 had flown a total of 24 690.52 hours and made 6791 landings. CU-T669 was purchased by another Cuban airline, Aerocaribbean and registered CU-T114. Currently she is in storage at Havana, Cuba. It is unlikely that she will fly again.

CU–P670

SERIES 310	VARIANT 318
Constructors No. 13437	Production No. 003
Built at Filton	First flight 2.4.59

CU-T670 at Luton airport during maintenance. (Aviation Photo News)

Ordered by Cubana de Aviacion, and completed to almost 320 series standard, she was wheeled out of the production hanger at Filton on 31 March 1959, registered CU-P670. Stored at Filton, while awaiting payment and finally delivered on 15 May 1959 and re-registered CU-T670 once in service.

Leased to Ceskoslovenske C.S.A. during 1963 and returned the same year. By the end of July 1978, CU-T670 had flown 15 554.44 hours and made 4138 landings. Withdrawn from service she was stored at Havana, Cuba. The aircraft is now reported as having been scrapped.

CU–P671

SERIES 310	VARIANT 318
Constructors No. 13515	Production No. 004
Built at Filton	First flight 29.4.59

Built to nearly 320 series standard, and ordered by Cubana de Aviacion then taken on charge from 2 July 1959. Initially she was stored at Filton while awaiting payment from Cubana.

CU-P671 at London (Heathrow) prior to delivery to Cubana. (Aviation Photo News)

CU-T671 a variant 318 at Luton airport. (Peter J Bish)

OK-MBB at London (Heathrow) airport. (Aviation Photo News)

Delivered via London (Heathrow) Airport on 26 August 1959 registered CU-P671, once in airline service re-registered CU-T671.

Leased to Ceskoslovenske C.S.A. in November 1963, in a revised livery and registered OK-MBB, she returned to Cubana in January 1969, and was repainted in their new livery and registered CU-T671. At the end of March 1981 a total of 30 317.14 hours had been flown and 7407 landings made. She was withdrawn from service by Cubana and is now stored in the open at Havana, Cuba. She may well be preserved by the Cubans for posterity in the Cubana livery.

PART EIGHT

Bristol Britannia Series 320 Specifications

VARIANT: 324 (Canadian Pacific Airlines). Other Britannias were brought up to general 320 standard.

POWERPLANT: Four Bristol Proteus 766 turbo-props developing 4445ehp. driving 16ft de Havilland four-blade hollow steel propellers. Later round-tipped Duralumin propeller blades were fitted which were less liable to stone damage whilst operating in reverse pitch. They were also more efficient.

DIMENSIONS:		
	Wingspan	142ft 3.5in.
	Overall length	124ft 3in.
	Height	37ft 6in.
	Wing area	2075sq. ft.

PAYLOAD & PERFORMANCE: Still air range, maximum payload (34 900lb) over 4268 statute miles at a cruising speed of 357mph

Still air range, maximum fuel (including reserves) 5340 statute miles at a cruising speed of 357mph with 23 524lb payload.

CREW: 4 – 7.

PASSENGER ACCOMMODATION: First class, 82. Mixed, 12 first class and 69 tourist class. Tourist, 110. Maximum coach, 139.

CARGO ACCOMMODATION: 900cu. ft.

FUEL CAPACITY: 8580 imperial gallons.

WEIGHTS: Empty 86 394lb (manufacturers).
93 100lb (operators).
All up weight (including fuel) 185 000lb.

Total built: 2.

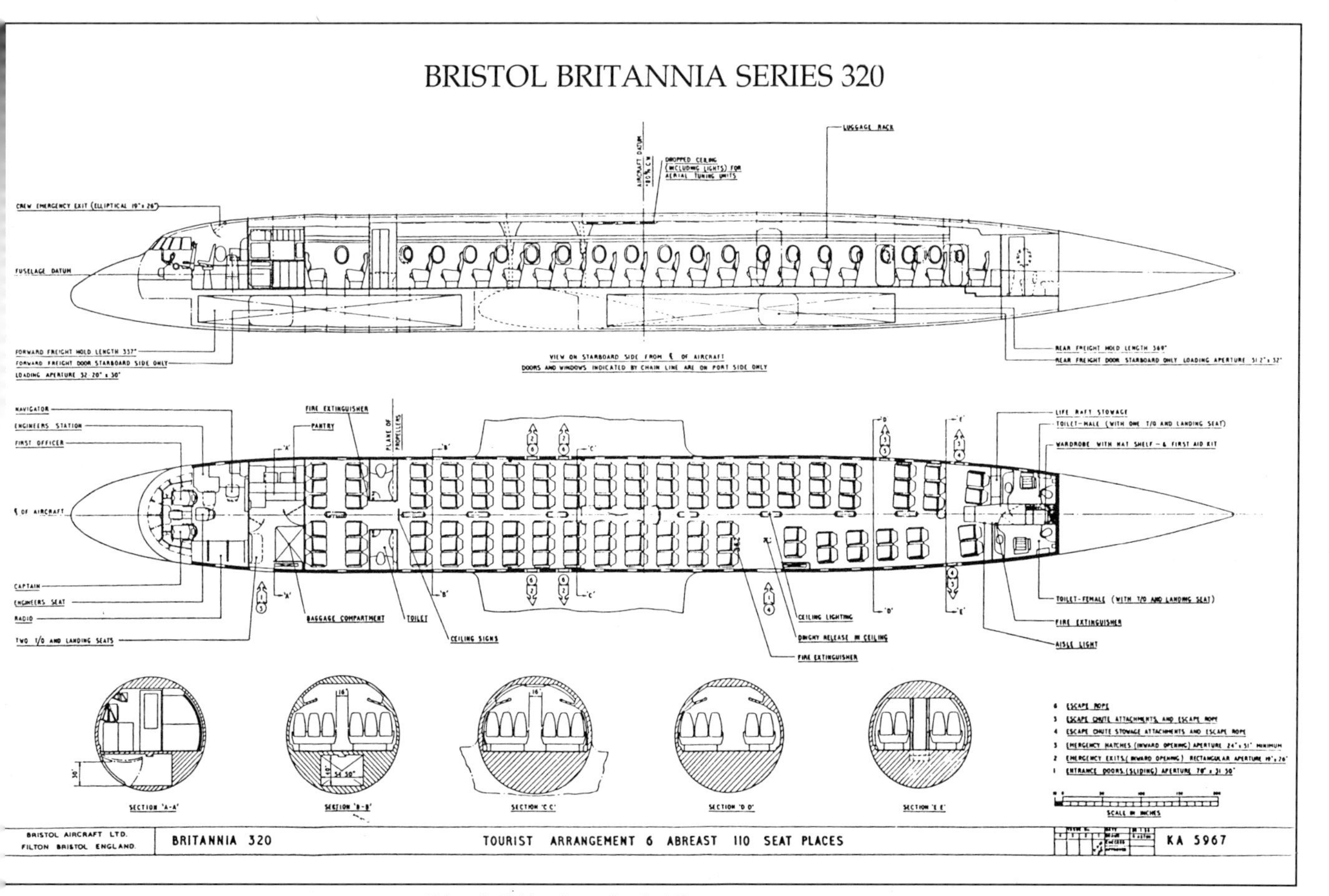

Britannia 324 interior seating for 110 passengers. (Manufacturer's)

BRITANNIA 320 GENERAL ARRANGEMENT DRAWING

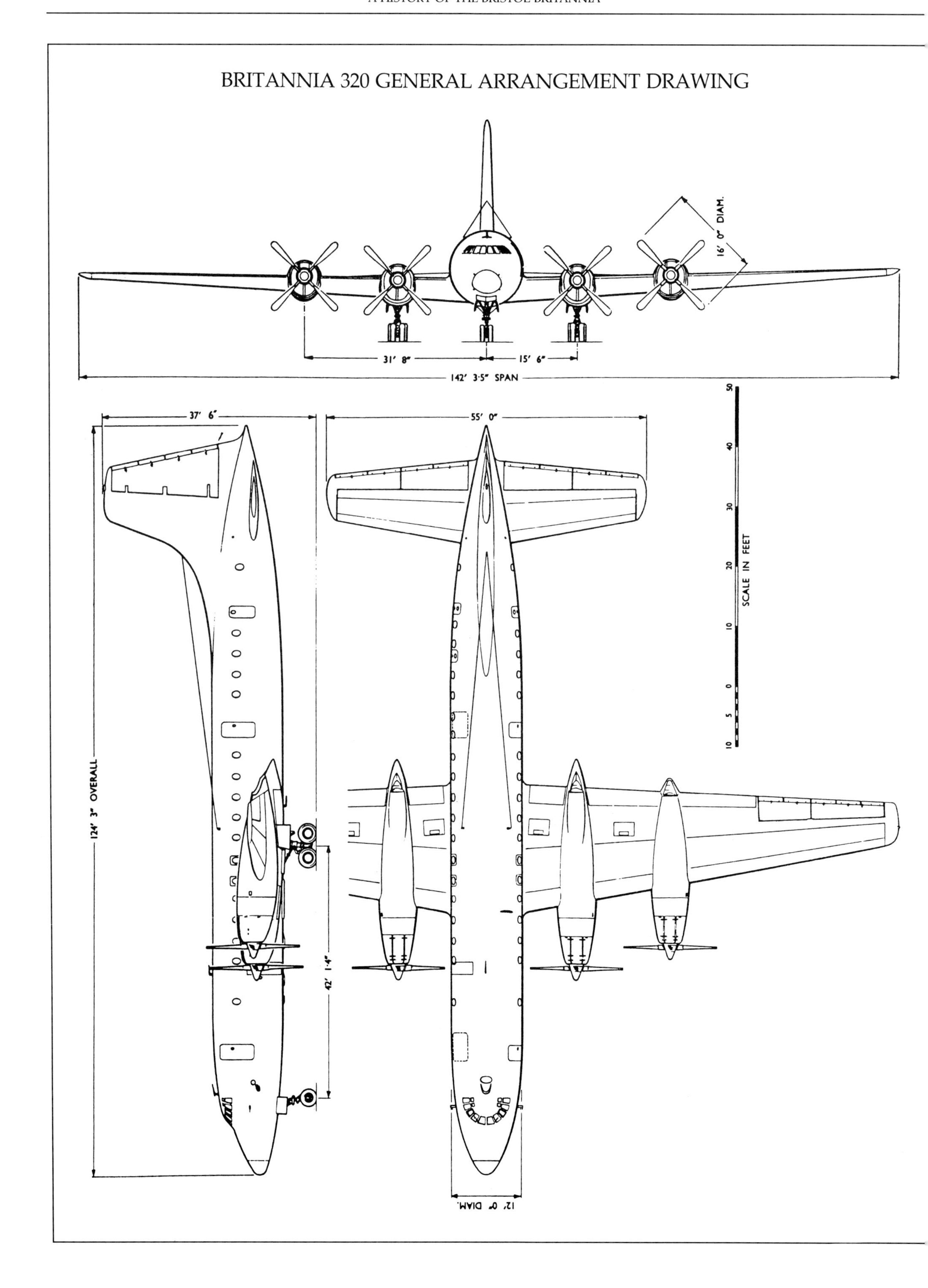

CF–CPD

SERIES 320	VARIANT 324
Constructors No. 13516	Production No. 001
Built at Filton	First flight 9.10.59
C of A: 9.3.61	

G-ARKA a variant 324 in the livery of Cunard Eagle Airways. (Aviation Photo News)

Ordered by Canadian Pacific Airlines in August 1959, and wheeled out of the hanger at Filton on 7th October 1959 as G-18-8 she was later registered CF-CPD, named 'Empress of Amsterdam', fleet numbered 527. Delivered to Canadian Pacific Airlines on 16 October 1959 on an 18-month lease. CF-CPD became surplus to requirements in January 1961 and was restored to the Bristol Aeroplane Company arriving back on 12 February 1961. Re-registered G-ARKA by Bristol Aircraft Limited on 15 February 1961. Repainted in the colours of Cunard Eagle Airways in February 1961 and delivered to them on 9 March 1961, named "Good Fortune" and granted her certificate of airworthiness on 9 March 1961.

Transferred to Bristol Aircraft Limited on 10 March 1964, she was leased by Cunard Eagle Airways the same day. With the new name of British Eagle International G-ARKA was purchased on 1 December 1967.

CCT Aircraft (Leasing) Limited purchased G-ARKA on 21 March 1969, but on 28 March 1969, G-ARKA was operated by Tellair of Switzerland. The company had hoped for the use of British Eagle Britannias on their tourist routes, but after the demise of British Eagle, Caledonian Airways operated ex-Eagle Britannias in Tellair's livery, using Caledonian cabin crews, etc., on charter flights from London (Heathrow) Airport. Registered HB-ITF, but this was never used. These charter flights ceased in October 1969 and in November 1969 G-ARKA was flown to Baginton, Coventry for storage and re-sale.

G-ARKA in Tellair livery. (Peter J Bish)

Purchased by Airline Engineering in June 1971. G-ARKA was used as a source for spares and scrapped at Baginton in October 1971.

CF–CPE

SERIES 320	VARIANT 324
Constructors No. 13517	Production No. 002
Built at Filton	First flight 4.11.59
C of A: 2.5.61	

CF-CPE as seen from another Britannia in flight. (Bristol Aeroplane Co Ltd/British Aerospace)

G-ARKB named 'Equality' while in service with British Eagle. (Military Aircraft Photographs)

Ordered by Canadian Pacific Airlines in August 1959 she was wheeled from the production hangar on 2 November 1959, painted in full livery, fleet numbered 528, named 'Empress of Mexico City'. Canadian registered CF-CPE and leased to Canadian Pacific Airlines on 13 November 1959.

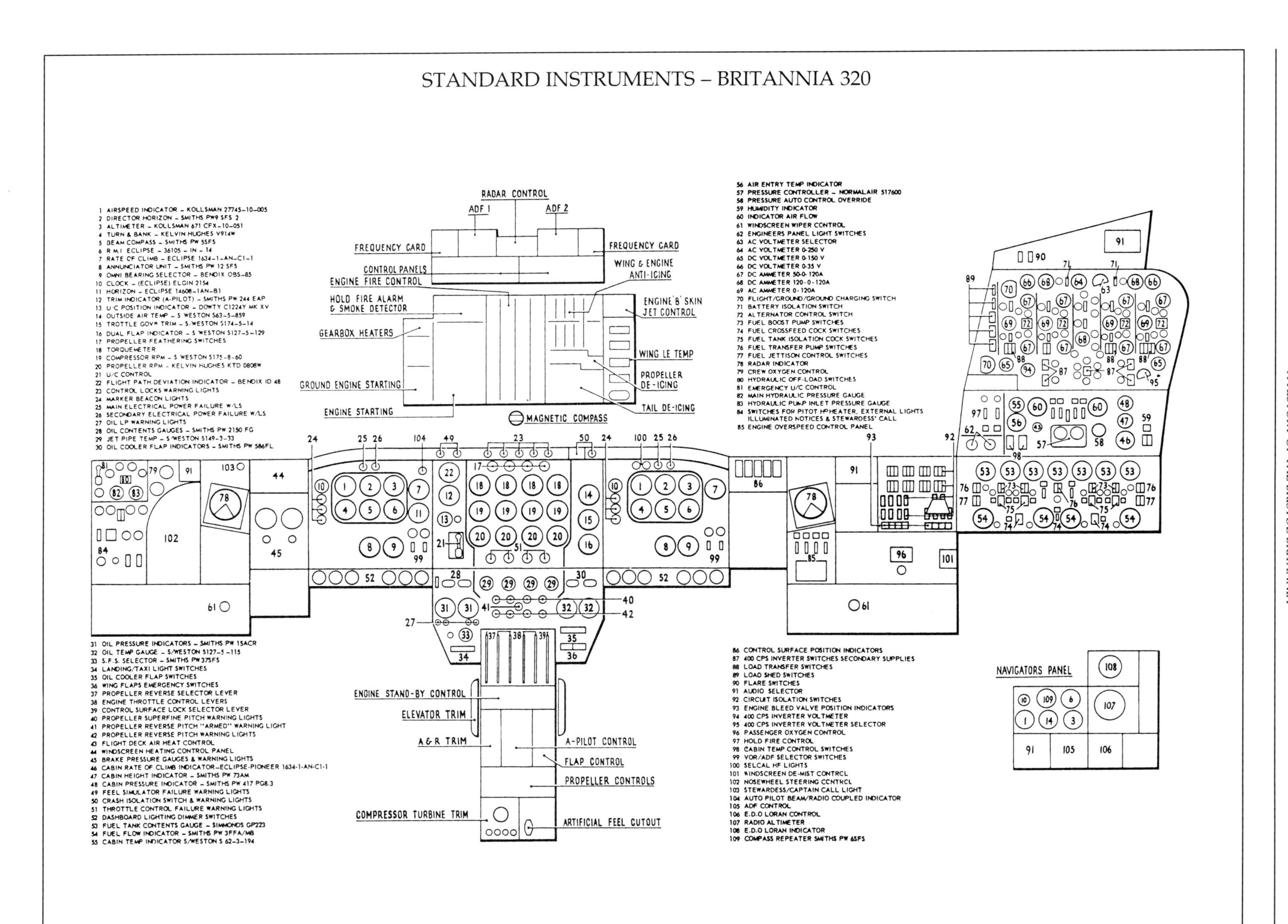
STANDARD INSTRUMENTS – BRITANNIA 320
RADAR CONTROL
ADF 1
ADF 2
FREQUENCY CARD
FREQUENCY CARD
CONTROL PANELS
ENGINE FIRE CONTROL
WING & ENGINE ANTI-ICING
HOLD FIRE ALARM & SMOKE DETECTOR
ENGINE 'B' SKIN JET CONTROL
GEARBOX HEATERS
WING LE TEMP
PROPELLER DE-ICING
GROUND ENGINE STARTING
ENGINE STARTING
TAIL DE-ICING
MAGNETIC COMPASS
ENGINE STAND-BY CONTROL
ELEVATOR TRIM
A & R TRIM
A-PILOT CONTROL
FLAP CONTROL
PROPELLER CONTROLS
COMPRESSOR TURBINE TRIM
ARTIFICIAL FEEL CUTOUT
NAVIGATORS PANEL
1 AIRSPEED INDICATOR – KOLLSMAN 27745-10-005
2 DIRECTOR HORIZON – SMITHS PW9 SFS 2
3 ALTIMETER – KOLLSMAN 671 CFX-10-051
4 TURN & BANK – KELVIN HUGHES V914W
5 BEAM COMPASS – SMITHS PW 5SFS
6 R.M.I. ECLIPSE – 36105 – IN – 14
7 RATE OF CLIMB – ECLIPSE 1634-1-AN-C1-1
8 ANNUNCIATOR UNIT – SMITHS PW 12 SFS
9 OMNI BEARING SELECTOR – BENDIX OBS-85
10 CLOCK – (ECLIPSE) ELGIN 2154
11 HORIZON – ECLIPSE 14608-1AN-B1
12 TRIM INDICATOR (A-PILOT) – SMITHS PW 244 EAP
13 U/C POSITION INDICATOR – DOWTY C1224Y MK XV
14 OUTSIDE AIR TEMP – S WESTON S63-5-859
15 TROTTLE GOVR TRIM – S/WESTON S174-5-14
16 DUAL FLAP INDICATOR – S WESTON S127-5-129
17 PROPELLER FEATHERING SWITCHES
18 TORQUEMETER
19 COMPRESSOR RPM – S WESTON S175-8-60
20 PROPELLER RPM – KELVIN HUGHES KTD 0808W
21 U/C CONTROL
22 FLIGHT PATH DEVIATION INDICATOR – BENDIX ID 48
23 CONTROL LOCKS WARNING LIGHTS
24 MARKER BEACON LIGHTS
25 MAIN ELECTRICAL POWER FAILURE W/LS
26 SECONDARY ELECTRICAL POWER FAILURE W/LS
27 OIL LP WARNING LIGHTS
28 OIL CONTENTS GAUGES – SMITHS PW 2150 FG
29 JET PIPE TEMP – S/WESTON S149-3-33
30 OIL COOLER FLAP INDICATORS – SMITHS PW 586FL
31 OIL PRESSURE INDICATORS – SMITHS PW 15ACR
32 OIL TEMP GAUGE – S/WESTON S127-5-115
33 S.F.S. SELECTOR – SMITHS PW 37SFS
34 LANDING/TAXI LIGHT SWITCHES
35 OIL COOLER FLAP SWITCHES
36 WING FLAPS EMERGENCY SWITCHES
37 PROPELLER REVERSE SELECTOR LEVER
38 ENGINE THROTTLE CONTROL LEVERS
39 CONTROL SURFACE LOCK SELECTOR LEVER
40 PROPELLER SUPERFINE PITCH WARNING LIGHTS
41 PROPELLER REVERSE PITCH "ARMED" WARNING LIGHT
42 PROPELLER REVERSE PITCH WARNING LIGHTS
43 FLIGHT DECK AIR HEAT CONTROL
44 WINDSCREEN HEATING CONTROL PANEL
45 BRAKE PRESSURE GAUGES & WARNING LIGHTS
46 CABIN RATE OF CLIMB INDICATOR–ECLIPSE-PIONEER 1634-1-AN-C1-1
47 CABIN HEIGHT INDICATOR – SMITHS PW 73AM
48 CABIN PRESSURE INDICATOR – SMITHS PW 417 PG8.3
49 FEEL SIMULATOR FAILURE WARNING LIGHTS
50 CRASH ISOLATION SWITCH & WARNING LIGHTS
51 THROTTLE CONTROL FAILURE WARNING LIGHTS
52 DASHBOARD LIGHTING DIMMER SWITCHES
53 FUEL TANK CONTENTS GAUGE – SIMMONDS GP223
54 FUEL FLOW INDICATOR – SMITHS PW 3FFA/MB
55 CABIN TEMP INDICATOR S/WESTON S 62-3-194
56 AIR ENTRY TEMP INDICATOR
57 PRESSURE CONTROLLER – NORMALAIR 517600
58 PRESSURE AUTO CONTROL OVERRIDE
59 HUMIDITY INDICATOR
60 INDICATOR AIR FLOW
61 WINDSCREEN WIPER CONTROL
62 ENGINEERS PANEL LIGHT SWITCHES
63 AC VOLTMETER SELECTOR
64 AC VOLTMETER 0-250 V
65 DC VOLTMETER 0-150 V
66 DC VOLTMETER 0-35 V
67 DC AMMETER 50-0-120A
68 DC AMMETER 120-0-120A
69 AC AMMETER 0-120A
70 FLIGHT/GROUND/GROUND CHARGING SWITCH
71 BATTERY ISOLATION SWITCH
72 ALTERNATOR CONTROL SWITCH
73 FUEL BOOST PUMP SWITCHES
74 FUEL CROSSFEED COCK SWITCHES
75 FUEL TANK ISOLATION COCK SWITCHES
76 FUEL TRANSFER PUMP SWITCHES
77 FUEL JETTISON CONTROL SWITCHES
78 RADAR INDICATOR
79 CREW OXYGEN CONTROL
80 HYDRAULIC OFF-LOAD SWITCHES
81 EMERGENCY U/C CONTROL
82 MAIN HYDRAULIC PRESSURE GAUGE
83 HYDRAULIC PUMP INLET PRESSURE GAUGE
84 SWITCHES FOR PITOT HP HEATER, EXTERNAL LIGHTS ILLUMINATED NOTICES & STEWARDESS' CALL
85 ENGINE OVERSPEED CONTROL PANEL
86 CONTROL SURFACE POSITION INDICATORS
87 400 CPS INVERTER SWITCHES SECONDARY SUPPLIES
88 LOAD TRANSFER SWITCHES
89 LOAD SHED SWITCHES
90 FLARE SWITCHES
91 AUDIO SELECTOR
92 CIRCUIT ISOLATION SWITCHES
93 ENGINE BLEED VALVE POSITION INDICATORS
94 400 CPS INVERTER VOLTMETER
95 400 CPS INVERTER VOLTMETER SELECTOR
96 PASSENGER OXYGEN CONTROL
97 HOLD FIRE CONTROL
98 CABIN TEMP CONTROL SWITCHES
99 VOR/ADF SELECTOR SWITCHES
100 SELCAL HF LIGHTS
101 WINDSCREEN DE-MIST CONTROL
102 NOSEWHEEL STEERING CONTROL
103 STEWARDESS/CAPTAIN CALL LIGHT
104 AUTO PILOT BEAM/RADIO COUPLED INDICATOR
105 ADF CONTROL
106 E.D.O LORAN CONTROL
107 RADIO ALTIMETER
108 E.D.O LORAN INDICATOR
109 COMPASS REPEATER SMITHS PW 6SFS

G-ARKB was operated by Caledonian Airways on behalf of Tellair. (Aviation Photo News)

She returned to Bristol Aircraft Limited on 11 April 1961 and was re-registered G-ARKB on 13 April 1961. Previously painted in the livery of Cunard Eagle Airways on 11 April 1961 she flew in these markings in May 1961. Delivered to Cunard Eagle on 1 May 1961. Transferred to Bristol Aircraft Services Limited on 10 March 1964 and re-leased to Cunard Eagle the same day named "Endeavour". British Eagle International, the original name of Cunard Eagle, operated G-ARKB from 23 December 1964 named 'Equality'. G-ARKB was re-named 'Resolution' in 1965.

Purchased by CCT Aircraft (Leasing) Limited on 11 April 1969 after the demise of British Eagle, G-ARKB was operated for the Swiss airline Tellair by Caledonian Airways. Delivery took place on 11 April 1969, but the Swiss registration HB-ITG was not taken up.

Withdrawn from service and stored at Baginton, Coventry from November 1969 until purchased by Airline Engineering in June 1971. She was used for spare parts and scrapped at Baginton in October 1971.

A truly nostalgic view of an early Variant 102 Britannia. (Peter Rushby)

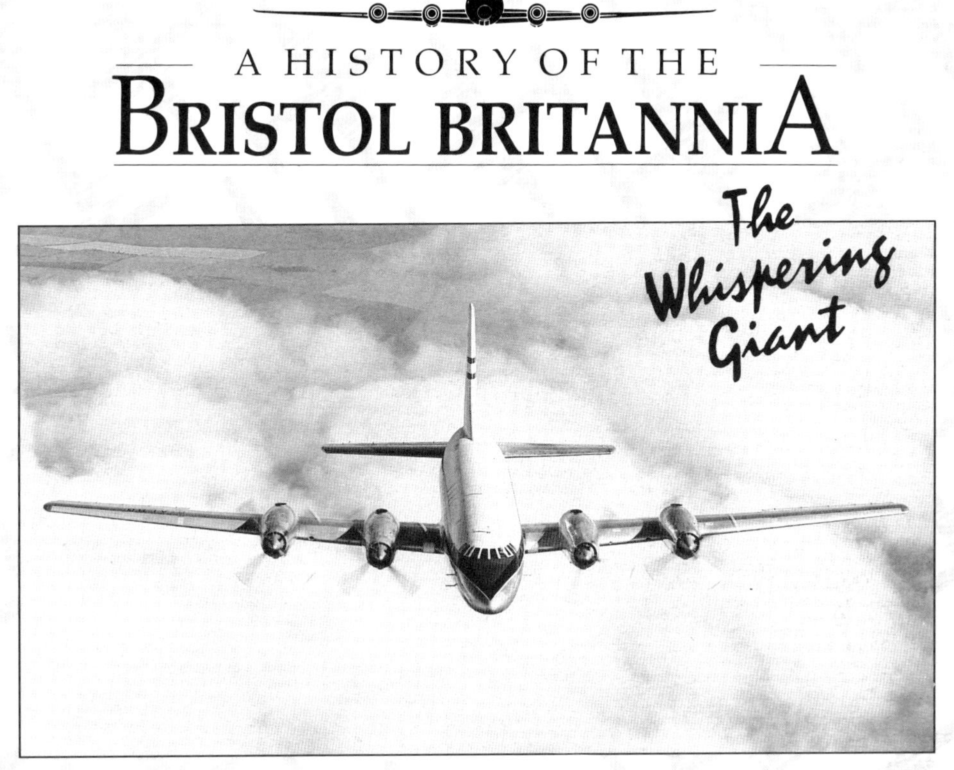

PICTORIAL REVIEW

G-BDUR
in a clean pose climbing with a touch of left rudder, after leaving Luton Airport.
(Stephen Piercey Collection)

9Q-CPX
at Luton Airport, now a 252F (J. Fielder)

EI-BBY
following her untimely ending during her approach to Shannon Airport.
(Stephen Piercey Collection)

G-AOVN
following her withdrawal from service was painted in Laker Airways colours and used for cabin staff training.
(Tom Singfield)

G-BDLZ
in the Ex-RAF livery of 'Air Faisel', in fact, the word 'FAISEL' should have been spelt 'FAISAL' which was eventually rectified.
(Via Tom Singfield)

G-BRAC
in a superb air to air pose – Redcoat Air Cargo certainly had an attractive livery.
(Stephen Piercey Collection)

G-ATLE
lying near the control tower at Gatwick Airport, she was used for various training activities before being burnt and scrapped.
(Tom Singfield)

HB-ITC
in Globeair's colourful livery, note the fuselage titles are slightly different to the one shown in the aircraft histories section.
(Via Tom Singfield)

OO-YCA
in Young Air Cargo livery sporting Arabian Red Crescent markings on her tail and forward fuselage roof.
(Via Tom Singfield)

G-BEMZ
ex Gaylan at Manston.
(Roger Hargreaves)

G-BRAC
in the 'Redair' livery seen at Cranfield on 5-1-80 when she was a television star in the BBC TV series 'Buccaneer'.
(Stephen Piercey Collection)

G-AOVT
at Luton Airport resplendent in Monarch Airlines livery. Note the Carvair in the background.
(Roger Hargreaves)

G-AOVS
in Lloyd International livery.
(Roger Hargreaves)

CU-T669
running her powerful Proteus engines at Luton Airport.
(Roger Hargreaves)

9G-ACE
under the apron lights at Luton.
(Stephen Piercey Collection)

EC-BFJ
wearing Air Spain livery.
(Roger Hargreaves)

9G-ACE
under the apron lights at Luton.
(Stephen Piercey Collection)

9Q-CPX
in Zaire Aero Service livery, a variant 252F.
(Flightlines International)

Heavylift's CL-44-0
'Guppy' departs Stansted and apart from its outsize fuselage the graceful Britannia 'roots' still shine through.
(Heavylift Cargo Airlines)

The Short Belfast
which started its days as the 'Britannic' freighter. G-BEPS is pictured at Rotterdam and is one of five Belfast freighters owned by Heavylift Cargo Airlines and although the aircraft differs considerably from the Britannia, it has a tailfin and wings similar to that of the Britannia.
(Heavylift Cargo Airlines – Richard Koster)

9Q-CHY
was the last serviceable Britannia to operate. She is shown at N'Djili Airport, Kinshasa, in the early livery of Business Cash Flow Aviation. Behind her is a spares source 9Q-CDT.
(Via Roger Hargreaves)

G-APLL
ex G-ANBG at London (Heathrow) in the lease markings of Nigerian Airways.
(Aviation Photo News)

G-ANBM
wore the livery of Treffield International during their lease, which incorporated the largest Union Jack ever worn on a Britannia.
(Tony Furlong)

9Q-CHU
in Katale Aero Transport titles.
(Flightlines International)

The flightdeck of G-AOVF undergoing restoration at the Aerospace Museum, RAF Cosford.
(Author)

G-AOVF
as she is seen now on show at Cosford, with the author looking out of the freight door. It is of interest that none of the BOAC Britannias ever operated with a freight door.
(Author)

G-ANBC
at London (Heathrow) Airport in the lease markings of Ghana Airways.
(Aviation Photo News)

G-ANBL
in open storage at London (Heathrow) following the proposed purchase by Paraense Transportes Aeroes S.A. not taking place.
(Aviation Photo News)

G-ANBK
in the later Northeast livery, with British Air Services on the forward fuselage. She is seen in company with a Vickers Viscount at Newcastle.
(Military Aircraft Photographs)

G-ANBC
at Filton following her return from Rangoon, showing the repaired areas of her nose section.
(Peter R March)

G-AOVG
at Paya Leba Airport 1966/67.
(Fred Hounslow)

G-AOVS
at London (Heathrow) Airport pre 1965.
(Fred Hounslow)

9Q-CHY
in Katale Aero Transport marks – the Boscombe Down livery very much in evidence.
(Stephen Piercey Collection)

PART NINE
APPENDIX ONE

Bristol Britannia G-AOVT (13427) Preserved Britannias

Duxford Aviation Society.
Imperial War Museum.
Duxford Airfield.
Cambridge.
CB2 4QR.

For information on events and other details relating to admission fees etc., telephone (0223) 835000 or (0223) 833963.

Among their extensive collection of civil and military aircraft, vehicles etc., can be found a variant 312 Britannia, G-AOVT. (13427). This aircraft is preserved by the Duxford Aviation Society, a band of extremely dedicated people who maintain this and other aircraft in tip top condition for the pleasure of the general public.

Not only is the Britannia maintained by the DAS but they are also assisted by the company who last operated her, Monarch Airlines of Luton, and it is in their livery that G-AOVT is exhibited.

On some days of the week, you are able to browse around the interior of G-AOVT, it is even possible to view the cockpit area. This is one of only three Britannia aircraft, complete in all respects and is certainly well worth the visit.

The museum is located near Cambridge, just 8 miles south on the M11 motorway at junction 11. The museum is open every day of the year with the exception of Christmas, Boxing and New Year's Day. Opening hours are between 10am and 5pm.

N.B. As with all long journeys to such places, it is advisable to ring to clarify opening times etc.

G-AOVT as preserved at Duxford Museum, Cambridge. (Duxford Museum)

Bristol Britannia G-AOVF (13237) Preserved Britannias

Aerospace Museum.
Cosford, Shifnal,
Shropshire. TF11 8UP.

For information on events and other details relating to admission fees etc., telephone (0902) 374112 or 374872.

The Aerospace museum at Cosford, has an extremely large collection of civil and military aircraft numbering around 70 or more. Among this interesting and varied collection is another Bristol Britannia, this time a variant 312F, G-AOVF (13237), displayed in the livery of BOAC.

The hardened Britannia purist, like the author, may feel disappointed to see this aircraft in the livery of BOAC, sporting the large forward freight door. BOAC operated 18 variant 312 Britannias and during their service with BOAC, none were fitted with this door. But this should not detract from our admiration at the effort and skills that have gone into the preservation of such a large aircraft.

An aircraft closely associated with the Bristol Britannia is also on display. The Short Belfast C.1, is displayed in the colours of Royal Air Force Air Support Command. Serialled XR-371 and named "Enceladus", with the c/n SH1825, this aircraft was one of ten built, although 12 were originally ordered.

Disposed of by the RAF along with the Britannia and Comet transport fleets, this aircraft shows the type of heavy lift aircraft that was used in the 1960s and early 70s.

To visit the Aerospace museum at Cosford, the main route would be the A41 north west of Wolverhampton, off junction 3 of the M54 motorway. The entrance is a mile from the motorway. There is also excellent rail access to the museum.

The museum is open all year round and the visiting hours are between 10am and 5pm every day, with the exception of Christmas, Boxing and New Year's Days. Special rates may apply to large group bookings or school parties. These groups would do well to telephone the above numbers in advance to book.

N.B. As with all long journeys to such places, it is advisable to ring to clarify opening times etc.

G-AOVF as preserved at Aerospace Museum, Cosford. (Aerospace Museum, Cosford)

APPENDIX TWO

Britannia Association

The Britannia Association exists for the benefit of members and ex-members of the Royal Air Force and the Women's Royal Air Force whose service was associated with the Bristol Britannia.

The Association was formed shortly after the disbandment of the RAF's Britannia fleet and was initially for members of the Sergeant's Mess. Later the doors were opened to all ranks. In spite of the finite number of potential members, the membership continues to grow as people qualified to join discover the Association's existance.

An annual reunion is held in the Swindon area and a regular magazine is distributed to members which is of great interest.

Anyone qualified and wishing to join should write for details to The Secretary, The Britannia Association, 112 Oxford Road, Calne, Wiltshire SN11 8AH.

Britannia Association's magazines published quarterly.

APPENDIX THREE

Bristol 175 Britannia – Fleet Lists Statistics (approx.)

FLYING HOURS: 3 287 410

LANDINGS: 703 213

AIRCRAFT WRITTEN-OFF

	FATALITIES:	SERIES:	W/O:
	92	100	3
	6	250	3
	15	300	2
	0	305	1
	245	310	5
	0	320	0
TOTAL	358		14

Total Collective Miles Flown: 620 000 000 (equal to 24 331 times around the world).

The Britannia's safety record is exampled by the fact that, between all 85 aircraft built, the total of fatalities is less than the number carried on one of today's wide bodied aircraft and that approximately 1 731 843 miles were flown in safety between each fatality.

Bristol 175 Britannia – Fleet Lists

The following fleet lists are for quick reference as to which company was associated with each Britannia aircraft. For individual dates concerning leases, ownership etc., refer to the individual aircraft histories.

A&AEE BOSCOMBE DOWN

C/N	Reg.	Variant
13421	XX-367	312F
13450	XN-392	C MK 2
13452	XN-404	C MK 2

AEROCARIBBEAN

C/N	Reg.	Variant
13433	CU-T114	318
13508	CU-T120	253F
13513	CU-T121	253F

AERONAVES DE MEXICO S.A.

C/N	Reg.	Variant
12818	XA-MEC	302
12919	XA-MED	302

AEROTRANSPORTES ENTRES RIOS

C/N	Reg.	Variant
13230	LV-PNJ	312F
13230	LV-JNL	312F

AER TURAS TEORANTE

C/N	Reg.	Variant
12921	EI-BAA	307F
13436	EI-BBH	253F
13448	EI-BDC	253F
13449	EI-BCI	253F
13450	XN-392	252F

AFREK LTD

C/N	Reg.	Variant
13508	G-BDUP	253F
13513	G-BDUR	253F

AFRICAN CARGO AIRWAYS

C/N	Reg.	Variant
12920	5Y-AYR	307F
12922	5Y-AZP	308F
13431	5Y-ALT	313

AFRICAN INTERNATIONAL

C/N	Reg.	Variant
13428	G-ATMA	314
13428	5Y-ANS	314

AFRICAN SAFARI AIRLINES

C/N	Reg.	Variant
12920	5Y-AYR	307F
12922	5Y-AZP	308F
13237	G-AOVF	312F
13393	5X-UVT	314
13393	5Y-ALP	314
13422	G-AOVN	312
13428	5Y-ANS	314
13431	5Y-ALT	313
13431	5X-UVH	313

AIR CHARTER LTD

C/N	Reg.	Variant
12920	G-ANCD	305
12921	G-ANCE	307

AIR FAISAL LTD

C/N	Reg.	Variant
12920	5Y-AYR	307F
13435	G-BDLZ	253F
13457	XL-660	253F
13457	G-BEMZ	253F
13511	G-BEPX	253F

AIR FRANCE

C/N	Reg.	Variant
12914	G-ANBM	102

AIR LINKS LTD

C/N	Reg.	Variant
13393	G-ATGD	314
13395	CF-CZC	314

AIR SPAIN

C/N	Reg.	Variant
13233	EC-WFL	313
13233	EC-BFL	313
13236	EC-WFK	312
13236	EC-BFK	312
13421	EC-BSY	312F
13429	G-AOVR	312
13429	EC-WFJ	312
13429	EC-BFJ	312

AIR CARRIERS OF ZAMBIA

C/N	Reg.	Variant
12915	G-ANBN	102

AIRLINE ENGINEERING LTD

C/N	Reg.	Variant
13207	G-AOVA	319
13419	G-AOVK	312
13426	G-APNB	317
13448	EI-BDC	253F
13455	EI-BBY	253F
13508	XM-496	253F
13508	G-BDUP	253F
13511	G-BEPX	253F
13513	XM-519	253F
13513	G-BDUR	253F
13516	G-ARKA	253F
13517	G-ARKB	253F

AIR WORKS INDIA LTD

C/N	Reg.	Variant
13435	G-BDLZ	253F

AIVEX HOLDINGS LTD

C/N	Reg.	Variant
12920	G-ANCD	307F
13430	G-AOVS	312F

ALL CARGO AIRLINES

C/N	Reg.	Variant
12920	5Y-AYR	307F

A.M.A.Z.

C/N	Reg.	Variant
13511	9Q-CAJ	253F

BKS AIR TRANSPORT LTD

C/N	Reg.	Variant
12905	G-ANBD	102
12908	G-APLL	102
12909	G-ANBH	102
12912	G-ANBK	102

BLACK ARROW LEASING LTD

C/N	Reg.	Variant
12920	5Y-AYR	307F
13457	G-BEMZ	253F

BRISTOL AEROPLANE CO. LTD

C/N	Reg.	Variant
12873	G-ALBO	101
12902	G-ANBA	102
12903	G-ANBB	102
12904	G-ANBC	102
12905	G-ANBD	102
12906	G-ANBE	102
12907	G-ANBF	102
12908	G-ANBG	102
12909	G-ANBH	102
12920	G-18-3	305
13207	G-AOVA	311
13516	G-18-8	324

BRISTOL AIRCRAFT LTD

C/N	Reg.	Variant
12902	G-ANBA	102
12918	G-ANCB	302
12918	G-18-1	302
12919	G-ANCC	302
12919	G-18-2	302
12920	G-ANCD	305
12920	4X-AGE	305
12921	G-ANCE	307
12922	G-ANCF	305
12922	G-18-4	305
12922	G-14-1	308
12923	G-ANCG	305
12923	G-14-2	308
12924	G-ANCH	309
13207	G-AOVA	311
13207	G-AOVA	319
13234	G-ARXA	313
13516	G-ARKA	324
13517	G-ARKB	324

BRISTOL AIRCRAFT SERVICES LTD

C/N	Reg.	Variant
13233	G-ARWZ	313

BRITISH EUROPEAN AIRWAYS

C/N	Reg.	Variant
13238	G-AOVG	312
13424	G-AOVP	312
13427	G-AOVT	312

BRITANNIA AIRWAYS

C/N	Reg.	Variant
12902	G-ANBA	102
12903	G-ANBB	102
12905	G-ANBD	102
12906	G-ANBE	102
12907	G-ANBF	102
12910	G-ANBI	102
12911	G-ANBJ	102
12913	G-ANBL	102
12915	G-ANBN	102
12916	G-ANBO	102

BRITISH & COMMONWEALTH SHIPPING & CO. (AVIATION) LTD

C/N	Reg.	Variant
13207	G-AOVA	311
13425	G-APNA	317
13426	G-APNB	317

BRITISH EAGLE INTERNATIONAL AIRLINES

C/N	Reg.	Variant
12922	G-ANCF	308
12922	G-ANCF	308F
12923	G-ANCG	308
12923	G-ANCG	308F
12924	G-ANCH	309
12925	G-AOVH	312
13207	G-AOVA	319
13230	G-AOVB	312
13230	G-AOVB	312F
13231	G-AOVC	312
13234	G-ARXA	313
13236	G-AOVE	312
13237	G-AOVF	312
13237	G-AOVF	312F
13238	G-AOVG	312
13419	G-AOVK	312
13420	G-AOVL	312
13421	G-AOVM	312
13421	G-AOVM	312F
13422	G-AOVN	312
13423	G-AOVO	312
13427	G-AOVT	312
13429	G-AOVR	312
13430	G-AOVS	312
13453	G-ASTF	314
13516	G-ARKA	324

BRITISH OVERSEAS AIRWAYS CORPORATION

C/N	Reg.	Variant
12902	G-ANBA	102
12903	G-ANBB	102
12904	G-ANBC	102
12905	G-ANBD	102
12906	G-ANBE	102
12907	G-ANBF	102
12908	G-ANBG	102
12908	G-APLL	102
12909	G-ANBH	102
12910	G-ANBI	102
12911	G-ANBJ	102
12912	G-ANBK	102
12913	G-ANBL	102
12914	G-ANBM	102
12915	G-ANBN	102
12916	G-ANBO	102
13207	G-AOVA	312
13230	G-AOVB	312
13231	G-AOVC	312
13235	G-AOVD	312
13236	G-AOVE	312
13237	G-AOVF	312
13238	G-AOVG	312
12925	G-AOVH	312
12926	G-AOVI	312
13418	G-AOVJ	312
13419	G-AOVK	312
13420	G-AOVL	312
13421	G-AOVM	312
13422	G-AOVN	312
13423	G-AOVO	312
13424	G-AOVP	312
13425	G-APNA	317
13427	G-AOVT	312
13429	G-AOVR	312
13430	G-AOVS	312

BRITISH UNITED AIRWAYS

C/N	Reg.	Variant
12920	G-ANCD	307F
12921	G-ANCE	307F
12924	G-ANCH	309
12926	G-AOVI	312
13207	G-AOVA	319
13232	G-ASFV	313
13233	G-ARWZ	313
13234	G-ARXA	313
13236	G-AOVE	312
13393	G-ATGD	314
13396	G-ATNZ	314
13425	G-APNA	317
13426	G-APNB	317
13431	G-ASFU	313

B.W.I.A.

C/N	Reg.	Variant
13230	G-AOVB	312
13418	G-AOVJ	312
13420	G-AOVL	312

BUSINESS CASH FLOW AVIATION

C/N	Reg.	Variant
13421	9Q-CHY	312F
13510	9Q-CDT	253F

CALEDONIAN AIRWAYS

C/N	Reg.	Variant
12925	G-AOVH	312
12926	G-AOVI	312
13207	G-AOVA	319
13396	G-ATNZ	314
13418	G-AOVJ	312
13428	G-ATMA	314
13453	G-ASTF	314
13516	G-ARKA	324
13517	G-ARKB	324

CANADIAN PACIFIC AIRWAYS

C/N	Reg.	Variant
13393	CF-CZA	314
13394	CF-CZB	314
13395	CF-CZC	314
13396	CF-CZD	314
13428	CF-CZX	314
13453	CF-CZW	314
13516	CF-CPD	324
13517	CF-CPE	324

CLANAIR LTD

C/N	Reg.	Variant
13425	G-APNA	317

CATHAY PACIFIC AIRWAYS

C/N	Reg.	Variant
12903	G-ANBB	102
12913	G-ANBL	102
12916	G-ANBO	102

CAPITAL AIRLINES

C/N	Reg.	Variant
12920	–	305
12921	–	305
12922	–	305
12923	–	305
12924	–	305

CCT AIRCRAFT LEASING LTD

C/N	Reg.	Variant
13207	G-AOVA	319
13419	G-AOVK	312
13516	G-ARKA	324
13517	G-ARKB	324

CENTRE AIR AFRIQUE

C/N	Reg.	Variant
13454	9U-BAD	253F

CESKOSLOVENSKE AEROLINIE

C/N	Reg.	Variant
13432	OK-MBA	318
13437	CU-T670	318
13515	OK-MBB	318

CUBANA DE AVIACION

C/N	Reg.	Variant
13432	CU-P668	318
13432	CU-T668	318
13433	CU-P669	318
13433	CU-T669	318
13437	CU-P670	318
13437	CU-T670	318
13515	CU-P671	318
13515	CU-T671	318

CUNARD EAGLE AIRWAYS

C/N	Reg.	Variant
13432	G-APPY	318
13516	G-ARKA	324
13517	G-ARKB	324

CYPRUS AIRWAYS

C/N	Reg.	Variant
13436	EI-BBH	253F
13448	EI-BDC	253F

DANTANA

C/N	Reg.	Variant
13457	G-BEMZ	253F

DOMAINE DE KATALE

C/N	Reg.	Variant
13399	9Q-CKG	253F
13399	9Q-CBT	253F
13451	9Q-CPX	252F
13510	9Q-CDT	253F

DONALDSON INTERNATIONAL AIRLINES

C/N	Reg.	Variant
13231	G-AOVC	312
13237	G-AOVF	312F
13418	G-AOVJ	312
13425	G-APNA	317
13426	G-APNB	317

E.A.A.C.

C/N	Reg.	Variant
12915	G-ANBN	102
12916	G-ANBO	102
12920	G-ANCD	307F
13230	G-AOVB	312
13423	G-AOVO	312
13424	G-AOVP	312F
13425	G-APNA	317
13427	G-AOVT	317

EAGLE AIRWAYS

C/N	Reg.	Variant
13432	G-APPY	318

El Al

C/N	Reg.	Variant
12920	4X-AGE	305
13232	4X-AGA	313
13233	4X-AGB	313
13234	4X-AGC	313
13430	G-AOVS	312F
13431	4X-AGD	313

EURAFRIC

C/N	Reg.	Variant
13448	EI-BDC	253F
13449	EI-BCI	253F

EUROWORLD

C/N	Reg.	Variant
13435	XM-490	253F
13451	XN-398	252F

GAYLAN AIR CARGO

C/N	Reg.	Variant
12920	5Y-AYR	307F
13457	G-BEMZ	253F
13457	A6-HMS	253F

GEMINI AIR TRANSPORT

C/N	Reg.	Variant
12920	G-ANCD	307F
13436	EI-BBH	253F
13514	9G-ACE	253F

GHANA AIRWAYS

C/N	Reg.	Variant
12904	G-ANBC	102
12906	G-ANBE	102
12910	G-ANBI	102
12924	9G-AAG	309
13207	9G-AAH	319

GLOBE AIR

C/N	Reg.	Variant
13232	HB-ITB	313
13431	HB-ITC	313

GUINNESS PEAT AVIATION

C/N	Reg.	Variant
13448	EI-BDC	253F

HUNTING CLAN AIR TRANSPORT

C/N	Reg.	Variant
13207	G-AOVA	311
13425	G-APNA	317
13426	G-APNB	317

IAC AIRLINES

C/N	Reg.	Variant
13237	9Q-CAZ	312F

INTERNATIONAL AVIATION SERVICES

C/N	Reg.	Variant
12919	G-ANCC	302
12920	G-ANCD	307F
12922	G-ANCF	308F
12924	G-ANCH	309
13233	EC-BFL	313

13237	G-AOVF	312F
13395	G-ATLE	314
13396	G-ATNZ	314
13424	G-AOVP	312F
13425	G-APNA	317
13428	5Y-ANS	314
13428	G-ATMA	314
13429	EC-BFJ	312
13430	G-AOVS	312F

INDONESIAN ANGKASA CIVIL AIR TRANSPORT

C/N	Reg.	Variant
12914	PK-ICA	102
12915	PK-ICB	102

INTERCONTINENTAL MEAT COMPANY

C/N	Reg.	Variant
13455	EI-BBY	253F

INVICTA INTERNATIONAL

C/N	Reg.	Variant
12922	G-ANCF	308F
13237	G-AOVF	312F
13427	G-AOVT	312
13430	G-AOVS	312F

KATALE AERO TRANSPORT

C/N	Reg.	Variant
13399	9Q-CKG	253F
13399	9Q-CBT	253F
13421	9Q-CHY	312F
13449	9Q-CHU	253F
13457	9Q-CGP	253F
13510	9Q-CDT	253F
13514	9Q-CUM	253F

LAKER AIRWAYS

C/N	Reg.	Variant
12914	G-ANBM	102
12915	G-ANBN	102

LIBERIA WORLD AIRWAYS

C/N	Reg.	Variant
13399	OO-YCH	253F
13399	EL-LWH	253F
13510	EL-LWG	253F

LLOYD INTERNATIONAL AIRLINES

C/N	Reg.	Variant
12920	G-ANCD	307
12921	G-ANCE	307F
13207	G-AOVA	319
13424	G-AOVP	312F
13425	G-APNA	317
13426	G-APNB	317
13430	G-AOVS	312F

LUKUM AIR SERVICES

C/N	Reg.	Variant
13514	9Q-CUM	253F

MALAYAN AIRWAYS

C/N	Reg.	Variant
12902	G-ANBA	102
12906	G-ANBE	102
12907	G-ANBF	102
12908	G-APLL	102
12910	G-ANBI	102
12911	G-ANBJ	102
12914	G-ANBM	102
12915	G-ANBN	102
12916	G-ANBO	102

MERCHANT AIR LTD

C/N	Reg.	Variant
13237	G-AOVF	312F
12922	G-ANCF	308F

MIDDLE EAST AIRLINES

C/N	Reg.	Variant
13236	G-AOVE	312

MINISTRY OF SUPPLY

C/N	Reg.	Variant
12873	VX-442	101
12873	WB-470	101
12873	G-ALBO	101
12874	VX-447	101
12874	WB-473	101
12874	G-ALRX	101
12917	G-ANCA	301
13450	G-APPE	252
13451	G-APPF	252
13452	G-APPG	252

MONARCH AIRLINES

C/N	Reg.	Variant
12915	G-ANBN	102
12921	G-ANCE	307F
12922	G-ANCF	308F
12924	G-ANCH	309
12925	G-AOVH	312
12926	G-AOVI	312
13234	G-ARXA	313
13237	G-AOVF	312F
13238	G-AOVG	312
13420	G-AOVL	312
13422	G-AOVN	312
13427	G-AOVT	312
13449	XL-640	253F
13454	XL-657	253F
13511	XM-517	253F

NATIONAL AERO LEASING

C/N	Reg.	Variant
12914	G-ANBM	102
12915	G-ANBN	102

NIGERIA AIRWAYS

C/N	Reg.	Variant
12902	G-ANBA	102
12903	G-ANBB	102
12906	G-ANBE	102
12907	G-ANBF	102
12908	G-APLL	102
12909	G-ANBH	102
12912	G-ANBK	102
12914	G-ANBM	102
12915	G-ANBN	102
13427	G-AOVT	312

NORTHEAST AIRLINES (NOT TAKEN UP)

C/N	Reg.	Variant
12920	N6595C	305
12921	N6596C	305
12922	N6597C	305
12923	N6598C	305
12924	N6599C	305

NORTHEAST AIRLINES

C/N	Reg.	Variant
12912	G-ANBK	102

PARAENSE TRANSPORTES AEROES SA (NOT TAKEN UP)

C/N	Reg.	Variant
12902	G-ANBA	102
12911	G-ANBJ	102
12913	G-ANBL	102

PAULING CONSTRUCTION COMPANY

C/N	Reg.	Variant
12921	G-ANCE	307F

PROTEUS AERO SERVICES

C/N	Reg.	Variant
12922	G-ANCF	308F

REDCOAT AIR CARGO LTD

C/N	Reg.	Variant
13430	G-AOVS	312F
13448	G-BRAC	253F
13449	G-BHAU	253F
13457	G-BEMZ	253F
13514	9G-ACE	253F

REDAIR (BBC TV SERIES.)

C/N	Reg.	Variant
13430	G-AOVS	312F
13430	G-BRAC	312F
13448	G-BRAC	253F
13449	G-BHAU	253F

ROYAL AIR MAROC

C/N	Reg.	Variant
12925	G-AOVH	312
12926	G-AOVI	312

ROYAL AIR FORCE

C/N	Reg.	Variant
13397	XL-635	C MK 1
13398	XL-636	C MK 1
13399	XL-637	C MK 1
13400	XL-638	C MK 1
13434	XM-489	C MK 1
13435	XM-490	C MK 1
13436	XM-491	C MK 1
13448	XL-639	C MK 1
13449	XL-640	C MK 1
13450	XN-392	C MK 2
13451	XN-398	C MK 2
13452	XN-404	C MK 2
13454	XL-657	C MK 1
13455	XL-658	C MK 1
13456	XL-659	C MK 1
13457	XL-660	C MK 1
13508	XM-496	C MK 1
13509	XM-497	C MK 1
13510	XM-498	C MK 1
13511	XM-517	C MK 1
13512	XM-518	C MK 1
13513	XM-519	C MK 1
13514	XM-520	C MK 1

SHACKLETON AVIATION

C/N	Reg.	Variant
12920	G-ANCD	307F
13452	XN-404	252F

SOUTHERN CROSS INTERNATIONAL

C/N	Reg.	Variant
12913	G-ANBL	102
13421	G-AOVM	312F

SWORDVALE AVIATION LTD

C/N	Reg.	Variant
13449	G-BHAU	253F
13457	G-BEMZ	253F

T.F. RICHTER & CO. LTD

C/N	Reg.	Variant
13457	G-BEMZ	253F

TELLAIR

C/N	Reg.	Variant
13516	G-ARKA	324
13517	G-ARKB	324

TRANSAIR CARGO

C/N	Reg.	Variant
13436	9Q-CMO	253F

TRANSCONTINENTAL S.A.

C/N	Reg.	Variant
12922	LV-PPJ	308
12922	LV-GJB	308
12923	LV-PPL	308
12923	LV-GJC	308

TRANSGLOBE AIRWAYS

C/N	Reg.	Variant
12929	G-ANCC	302
12924	G-ANCH	309
13393	G-ATGD	314
13395	G-ATLE	314

TRANSGULF AIR CARGO

C/N	Reg.	Variant
12920	5Y-AYR	307F
13457	XL-660	253F

TREFFIELD INTERNATIONAL

C/N	Reg.	Variant
12914	G-ANBM	102

TREK AIRWAYS

C/N	Reg.	Variant
13395	G-ATLE	314

VICKERS ARMSTRONG (AIRCRAFT) LTD

C/N	Reg.	Variant
13207	G-AOVA	319

WESTWING AVIATION

C/N	Reg.	Variant
12920	5Y-AYR	307F

YOUNG AIR CARGO

C/N	Reg.	Variant
13397	OO-YCA	253F
13398	OO-YCE	253F
13399	OO-YCH	253F
13434	OO-YCC	253F
13456	OO-YCB	253F
13509	XM-497	253F
13510	OO-YCG	253F
13512	OO-YCD	253F

APPENDIX FOUR

Bristol Britannia registration cross reference

P/N	C/N	REGISTRATIONS
(001)	12873	G-ALBO 7708M (VX-442. WB-470)
(002)	12874	G-ALRX (VX-447. WB-473)
(007)	12902	G-ANBA
(013)	12903	G-ANBB
(003)	12904	G-ANBC
(004)	12905	G-ANBD
(005)	12906	G-ANBE
(006)	12907	G-ANBF
(007)	12908	G-ANBG G-APLL
(008)	12909	G-ANBH
(009)	12910	G-ANBI
(011)	12911	G-ANBJ
(012)	12912	G-ANBK
(014)	12913	G-ANBL
(015)	12914	G-ANBM PK-ICA
(016)	12915	G-ANBN PK-ICB
(017)	12916	G-ANBO
(001)	12917	G-ANCA
(019)	12918	G-18-1 G-ANCB XA-MEC
(021)	12919	G-18-2 G-ANCC XA-MED G-ANCC
(023)	12920	G-18-3 G-ANCD 4X-AGE G-ANCD 5Y-AYR (N6595C)
(002)	12921	G-ANCE EI-BAA (N6596C)
(003)	12922	G-18-4 G-14-1 LV-PPJ LV-GJB G-ANCF 5Y-AZP G-ANCF (N6597C)
(004)	12923	G-14-2 LV-PPL LV-GJC G-ANCG (N6598C)
(001)	12924	G-ANCH 9G-AAG G-41 G-ANCH (N6599C)
(038)	12925	G-AOVH
(003)	13399	XL-637 OO-YCH EL-LWH OO-YCH 9Q-CKG
(004)	13400	XL-638
(041)	13418	G-AOVJ (G-AOFJ)
(043)	13419	G-AOVK
(045)	13420	G-AOVL
(048)	13421	G-AOVM EC-BSY XX-367 9Q-CHY
(013)	13422	G-AOVN
(014)	13423	G-AOVO
(015)	13424	G-AOVP
(001)	13425	G-APNA
(002)	13426	G-APNB
(018)	13427	G-AOVT
(006)	13428	CF-CZX G-ATMA 5Y-ANS G-ATMA
(016)	13429	G-AOVR EC-WFJ EC-BFJ
(017)	13430	G-AOVS G-BRAC G-AOVS
(004)	13431	4X-AGD G-ASFU 4X-AGD HB-ITC 5X-UVH 5Y-ALT
(001)	13432	CU-P668 CU-T668 G-APYY CU-T668 OK-MBA CU-T668
(002)	13433	CU-P669 CU-T669 CU-T114
(011)	13434	XM-489 OO-YCC
(012)	13435	XM-490 G-BDLZ
(013)	13436	XM-491 EI-BBH 9Q-CMO
(003)	13437	CU-P670 CU-T670
(005)	13448	XL-639 EI-BDC G-BRAC
(006)	13449	XL-640 EI-BCI G-BHAU 9Q-CHU
(001)	13450	G-APPE XN-392
(002)	13451	G-APPF XN-398 9Q-CPX
(003)	13452	G-APPG XN-404

(040)	12926	G-AOVI
(018)	13207	G-AOVA 9G-AAH G-AOVA (G-AMYK. G-AOFA)
	13208	(G-AMYL. G-AOFB)
(022)	13230	G-AOVB LV-PNJ LV-JNL
(029)	13231	G-AOVC (G-AOFC)
(024)	13232	4X-AGA G-ASFV 4X-AGA HB-ITB
(025)	13233	4X-AGB G-ARWZ 4X-AGB EC-WFL EC-BFL
(027)	13234	4X-AGC G-ARXA 4X-AGC G-ARXA (G-ANGK)
(030)	13235	G-AOVD (G-AOFD)
(032)	13236	G-AOVE EC-WFK EC-BFK (G-AOFE)
(034)	13237	G-AOVF 9Q-CAZ G-AOVF (G-AOFF)
(037)	13238	G-AOVG (G-AOFG)
(033)	13393	CF-CZA G-ATGD 5X-UVT 5Y-ALP
(036)	13394	CF-CZB
(039)	13395	CF-CZC G-ATLE
(004)	13396	CF-CZD G-ATNZ
(001)	13397	XL-635 OO-YCA
(002)	13398	XL-636 OO-YCE

Above are all known registrations appertaining to the Bristol Britannia. Each airframe construction number is listed in numerical order with all registrations allocated to that particular aircraft being listed in order of allocation and re-allocation. Those registrations listed in brackets were allocated but not worn. The number within brackets is the production number allocated to that airframe.

(005)	13453	CF-CZW G-ASTF CF-CZW G-ASTF
(007)	13454	XL-657 9U-BAD
(008)	13455	XL-658 EI-BBY
(009)	13456	XL-659 OO-YCB
(010)	13457	XL-660 G-BEMZ A6-HMS G-BEMZ 9Q-CGP
(014)	13508	XM-496 G-BDUP CU-T120
(015)	13509	XM-497 OO-YCF
(001)	13510	XM-498 OO-YCG EL-LWG 9Q-CDT
(002)	13511	XM-517 9Q-CAJ G-BEPX
(003)	13512	XM-518 OO-YCD
(004)	13513	XM-519 G-BDUR CU-T121
(005)	13514	XM-520 9G-ACE
(004)	13515	CU-P671 CU-T671 OK-MBB CU-T671
(001)	13516	G-18-8 CF-CPD G-ARKA (HB-ITF)
(002)	13517	CF-CPE G-ARKB (HB-ITG)

APPENDIX FIVE

Bristol Britannia registration cross reference

Britannia registrations with constructors number

ARGENTINA

LV-GJB	12922
LV-GJC	12923
LV-JNL	13230
LV-PNJ	13230
LV-PPJ	12922
LV-PPL	12923

BELGIUM

OO-YCA	13397
OO-YCB	13456
OO-YCC	13434
OO-YCD	13512
OO-YCE	13398
OO-YCF	13508*
OO-YCG	13510
OO-YCH	13399

BURUNDI

9U-BAD	13454

CANADA

CF-CPD	13516
CF-CPE	13517
CF-CZA	13393
CF-CZB	13394
CF-CZC	13395
CF-CZD	13396
CF-CZW	13453
CF-CZX	13428

CUBA

CU-P668	13432
CU-P669	13433
CU-P670	13437
CU-P671	13515
CU-T114	13433
CU-T120	13508
CU-T121	13513
CU-T668	13432
CU-T669	13433
CU-T670	13437
CU-T671	13515

CZECHOSLOVAKIA

OK-MBA	13432
OK-MBB	13515

GHANA

9G-AAG	12924
9G-AAH	13207
9G-ACE	13514

GREAT BRITAIN

G-ALBO	12873
G-ALRX	12874
G-AMYK	13207*
G-AMYL	13208*
G-ANBA	12902
G-ANBB	12903
G-ANBC	12904
G-ANBD	12905
G-ANBE	12906
G-ANBF	12907
G-ANBG	12908
G-ANBF	12909
G-ANBI	12910
G-ANBJ	12911
G-ANBK	12912
G-ANBL	12913
G-ANBM	12914
G-ANBN	12915
G-ANBO	12916
G-ANCA	12917
G-ANCB	12918
G-ANCC	12919
G-ANCD	12920
G-ANCE	12921
G-ANCF	12922
G-ANCG	12923
G-ANCH	12924
G-ANGK	13234*
G-AOFA	13207*
G-AOFB	13208*
G-AOFC	13231*
G-AOFD	13235*
G-AOFE	13236*
G-AOFF	13237*
G-AOFG	13238*
G-AOFJ	13418*
G-AOVA	13207*
G-AOVB	13230
G-AOVC	13231
G-AOVD	13235
G-AOVE	13236
G-AOVF	13237
G-AOVG	13238
G-AOVH	12925
G-AOVI	12926
G-AOVJ	13418
G-AOVK	13419
G-AOVL	13420
G-AOVM	13421
G-AOVN	13422
G-AOVO	13423
G-AOVP	13424
G-AOVR	13429
G-AOVS	13430
G-AOVT	13427
G-APLL	12908
G-APNA	13425
G-APNB	13426
G-APPE	13450
G-APPF	13451
G-APPG	13452
G-APYY	13432
G-ARKA	13516
G-ARKB	13517
G-ARWZ	13233
G-ARXA	13234
G-ASFU	13431
G-ASFV	13232
G-ASTF	13453
G-ATGD	13393
G-ATLE	13395
G-ATMA	13428
G-ATNZ	13396
G-BDLZ	13435
G-BDUP	13508
G-BDUR	13513
G-BEMZ	13457
G-BEPX	13511
G-BHAU	13449
G-BRAC	13448
G-14-1	12922
G-18-1	12918
G-18-2	12919
G-18-4	12922
G-18-8	13516
G-41	12924
VX 442	12873*
VX 447	12874*
VX 454	12875*
WB 470	12873*
WB 473	12874*
XL 635	13397
XL 636	13398
XL 637	13399
XL 638	13400
XL 639	13448
XL 640	13449
XL 657	13454
XL 658	13455
XL 659	13456
XL 660	13457
XM 489	13434
XM 490	13435
XM 491	13436
XM 496	13508
XM 497	13509
XM 498	13510
XM 517	13511
XM 518	13512
XM 519	13513
XM 520	13514
XN 392	13450
XN 398	13451
XN 404	13452
XX 367	13421
7708M	12873

INDONESIA

PK-ICA	12914
PK-ICB	12915

IRELAND

EI-BAA	12921
EI-BBH	13436
EI-BBY	13455
EI-BCI	13449
EI-BDC	13448

ISRAEL

4X-AGA	13232
4X-AGB	13233
4X-AGC	13234
4X-AGD	13431
4X-AGE	12920

KENYA

5Y-ALP	13393
5Y-ALT	13431
5Y-ANS	13428
5Y-AYR	12920
5Y-AZP	12922

LIBERIA

EL-LWG	13510
EL-LWH	13399

MEXICO

XA-MEC	12918
XA-MED	12919

SPAIN

EC-BFJ	13429
EC-BFK	13236
EC-BFL	13233
EC-BSY	13421
EC-WFJ	13429
EC-WFK	13236
EC-WFL	13233

SWITZERLAND

HB-ITB	13232
HB-ITC	13431
HB-ITF	13516*
HB-ITG	13517*

UGANDA

5X-UVH	13431
5X-UVT	13393

UNITED ARAB EMIRATES

A6-HMS	13457

UNITED STATES OF AMERICA

N6595C	12920*
N6596C	12921*
N6597C	12922*
N6598C	12923*
N6599C	12924*

ZAIRE

9Q-CAJ	13511
9Q-CAZ	13237
9Q-CBT	13399
9Q-CDT	13510
9Q-CGP	13457
9Q-CHU	13449
9Q-CHY	13421
9Q-CKG	13399
9Q-CMO	13436
9Q-CPX	13451
9Q-CUM	13514

NB. All registrations marked* were not worn by that aircraft. The total number of registrations allocated to the Bristol Britannia world wide, including those not worn, is 205.

APPENDIX SIX
QUICK REFERENCE TABLES

No. 1

REG	C/N	OPERATOR	D/D		VARIANT
VX-442	12873	MINISTRY OF SUPPLY	(NTU)		
WB-470		MINISTRY OF SUPPLY	(NTU)		
G-ALBO		BAC	11.6.48		101
7708M		RAF MAINTENANCE COMM'D.	30.10.60		

Broken up and burnt on 12 June 1968, although forward fuselage placed on Brize Norton's airfield dump in March 1978.

No. 2

REG	C/N	OPERATOR	D/D		VARIANT
VX-447	12874	MINISTRY OF SUPPLY	(NTU)		
WB-473		MINISTRY OF SUPPLY	(NTU)		
G-ALRX		MINISTRY OF SUPPLY	25.6.51		101
Written off 4 February, 1954 in River Severn Estuary.					
SIRIUS II		A&AEE BOSCOMBE DOWN	CURRENT MID 1992		

No. 3

REG	C/N	OPERATOR	D/D		VARIANT
G-ANBA	12902	BAC	7.1.54		102
		BRISTOL AIRCRAFT LTD.	9.3.56	T	
		BOAC	12.8.57	P	
		NIGERIA AIRWAYS	13.4.59	L	
		BOAC	1960	R	
		MALAYAN AIRWAYS	9.12.61	L	
		BOAC	17.1.62	R	
		PARAENSE TRANSPORTES AEROES SA. (NTU)			
		BRITANNIA AIRWAYS	26.3.65	P	

Withdrawn from service at Luton November 1969 and scrapped June 1970.

No. 4

REG	C/N	OPERATOR	D/D		VARIANT
G-ANBB	12903	BAC	7.1.54		102
		BOAC	18.6.57	P	
		NIGERIA AIRWAYS	6.59	L	
		BOAC	1960	R	
		CATHAY PACIFIC AIRWAYS	12.1.61	L	
		BOAC	31.1.61	R	
		BRITANNIA AIRWAYS	18.11.64	L	

Crashed on approach to Ljublijana Airport, Yugoslavia 1.9.66.

No. 5

REG	C/N	OPERATOR	D/D		VARIANT
G-ANBC	12904	BAC	7.1.54		102
		BOAC	30.12.55	P	
		GHANA AIRWAYS	Early 1960	L	
		BOAC	Late 1960	R	

Written off at Khartoum Airport, on 11 November 1960.

No. 6

REG	C/N	OPERATOR	D/D		VARIANT
G-ANBD	12905	BAC	7.1.54		102
		BOAC	30.12.55	P	
		BKS AIR TRANSPORT	16.11.65	L	
		BRITANNIA AIRWAYS	27.4.68	SL	
		BKS AIR TRANSPORT	1.10.68	R	

Withdrawn from service and stored at Southend Airport, Essex in January 1970, later broken up and scrapped in May 1970.

No. 7

REG	C/N	OPERATOR	D/D		VARIANT
G-ANBE	12906	BAC	18.1.56		102
		BOAC	2.3.56	P	
		NIGERIA AIRWAYS	April 1958	L	
		BOAC	Returned		
		GHANA AIRWAYS	1960	L	
		BOAC	Returned		
		MALAYAN AIRWAYS	2/3.1963	L	
		BOAC	3.4.63	R	
		BRITANNIA AIRWAYS	1.2.66	L	
		BRITANNIA AIRWAYS	16.3.70	P	

Withdrawn from use by Britannia Airways and stored at Luton Airport from December 1970. Scrapped in July 1972.

No. 8

REG	C/N	OPERATOR	D/D		VARIANT
G-ANBF	12907	BAC	18.1.56		102
		BOAC	14.3.56	P	
		MALAYAN AIRWAYS	18.10.61	L	
		BOAC	14.11.61	R	
		NIGERIA AIRWAYS	Nov. 1961	L	
		BOAC	20.11.61	R	
		MALAYAN AIRWAYS	22.11.62	L	
		BOAC	12.12.62	R	
		BRITANNIA AIRWAYS	12.2.65	L	
		BRITANNIA AIRWAYS	Purchased		

Withdrawn from service by Britannia Airways and stored at Luton Airport October 1969. Broken up in May 1970.

No. 9

REG	C/N	OPERATOR	D/D		VARIANT
G-ANBG	12908	BAC	18.1.56		102
		BOAC	8.5.56	P	
G-APLL		BOAC	19.3.58	RR	
		NIGERIA AIRWAYS	Early 1959	L	
		BOAC	Late 1959	R	
		BUA	1960	L	
		BOAC	1960	R	
		MALAYAN AIRWAYS	10.5.62	L	
		BOAC	6.6.62	R	
		MALAYAN AIRWAYS	3.7.62	L	
		BOAC	1.8.62	R	
		BKS AIR TRANSPORT	16.11.65	P	

Withdrawn from use and stored at Newcastle Airport 2.69 and scrapped during 9.69.

No. 10

REG	C/N	OPERATOR	D/D		VARIANT
G-ANBH	12909	BAC	18.1.56		102
		BOAC	24.7.57	P	
		NIGERIA AIRWAYS	1958	L	
		BOAC	1958	R	
		BKS AIR TRANSPORT	10.3.65	L	
		BKS AIR TRANSPORT	30.9.65	P	

Scrapped, Southend Airport during September 1969.

No. 11

REG	C/N	OPERATOR	D/D		VARIANT
G-ANBI	12910	BOAC	29.6.56		102
		GHANA AIRWAYS	4.60	L	
		BOAC	1960	R	
		MALAYAN AIRWAYS	12.4.62	L	
		BOAC	9.5.62	R	
		BRITANNIA AIRWAYS	3.2.66	L	
		BRITANNIA AIRWAYS	29.4.66	P	

Withdrawn from service and scrapped at Luton Airport, February 1970.

No. 12

REG	C/N	OPERATOR	D/D		VARIANT
G-ANBJ	12911	BOAC	21.2.57		102
		MALAYAN AIRWAYS	8.2.62	L	
		BOAC	7.3.62	R	
		MALAYAN AIRWAYS	5.6.62	L	
		BOAC	4.7.62	R	
		PARAENSE TRANSPORTES-AEROES S.A.	(NTU)		
		EURAVIA	11.64	L	
		BRITANNIA AIRWAYS	5.5.65	P	

Withdrawn from service and stored at Luton Airport October 1970, and later scrapped during March 1971.

No. 13

REG	C/N	OPERATOR	D/D		VARIANT
G-ANBK	12912	BOAC	8.1.56		102
		NIGERIAN AIRWAYS	Early 1961	L	
		BOAC	Late 1961	R	
		BKS AIR TRANSPORT	11.4.64	L	
		BKS AIR TRANSPORT	4.70	P	
		NORTHEAST AIRLINES (UK)	1.11.70	NN	

Scrapped at Woolsington, Newcastle during July 1972.

No. 14

REG	C/N	OPERATOR	D/D		VARIANT
G-ANBL	12913	BOAC	2.3.57		102
		CATHAY PACIFIC AIRWAYS	18.12.60	L	
		BOAC	31.1.61	R	
		PARAENSE TRANSPORTES-AEROES S.A.	(NTU)		
		BRITANNIA AIRWAYS	26.6.65	L	
		SOUTHERN CROSS INTERNATIONAL	20.5.70	SL	
		BRITANNIA AIRWAYS	Mid-June 1970	R	

Withdrawn from use at Luton Airport in December 1970, and later scrapped in July 1972.

No. 15

REG	C/N	OPERATOR	D/D		VARIANT
G-ANBM	12914	BOAC	11.3.57		102
		NIGERIA AIRWAYS	11.59	L	
		BOAC	1960	R	
		MALAYAN AIRWAYS	15.11.61	L	
		BOAC	18.12.61	R	
		MALAYAN AIRWAYS	18.1.62	L	
		BOAC	7.2.62	R	
		MALAYAN AIRWAYS	25.9.62	L	
		BOAC	24.10.62	R	
		LAKER AIRWAYS	8.4.66	L	
		AIR FRANCE	29.7.66	SL	
		LAKER AIRWAYS	25.9.66	R	
		TREFFIELD INTERNATIONAL	29.4.67	SL	
		LAKER AIRWAYS	11.6.67	R	
		NATIONAL AERO LEASING	19.1.69	P	
PK-ICA		INDONESIA ANGKASA C.A.T.	11.2.69	P NR	

Withdrawn from use at Jakarta, Indonesia in June 1970, finally broken up and scrapped in December 1971.

No. 16

REG	C/N	OPERATOR	D/D		VARIANT
G-ANBN	12915	BOAC	4.5.57		102
		EAAC	1958	L	
		BOAC	1958	R	
		NIGERIA AIRWAYS	1.10.60	L	
		BOAC	1961	R	

No. 16 *(continued)*

REG	C/N	OPERATOR	D/D		VARIANT
G-ANBN	12915	MALAYAN AIRWAYS	8.3.62	L	
		BOAC	11.4.62	R	
		MALAYAN AIRWAYS	28.8.62	L	
		BOAC	26.9.62	R	
		MALAYAN AIRWAYS	23.10.62	L	
		BOAC	15.1.63	R	
		LAKER AIRWAYS	21.4.66	L	
		AIR CARRIERS OF ZAMBIA	16.11.67	SL	
		LAKER AIRWAYS	23.1.68	R	
		MONARCH AIRLINES	1968	L	
		LAKER AIRWAYS	1968	R	
		BRITANNIA AIRWAYS	16.4.68	SL	
		LAKER AIRWAYS	17.10.68	R	
		NATIONAL AERO LEASING	21.1.69	P	
PK-ICB		INDONESIA ANGKASA C.A.T.	11.2.69	P	

Withdrawn from use at Jakarta, Indonesia in June 1970. Broken up and scrapped in December 1971.

No. 17

REG	C/N	OPERATOR	D/D		VARIANT
G-ANBO	12916	BOAC	31.5.57	P	102
		CATHAY PACIFIC AIRWAYS	12.60	L	
		BOAC	1961	R	
		MALAYAN AIRWAYS	2.9.61	L	
		BOAC	18.10.61	R	
		EAAC	1961	L	
		BOAC		Returned	
		MALAYAN AIRWAYS	31.7.62	L	
		BOAC	29.8.62	R	
		BRITANNIA AIRWAYS	4.1.65	L	
		BRITANNIA AIRWAYS	16.3.70	P	

Withdrawn from service and stored at Luton Airport, in October 1970. Broken up and scrapped in May 1971.

No. 18

REG	C/N	OPERATOR	D/D		VARIANT
G-APPE	13450	MINISTRY OF SUPPLY	31.10.58		252
XN-392		A&AEE BOSCOMBE DOWN	3.59		
		RAF No. 99 SQDN.	18.9.59		C.MK.2
		RAF Nos. 99/511 SQDNs.	29.3.61	T	
		AER TURAS TEORANTE	18.12.75	P	

Scrapped at Baginton, Coventry in May 1976.

No. 19

REG	C/N	OPERATOR	D/D		VARIANT
G-APPF	13451	MINISTRY OF SUPPLY	28.11.58		252
XN-398		RAF No. 99 SQDN.	19.3.59		C.MK.2
		RAF Nos. 99/511 SQDNs.	17.5.61	T	
		EUROWORLD	11.9.75	P	252F
9Q-CPX		ZAIRE AERO SERVICE	1.2.77	P	
		DOMAINE DE KATALE	11.77	L	
		ZAIRE AERO SERVICE	Returned		
		DOMAINE DE KATALE	Leased		
		KATALE AERO TRANSPORT	Returned		

No longer in service, scrapped at Goma, Zaire.

No. 20

REG	C/N	OPERATOR	D/D		VARIANT
G-APPG	13452	MINISTRY OF SUPPLY	28.11.58	252	
XN-404		A&AEE BOSCOMBE DOWN	8.4.59		
		RAF No. 99 SQDN.	6.4.59		C.MK.2
		RAF Nos. 99/511 SQDNs.	27.2.61	T	
		SHACKLETON AVIATION	17.12.75		
		AIR FAISAL	(NTU)		

Broken up and scrapped at Luton Airport, November 1976.

No. 21

REG	C/N	OPERATOR	D/D		VARIANT
XL-635	13397	RAF No. 99 SQDN.	30.1.60		C.MK.1
		RAF Nos. 99/511 SQDNs.	22.12.60	T	
		YOUNG AIR CARGO	5.9.75	P C	253F
OO-YCA		YOUNG AIR CARGO	11.9.75	NR	

Scrapped at Stansted Airport, Essex in July 1977.

No. 22

REG	C/N	OPERATOR	D/D		VARIANT
XL-636	13398	RAF No. 99 SQDN.	4.6.59		C.MK.1
		RAF Nos. 99/511 SQDNs.	2.11.60	T	
OO-YCE		YOUNG AIR CARGO	6.5.76	P NR C	253F

Broken up and scrapped at Ostend, Belgium during August 1978.

No. 23

REG	C/N	OPERATOR	D/D		VARIANT
XL-637	13399	RAF No. 99 SQDN.	28.6.59		C.MK.1
		RAF No's 99/511 SQDN's.	9.9.60	T	
		CAPT. J. DE BRY	8.3.76	P C	253F

No. 23 *(continued)*

REG	C/N	OPERATOR	D/D		VARIANT
OO-YCH		YOUNG AIR CARGO	8.76	P NR	
		LIBERIA WORLD AIRWAYS	8.77	L	
EL-LWH		LIBERIA WORLD AIRWAYS		RR	
OO-YCH		YOUNG AIR CARGO	9.77	R	
9Q-CKG		DOMAINE DE KATALE	27.4.79	P NR	
9Q-CBT		DOMAINE DE KATALE	NR		

Reportedly broken up and scrapped in Zaire.

No. 24

REG	C/N	OPERATOR	D/D		VARIANT
XL-638	13400	RAF No. 99 SQDN.	5.8.59		C.MK.1
		RAF No's 99/511 SQDNs.	30.6.60	T	

Written off at RAF Khormaksar, Aden on 12 October 1967.

No. 25

REG	C/N	OPERATOR	D/D		VARIANT
XL-639	13448	RAF No. 99 SQDN.	8.10.59		C.MK.1
		RAF No's 99/511 SQDNs	12.10.60	T	
		GUINNESS PEAT AVIATION	10.2.76	P C	253F
EI-BDC		GUINNESS PEAT AVIATION		NR	
		AIRLINE ENGINEERING	10.2.77	P	
		AER TURAS TEORANTE	18.6.77	L	
		CYPRUS AIRWAYS	19.6.77	SL	
		AER TURAS TEORANTE	5.7.77	R	
		AIRLINE ENGINEERING	9.77	R	
		CYPRUS AIRWAYS	17.9.77	L	
		AIRLINE ENGINEERING	8.10.77	R	
		CYPRUS AIRWAYS	10.77	L	
		AIRLINE ENGINEERING	7.11.77	R	
		EURAFRIC	20.1.78	P	
G-BRAC		REDCOAT AIR CARGO	4.6.78	P NR	
		REDAIR (BBC TV SERIES)			

Written off near Billerica, Mass., 16 February, 1980 after take-off from Logan Airport.

No. 26

REG	C/N	OPERATOR	D/D		VARIANT
XL-640	13449	RAF No. 511 SQDN.	2.11.59		C.MK.1
		RAF Nos. 99/511 SQDNs.	16.1.61	T	
		MONARCH AIRLINES	13.1.76	P C	253F
		AER TURAS TEORANTE		(NTU)	
		EURAFRIC	3.77	(NTU)	
EI-BCI		AER TURAS TEORANTE	4.4.77	L NR	
		EURAFRIC	10.4.78	R	
		AER TURAS TEORANTE	25.5.78	L	
		EURAFRIC	6.9.78	R	
G-BHAU		REDCOAT AIR CARGO	13.8.79	L NR	
		SWORDVALE AVIATION	2.12.81	P	
9Q-CHU		KATALE AERO TRANSPORT	4.82	P NR	

Broken up and scrapped in Kinshasa, Zaire during 1986.

No. 27

REG	C/N	OPERATOR	D/D		VARIANT
XL-657	13454	RAF No. 511 SQDN.	23.12.59		C.MK.1
		RAF No's 99/511 SQDNS.	24.2.61	T	
		MONARCH AIRLINES	31.12.75	P C	253F
9U-BAD		CENTRE AIR AFRIQUE	10.3.76	P NR	

Withdrawn from use at Charleroi, Belgium 25.2.77 and later broken up and scrapped.

No. 28

REG	C/N	OPERATOR	D/D		VARIANT
XL-658	13455	RAF No.511 SQDN.	5.2.60		C.MK.1
		RAF No's 99/511 SQDNs.		T	
EI-BBY		AIRLINE ENGINEERING	26.5.76	P NR C	253F
		INTERCONTINENTAL MEAT COMPANY	10.8.76	P	

Written off at Shannon Airport on 30 September, 1977.

No. 29

REG	C/N	OPERATOR	D/D		VARIANT
XL-659	13456	RAF No. 511 SQDN.	4.3.60		C.MK.1
		RAF No's 99/511 SQDN's.		T	
		YOUNG AIR CARGO	5.9.75	P C	253F
OO-YCB		YOUNG AIR CARGO	11.9.75	NR	

Scrapped at Ostend, Belgium in December, 1977.

No. 30

REG	C/N	OPERATOR	D/D		VARIANT
XL-660	13457	RAF No.511 SQDN.	23.4.60		C.MK.1
		RAF No.99 SQDN.	1.5.60	T	
		RAF Nos 99/511 SQDNs.	9.60	T	
		AIR FAISAL	14.5.76	P C	253F
		TRANSGULF AIR CARGO	5.76	P	
G-BEMZ		AIR FAISAL	11.2.77	NR	
		T.F. RICHTER & CO LTD.	13.9.79	P	
		BLACK ARROW LEASING	14.2.80	P	
A6-HMS		GAYLAN AIR CARGO	9.4.80	L NR	
G-BEMZ		GAYLAN AIR CARGO	3.4.81	RR	
		REDCOAT AIR CARGO/DANTANA	22.9.81	L	
		SWORDVALE AVIATION	2.12.81	P	
9Q-CGP		KATALE AERO TRANSPORT	11.82	P NR	

Withdrawn from use and reportedly broken up.

No. 31

REG	C/N	OPERATOR	D/D		VARIANT
XM-489	13434	RAF No. 511 SQDN.	4.5.60		C.MK.1
		RAF Nos. 99/511 SQDNs.	9.60	T	
OO-YCC		YOUNG AIR CARGO	10.2.76	P NR C	253F

Scrapped during 1978 at Gosselies, Belgium.

No. 32

REG	C/N	OPERATOR	D/D		VARIANT
XM-490	13435	RAF No.99 SQUADRON	9.6.60		C.MK.1
		RAF No's 99/511 SQDNS.	7.11.60	T	
		EUROWORLD	29.10.75	P C	253F
G-BDLZ		AIR FAISAL	17.11.75	P NR	
		AIR WORKS INDIA	12.76	L	
		AIR FAISAL	1977 Returned		

Withdrawn from use at Luton Airport in May 1979 and broken up in Setember 1979.

No. 33

REG	C/N	OPERATOR	D/D		VARIANT
XM-491	13436	RAF No. 511 SQUADRON	7.7.60		C.MK.1
		RAF No's 99/511 SQDNs.	15.5.61	T	
EI-BBH		AER TURAS TEORANTE	8.9.75	P NR C	253F
		CYPRUS AIRWAYS	9.9.76	L	
		AER TURAS TEORANTE	12.4.78	R	
		GEMINI AIR TRANSPORT	23.3.79	L	
		AER TURAS TEORANTE	23.5.79	R	
9Q-CMO		KATALE AERO TRANSPORT	11.81	P NR	

No longer in service, possibly a spares source.

No. 34

REG	C/N	OPERATOR	D/D		VARIANT
XM-496	13508	RAF Nos. 99/511 SQDNs.	19.9.60		C.MK.1
		MONARCH AIRLINES ENGINEERING LTD.	6.1.76	P C	253F
G-BDUP		MONARCH AIRLINES ENGINEERING LTD.	31.3.76	NR	
		AFREK	21.5.76	P	
		MONARCH AIRLINES ENGINEERING LTD.	30.7.84	P	
CU-T120		AEROCARIBBEAN	8.84	P NR	

Still in service to date (grounded due to lack of spares in Cuba, 10.90). Mid 1992 still in open storage, Havana, Cuba.

No. 35

REG	C/N	OPERATOR	D/D		VARIANT
XM-497	13509	RAF Nos. 99/511 SQDNs.	5.12.60		C.MK.1
		YOUNG AIR CARGO	23.4.76	P C	253F
OO-YCF		YOUNG AIR CARGO	5.5.76	NR	(NTU)

Broken up at Stansted Airport, Essex and remains used by BAA Fire School until burnt out in May 1981.

No. 36

REG	C/N	OPERATOR	D/D		VARIANT
XM-498	13510	RAF No. 99 SQDN.	19.10.59		C.MK.1
		RAF Nos. 99/511 SQDNs.	7.7.61	T	
OO-YCG		YOUNG AIR CARGO	11.6.76	P NR C	253F
EL-LWG		LIBERIA WORLD AIRWAYS	11.7.76	L NR	
9Q-CDT		KATALE AERO TRANSPORT	8.5.79	P NR	
		BUSINESS CASH FLOW AVI'	7.88	P	

Used as a source of spares for 9Q-CHY by BCF, scrapped in January 1992.

No. 37

REG	C/N	OPERATOR	D/D		VARIANT
XM-517	13511	RAF No. 511 SQDN.	3.12.59		C.MK.1
		RAF Nos. 99/511 SQDNs.	20.2.61	T	
		MONARCH AIRLINES	21.10.75	P C	253F
9Q-CAJ		AMAZ	8.76	P NR	
G-BEPX		AIRLINE ENGINEERING	14.4.77	P NR	

Withdrawn from use and broken up at Luton Airport April 1980.

No. 38

REG	C/N	OPERATOR	D/D		VARIANT
XM-518	13512	RAF No. 511 SQDN.	30.12.59		C.MK.1
		RAF Nos. 99/511 SQDNs.	23.11.60	T	
OO-YCD		YOUNG AIR CARGO	4.3.76	P NR C	253F

Broken up for spares at Gosselies, Belgium and scrapped during 1978.

No. 39

REG	C/N	OPERATOR	D/D		VARIANT
XM-519	13513	RAF No. 511 SQDN.	8.2.60		C.MK.1
		RAF Nos. 99/511 SQDNs.	28.11.60	T	
		AIRLINE ENGINEERING	13.2.76	P C	253F
G-BDUR		AIRLINE ENGINEERING	31.3.76	NR	
		AFREK	2.7.76	P	
		AIRLINE ENGINEERING	30.7.84	P	
CU-T121		AEROCARIBBEAN	8.84	P NR	

In open storage since October 1990 at Havana, Cuba.

No. 40

REG	C/N	OPERATOR	D/D		VARIANT
XM-520	13514	RAF No. 511 SQDN.	21.3.60		C.MK.1
		RAF Nos. 99/511 SQDNs.	22.3.61	T	
9G-ACE		GEMINI AIR TRANSPORT	16.9.75	P NR C	253F
		REDCOAT AIR CARGO	5.76	L	
		GEMINI AIR TRANSPORT	1977	R	

No. 40 *(continued)*

REG	C/N	OPERATOR	D/D		VARIANT
9Q-CUM		LUKUM AIR SERVICES	9.81	P NR	
		KATALE AERO TRANSPORT	7.86	P	

Broken up for spares at Kinshasa, Zaire for Katale Aero Transport in July 1986.

No. 41

REG	C/N	OPERATOR	D/D		VARIANT
G-ANCA	12917	BAC	11.3.55		301
		MINISTRY OF SUPPLY	26.3.56	T	
		BAC	31.7.56	R	

Whilst on test flight, crashed at Downend near Bristol 6.11.57, killing all 15 persons aboard.

No. 42

REG	C/N	OPERATOR	D/D		VARIANT
	12918	BOAC	(NTU)		302
G-ANCB		BRISTOL AIRCRAFT LTD.	20.1.56		
G-18-1		BRISTOL AIRCRAFT LTD.	6.57	NR	
XA-MEC		AERONAVES DE MEXICO.	31.5.57	P NR	
		AERONAVES DE MEXICO.	1.11.57	D	

Written off at Tijuana, Mexico on 9 July, 1965.

No. 43

REG	C/N	OPERATOR	D/D		VARIANT
	12919	BOAC	(NTU)		302
G-ANCC		BRISTOL AIRCRAFT LTD.	8.1.57		
G-18-2		BRISTOL AIRCRAFT LTD.	24.7.57	NR	
XA-MED		AERONAVES DE MEXICO	31.5.57	P NR	
		AERONAVES DE MEXICO	15.12.57	D	
G-ANCC		TRANSGLOBE AIRWAYS	12.5.66	P RR	
		IAS CARGO AIRLINES	1968	P	

Withdrawn from use at Biggin Hill, Kent in May 1970. Later broken up for scrap during August 1970.

No. 44

REG	C/N	OPERATOR	D/D		VARIANT
	12920	BOAC	(NTU)		302
		CAPITAL AIRLINES U.S.A.	(NTU)		305
G-18-3		BAC	1.6.57		
G-ANCD		BRISTOL AIRCRAFT LTD.	3.1.58	T NR	
N6595C		NORTHEAST AIRLINES USA.	(NTU)		
G-ANCD		NORTHEAST AIRLINES USA.	29.1.58	RR	
		CUBANA (SALES TOUR)	4.6.58		
4X-AGE		EL AL	8.7.58	L NR	

No. 44 *(continued)*

REG	C/N	OPERATOR	D/D		VARIANT
4X-AGE		EL AL	17.7.58	D	
		BRISTOL AIRCRAFT LTD.	6.3.59	R	
G-ANCD		BRISTOL AIRCRAFT LTD.	20.3.59	RR	
		AIR CHARTER LTD.	24.3.59	L	
		AIR CHARTER LTD.	6.59	C	307
		BUA	1.7.60	MERGED	
		AIR CHARTER LTD.	23.8.60	P	
		LLOYD INTERNATIONAL	17.2.69	L	
		LLOYD INTERNATIONAL	2.69	C	307F
		LLOYD INTERNATIONAL EAST AFRICAN AIRWAYS	2.69	SL	
		AIVEX HOLDINGS LTD.	27.7.73		
		SHACKLETON AVIATION	7.73		
		IAS CARGO AIRLINES	22.9.73	L	
5Y-AYR		AFRICAN CARGO AIRWAYS	13.5.75	L NR	
		WESTWING AVIATION SERVICES	1.2.77	L	
		BLACK ARROW FINANCE	5.77		
		TRANSGULF AIR CARGO	11.77	L	
		AIR FAISAL	1978	SL	
		ALL CARGO AIRLINES	12.78	L	
		GAYLAN AIR CARGO	8.79	L	

Withdrawn from use and stored at Hurn Airport, Bournemouth from October 1982, later broken up and scrapped.

No. 45

REG	C/N	OPERATOR	D/D		VARIANT
	12921	BOAC	(NTU)		305
		CAPITAL AIRLINES USA	(NTU)		
N6596C		NORTHEAST AIRLINES USA	(NTU)		
G-ANCE		BRISTOL AIRCRAFT LTD.	3.1.58	C	307
		AIR CHARTER	12.9.58	P	
		BUA	1.7.60	P C	307F
		LLOYD INTERNATIONAL	26.2.69	L	
		MONARCH AIRLINES	22.6.73	P	
		IAS CARGO AIRLINES	20.1.74	L	
		MONARCH AIRLINES	31.1.74	R	
EI-BAA		AER TURAS TEORANTE	6.5.74	L NR	
		PAULING CONSTRUCTION CO.	17.11.74	L	
		AER TURAS TEORANTE	17.1.75	R	

Withdrawn from use and scrapped at Dublin Airport, after being used as spares source from May 1981.

No. 46

REG	C/N	OPERATOR	D/D		VARIANT
	12922	BOAC	(NTU)		305
		CAPITAL AIRLINES (USA)	(NTU)		
N6597C		NORTHEAST AIRLINES (USA)	(NTU)		
G-ANCF		BRISTOL AIRCRAFT LTD.	3.1.58	NR	
G-18-4		BRISTOL AIRCRAFT LTD.	11.58	NR	
G-14-1		BRISTOL AIRCRAFT LTD.	10.59	NR C	308
LV-PPJ		TRANSCONTINENTAL S.A.	24.8.59	P NR	
		TRANSCONTINENTAL S.A.	16.12.59	D	
LV-GJB		TRANSCONTINENTAL S.A.	1960	NR	
		BRITISH EAGLE	16.1.64	P	

No. 46 *(continued)*

REG	C/N	OPERATOR	D/D		VARIANT
G-ANCF		BRITISH EAGLE	2.3.64	RR	
		BRITISH EAGLE	7.64.	C	308F
		MONARCH AIRLINES	6.12.68	P	
		MONARCH AIRLINES	12.12.68	D	
		IAS CARGO AIRLINES	31.12.73	L	
		MONARCH AIRLINES	23.1.74	R	
5Y-AZP		AFRICAN CARGO AIRLINES	1.2.76	L NR	
		INVICTA INTERNATIONAL	14.6.76	SL	
G-ANCF		INVICTA INTERNATIONAL	7.1.77	P RR	
		PROTEUS AERO SERVICES	1984	P	

Withdrawn from use at Manston, Kent 1981, purchased by Proteus Aero Services for preservation, possibly at the new Bristol Aero Collection at Filton in British Eagle livery, and now owned by the Britannia Aircraft Preservation Trust.

No. 47

REG	C/N	OPERATOR	D/D		VARIANT
	12923	BOAC	(NTU)		305
		CAPITAL AIRLINES USA	(NTU)		
N6598C		NORTHEAST AIRLINES USA	(NTU)		
G-ANCG		BRISTOL AIRCRAFT LTD.	3.1.58	NR	
G-14-2		BRISTOL AIRCRAFT LTD.	20.11.59	NR C	308
LV-PPL		TRANSCONTINENTAL S.A.	17.12.59	P NR	
LV-GJC		TRANSCONTINENTAL S.A.	1959	NR	
		BRITISH EAGLE	23.2.64	P	
G-ANCG		BRITISH EAGLE	6.4.64	RR C	308F

Damaged beyond repair following a wheels up landing at Manston Airport, Kent on 20 April, 1967.

No. 48

REG	C/N	OPERATOR	D/D		VARIANT
	12924	BOAC	(NTU)		305
		CAPITAL AIRLINES (USA)	(NTU)		
N6599C		NORTHEAST AIRLINES (USA)	(NTU)		
G-ANCH		BRISTOL AIRCRAFT LTD.	3.1.58	NR C	309
9G-AAG		GHANA AIRWAYS	16.8.60	L NR	
G-41		GHANA AIRWAYS	1.6.65	NR	
G-ANCH		BUA	4.6.65	L RR	
		BRISTOL AIRCRAFT LTD.	Returned		
		GHANA AIRWAYS	7.10.65	L	
		TRANSGLOBE AIRWAYS	6.12.66	L	
		GHANA AIRWAYS	30.9.67	R	
		BRITISH EAGLE	(NTU)		
		GHANA AIRWAYS	3.68	R	
		MONARCH AIRLINES	25.9.68	L	
		GHANA AIRWAYS	4.5.72	R	
		IAS CARGO AIRLINES	12.72	P	

Scrapped at Biggin Hill, Kent in August 1983.

No. 49

REG	C/N	OPERATOR	D/D		VARIANT
G-AMYK	13207	BAC	(NTU)		200
G-AOFA		BAC	(NTU)		300LR
G-AOVA		BAC	21.11.56		311
		BOAC	15.7.57	L C	312
		BRISTOL AIRCRAFT LTD.	4.58	R C	311
		HUNTING CLAN AIR TRANSPORT	1.59	L	
		BRISTOL AIRCRAFT LTD.	1959	R C	319
9G-AAH		GHANA AIRWAYS	9.60	P NR	
		GHANA AIRWAYS	9.11.60	D	
G-AOVA		VICKERS ARMSTRONG(AIRCRAFT)LTD.	1963	P RR	
		BRISTOL AIRCRAFT SERVICES	31.12.63	P	
		BRITISH EAGLE	1.1.64	L	
		BUA	12.2.64	L	
		BRISTOL AIRCRAFT SERVICES	19.4.64	R	
		BRITISH EAGLE	25.4.64	L	
		BRITISH EAGLE	29.12.67	P	
		CCT AIRCRAFT LEASING	25.3.69	P	
		CALEDONIAN AIRWAYS	25.3.69	L	
		CCT AIRCRAFT LEASING	11.69	R	
		LLOYD INTERNATIONAL	13.12.69	L	
		CALEDONIAN AIRWAYS	13.12.69	SL	
		CCT AIRCRAFT LEASING	2.70	R	
		AIRLINE ENGINEERING	6.71	P	

Withdrawn from use at Baginton Airport, Coventry 2.70 an used for spares 10.71. Later scrapped.

No. 50

REG	C/N	OPERATOR	D/D		VARIANT
G-AOVB	13230	BOAC	10.9.57		312
		EAAC	5.11.58	L	
		BOAC	early 59	R	
		BWIA	1960	L	
		BOAC	1960	R	
		BRITISH EAGLE	15.10.63	L	
		BRITISH EAGLE		C	312F
		BOAC	11.68	R	
	LV-PNJ	AER ARGENTINA	9.10.69	P NR	
	LV-JNL	AER ARGENTINA	2.70	NR	

Written off 12 July, 1970 near Ezeiza, Argentina whilst landing in fog.

No. 51

REG	C/N	OPERATOR	D/D		VARIANT
G-AOFC	13231	BAC	22.11.55	(NTU)	300LR
G-AOVC		BOAC	15.11.57	P	312
		BRITISH EAGLE	15.5.64	L	
		DONALDSON INTERNATIONAL	20.5.69	P	

Withdrawn from service on 28 September 1970 and scrapped at Stansted Airport, Kent.

No. 52

REG	C/N	OPERATOR	D/D		VARIANT
G-AOFD	13235	BAC	(NTU)		300LR
G-AOVD		BOAC	6.12.57		312

Crashed and written off near Christchurch on 24.12.57

No. 53

REG	C/N	OPERATOR	D/D		VARIANT
G-AOFE	13236	BAC	(NTU)		300LR
G-AOVE		BOAC	21.12.57	P	312
		BUA	27.9.61	L	
		MEA	21.4.64	SL	
		BUA	21.5.64	R	
		BOAC	21.5.65	R	
		BRITISH EAGLE	6.6.64	L	
		BRITISH EAGLE	30.11.66	P	
EC-WFK		AIR SPAIN	11.66	P NR	
EC-BFK		AIR SPAIN	11.66	NR	
		IAS CARGO AIRLINES	9.73	P	

Withdrawn from service and scrapped for spares in 1974 at Palma.

No. 54

REG	C/N	OPERATOR	D/D		VARIANT
G-AOFF	13237	BAC	(NTU)		300LR
G-AOVF		BOAC	2.1.58	P	312
		BRITISH EAGLE	4.3.64	L	
		BRITISH EAGLE	1968	C	312F
		BOAC	27.11.68	R	
		MONARCH AIRLINES	22.1.70	P	
		DONALDSON INTERNATIONAL	21.4.70	L	
		DONALDSON INTERNATIONAL	24.7.72	P	
		IAS	31.10.72	P	
		AFRICAN SAFARI AIRLINES	1.11.72	L	
		IAS CARGO AIRLINES	19.12.72	R	
		INVICTA (1976) LTD.	4.76	L	
		IAS CARGO AIRLINES	RETURNED		
		REDCOAT AIR CARGO	3.8.79	L	
		INVICTA INTERNATIONAL	RETURNED		
9Q-CAZ		IAC CARGO AIRLINES	6.1.81	L NR	
		INVICTA INTERNATIONAL	4.6.81	R	
		MERCHANT AIR	21.2.84	P	
G-AOVF		BOAC (PRESERVED COSFORD MUSEUM)	MAY 1984.		

No. 55

REG	C/N	OPERATOR	D/D	VARIANT
G-AOFG	13238	BAC	(NTU)	300LR

No. 55 *(continued)*

REG	C/N	OPERATOR	D/D		VARIANT
G-AOVG		BOAC	19.3.58	P	312
		BEA	4-5.61	L	
		BOAC	5.61	R	
		BRITISH EAGLE	3.4.64	L	
		MONARCH AIRLINES	10.10.69	P	

Withdrawn from use at Luton Airport and scrapped August 1974.

No. 56

REG	C/N	OPERATOR	D/D		VARIANT
G-ANCI	12925	BAC	(NTU)		305
G-AOVH		BOAC	11.2.58		312
		BRITISH EAGLE	6.11.64	L	
		CALEDONIAN AIRWAYS	7.3.65	P	
		ROYAL AIR MAROC	14.3.65	L	
		CALEDONIAN AIRWAYS	5.5.65	R	
		MONARCH AIRLINES	1.4.68	P	

Withdrawn from service and used as a cabin crew trainer at Luton Airport from November 1971. Scrapped in June 1972.

No. 57

REG	C/N	OPERATOR	D/D		VARIANT
G-ANCJ	12926	BAC	(NTU)		305
G-AOVI		BOAC	10.4.58		312
		BUA	22.9.61	L	
		BOAC	1.7.64	R	
		CALEDONIAN AIRWAYS	18.12.64	L	
		CALEDONIAN AIRWAYS	19.1.65	P	
		ROYAL AIR MAROC	4.66	L	
		CALEDONIAN AIRWAYS	1966	R	
		MONARCH AIRLINES	14.2.68	P	
		CALEDONIAN AIRWAYS	17.2.68	L	
		MONARCH AIRLINES	29.3.68	R	

Withdrawn from use and stored at Luton Airport from January 1972. Broken up and scrapped from April 1972.

No. 58

REG	C/N	OPERATOR	D/D		VARIANT
G-AOFJ	13418	BAC	(NTU)		300LR
G-AOVJ		BOAC	23.4.58		312
		BWIA	1961	L	
		BOAC	1961	R	
		CALEDONIAN AIRWAYS	28.4.65	L	
		CALEDONIAN AIRWAYS	12.11.69	P	
		DONALDSON INTERNATIONAL	11.70	P	

Withdrawn from use at Stansted Airport in December 1970 for spares, then to airfield fire dump for training.

No. 59

REG	C/N	OPERATOR	D/D		VARIANT
G-AOVK	13419	BOAC	11.5.58	P	312
		BRITISH EAGLE	31.5.65	L	
		BRITISH EAGLE	1.12.67	P	
		CCT AIRCRAFT LEASING	11.4.69	P	
		MONARCH AIRLINES/AIRLINE ENGINEERING	24.5.69	P	

Withdrawn from use, broken up and scrapped at Luton Airport from February 1970.

No. 60

REG	C/N	OPERATOR	D/D		VARIANT
G-AOVL	13420	BOAC	20.5.58		312
		BWIA	1958	L	
		BOAC	1958	R	
		BRITISH EAGLE	30.4.65	L	
		BRITISH EAGLE	18.4.68	P	
		MONARCH AIRLINES	17.2.69	L	
		MONARCH AIRLINES	31.7.69	P	

Withdrawn from use at Luton Airport and scrapped during July 1971.

No. 61

REG	C/N	OPERATOR	D/D		VARIANT
G-AOVM	13421	BOAC	10.6.58		312
		BRITISH EAGLE	28.3.64	L	
		BRITISH EAGLE	12.67	P C	312F
		SOUTHERN CROSS INTERNATIONAL		(NTU)	
		AIR SPAIN	6.3.69	P	
EC-BSY		AIR SPAIN	1.12.69	NR	
XX-367		M.O.D.(P.E.)	11.71	P NR	
		A&AEE BOSCOMBE DOWN	3.5.72	T	
9Q-CHY		KATALE AERO TRANSPORT	3.84	P NR	
		BUSINESS CASH FLOW	4.89	P	

No longer in service to date, although now up for sale.

No. 62

REG	C/N	OPERATOR	D/D		VARIANT
G-AOVN	13422	BOAC	4.7.58		312
		BRITISH EAGLE	2.6.64	L C	312F
		MONARCH AIRLINES	6.3.69	P	
		AFRICAN SAFARI AIRWAYS	28.9.72	L	
		MONARCH AIRLINES	2.11.72	R	

Withdrawn from use at Luton Airport in November 1973 and scrapped during February 1974.

No. 63

REG	C/N	OPERATOR	D/D		VARIANT
G-AOVO	13423	BOAC	4.9.58	P	312
		EAAC	1958/1959	L	
		BOAC	1959	R	
		BRITISH EAGLE	17.1.64	L	

Crashed into Clungezer mountain in the Austrian Alps on approach to Innsbruck on 29 February 1964.

No. 64

REG	C/N	OPERATOR	D/D		VARIANT
G-AOVP	13424	BOAC	15.9.58		312
		BEA	4/5 1961	L	
		BOAC	5.61	R	
		LLOYD INTERNATIONAL AIRLINES	15.4.65	LC	312F
		EAST AFRICAN AIRWAYS	1968	SL	
		LLOYD INTERNATIONAL AIRLINES	17.1.69	P	
		IAS CARGO AIRLINES	10.7.73	P	

Scrapped at Biggin Hill, Kent from June 1977.

No. 65

REG	C/N	OPERATOR	D/D		VARIANT
G-AOVR	13429	BOAC	3.10.58		312
		BRITISH EAGLE	22.2.65	P	
EC-WFJ		AIR SPAIN	20.10.66	P NR	
EC-BFJ		AIR SPAIN	10.66	NR	
		IAS CARGO AIRLINES	4.73	P	

Withdrawn from use at Biggin Hill, Kent April 1973 and finally scrapped during August 1975.

No. 66

REG	C/N	OPERATOR	D/D		VARIANT
G-AOVS	13430	BOAC	29.10.58		312
		LLOYD INTERNATIONAL	4.7.65	L	
		BOAC	7.65	R	
		BRITISH EAGLE	7.65	SL	
		LLOYD INTERNATIONAL	12.65	R	
		LLOYD INTERNATIONAL	6.66	PC	312F
		El-Al	12.70	L	
		LLOYD INTERNATIONAL	6.71	R	
		IAS CARGO AIRLINES	18.1.73	L	
		AIVEX HOLDINGS	28.12.73	P	
		IAS CARGO AIRLINES	28.12.73	L	
		WESTWINGS AVIATION	14.10.74	P	
		INVICTA (1976) LTD.	1.1.76	L	
		IAS CARGO AIRLINES	13.6.76	R	
		AIVEX HOLDINGS	21.3.77	P	
		REDCOAT AIR CARGO	5.77	L	
		REDCOAT AIR CARGO	4.4.79	P	
G-BRAC		REDAIR (BBC TV)	1980		

Fuselage on fire ground at Luton Airport for non-destructive fire training, August 1990. Tail and wings have been removed. At the end of May 1992, she is used by Airport Fire Service.

No. 67

REG	C/N	OPERATOR	D/D		VARIANT
G-AOVT	13427	BOAC	1.1.59		312
		EAAC	1959	L	
		BEA	4-5.61	L	
		BOAC	5.61	R	
		NIGERIAN AIRWAYS	1961	L	
		BRITISH EAGLE	13.9.63	L	
		MONARCH AIRLINES	18.8.69	P	
		INVICTA INTERNATIONAL AIRLINES	13.12.74	L	
		MONARCH AIRLINES	10.3.75	R	

Monarch Airlines donated G-AOVT to the Duxford Aviation Society, Cambridge for preservation and public display. Delivered on 29 June 1975.

No. 68

REG	C/N	OPERATOR	D/D		VARIANT
4X-AGA	13232	El-Al	5.9.57		313
G-ASFV		BUA for El-Al	19.3.63	L NR	
4X-AGA		El-Al	1.4.63	R RR	
HB-ITB		GLOBE AIR	3.4.64	P NR	

Undershot runway whilst landing at Nicosia, Cyprus on 19 April, 1964 and was written off killing 126 persons aboard.

No. 69

REG	C/N	OPERATOR	D/D		VARIANT
4X-AGB	13233	El-Al	19.10.57		313
G-ARWZ		BRISTOL AIRCRAFT SERVICES LTD.	13.2.62	L NR	
		BUA	14.2.62	L	
4X-AGB		El-Al	26.3.65	R RR	
EC-WFL		AIR SPAIN	3.67	P NR	
EC-BFL		AIR SPAIN	3.67	NR	
		IAS CARGO AIRLINES	9.73	P	

Scrapped at Palma during 1974.

No. 70

REG	C/N	OPERATOR	D/D		VARIANT
G-ANGK	13234	BAC	23.11.53		250
4X-AGC	13234	El-Al	28.11.57	P NR	313
G-ARXA		BRISTOL AIRCRAFT LTD.	14.3.62	T NR	
		BUA	12.3.64	SL	
4X-AGC		El-Al	27.9.64	R RR	
G-ARXA		BRITISH EAGLE	22.4.66	L RR	
4X-AGC		El-Al	8.11.68	SL RR	
G-ARXA		MONARCH AIRLINES	11.70	P RR	

Scrapped at Luton Airport during November 1970.

No. 71

REG	C/N	OPERATOR	D/D		VARIANT
4X-AGD	13431	El-Al	7.3.59		313
G-ASFU		BUA during strike for El-Al	18.3.63	NR	
4X-AGD		El-Al	8.4.63	R RR	
HB-ITC		GLOBE AIR	8.3.65	P NR	
5X-UVH		AFRICAN SAFARI AIRWAYS	26.12.67	P NR	
5Y-ALT		AFRICAN SAFARI AIRWAYS	25.5.70	NR	
		AFRICAN CARGO AIRWAYS	11.73	P	

Withdrawn from service and scrapped during 1975 at Stansted Airport.

No. 72

REG	C/N	OPERATOR	D/D		VARIANT
CF-CZA	13393	CANADIAN PACIFIC AIRLINES	9.4.58		314
		AIR LINKS LTD.	5.65	P	
G-ATGD		AIR LINKS LTD.	9.7.65	NR	
		BUA	7.65	L	
		TRANSGLOBE AIRWAYS	9.8.65		
5X-UVT		AFRICAN SAFARI AIRLINES	16.9.69	P NR	
5Y-ALP		AFRICAN SAFARI AIRLINES	26.4.70	NR	

Withdrawn from use and scrapped at Biggin Hill, Kent in December 1971.

No. 73

REG	C/N	OPERATOR	D/D	VARIANT
CF-CZB	13394	CANADIAN PACIFIC AIRLINES	24.9.58	314

Written off whilst attempting an overshoot at Hickham Field, Honolulu, Hawaii on 22 July, 1962 and damaged beyond repair.

No. 74

REG	C/N	OPERATOR	D/D		VARIANT
CF-CZC	13395	CANADIAN PACIFIC AIRLINES	20.5.58		314
		AIR LINKS LTD.	6.65	P	
G-ATLE		TRANSGLOBE AIRWAYS	30.11.65	L NR	
		TREK AIRWAYS	6.68	L	
		IAS CARGO AIRLINES	30.12.69	P	

Scrapped at Gatwick in March 1984.

No. 75

REG	C/N	OPERATOR	D/D		VARIANT
CF-CZD	13396	CANADIAN PACIFIC AIRLINES	27.6.58		314
G-ATNZ		CALEDONIAN AIRWAYS	31.1.66	P NR	
		CALEDONIAN / BUA	17.5.66		
		IAS CARGO AIRLINES	10.3.71	L	
		IAS CARGO AIRLINES	20.4.71	P	

Scrapped at Biggin Hill, Kent during June 1972.

No. 76

REG	C/N	OPERATOR	D/D		VARIANT
CF-CZW	13453	CANADIAN PACIFIC AIRLINES	7.8.58		314
G-ASTF		BRITISH EAGLE	20.5.64	L NR	
CF-CZW		CANADIAN PACIFIC AIRLINES	15.10.64	R RR	
G-ASTF		CALEDONIAN AIRWAYS	27.1.66	L RR	

Withdrawn from use and stored at Gatwick Airport in November 1969. Scrapped during October 1970.

No. 77

REG	C/N	OPERATOR	D/D		VARIANT
CF-CZX	13428	CANADIAN PACIFIC AIRLINES	3.7.58		314
G-ATMA		CALEDONIAN AIRWAYS	28.12.65	P NR	
CF-CZX		CANADIAN PACIFIC AIRLINES	31.10.69	R RR	
5Y-ANS		AFRICAN SAFARI AIRWAYS	12.69	L NR	
		IAS CARGO AIRLINES	5.4.71	P	
		AFRICAN SAFARI AIRWAYS	4.71	L	
G-ATMA		IAS CARGO AIRLINES	11.71	R RR	
5Y-ANS		AFRICAN INTERNATIONAL	9.2.72	L RR	
G-ATMA		AFRICAN INTERNATIONAL		RR	
		IAS CARGO AIRLINES	18.5.72	R	

Scrapped at Biggin Hill, Kent, August 1975.

No. 78

REG	C/N	OPERATOR	D/D		VARIANT
G-APNA	13425	CLANAIR LTD.	Late 1957	317	
		BRITISH & COMMONWEALTH SHIPPING COMPANY LTD.	11.12.58		
		BRITISH & COMMONWEALTH SHIPPING COMPANY (AVIATION) LTD.	21.4.59		
		BOAC	1960-61	L	
		EAAC	1960-61	L	
		BEA	1960-61	L	
		BUA	1960 Merger		
		DONALDSON INTERNATIONAL DIA	2.10.67	P	
		LLOYD INTERNATIONAL AIRLINES	10.67	L	
		DONALDSON INTERNATIONAL DIA	5.69	R	
		IAS CARGO AIRLINES	10.72	P	

Withdrawn from use and scrapped at Baginton, Coventry in July 1973.

No. 79

REG	C/N	OPERATOR	D/D		VARIANT
G-APNB	13426	CLANAIR LTD.	(NTU)		317
		BRITISH & COMMONWEALTH SHIPPING CO. LTD.	30.4.59		
		BRITISH & COMMONWEALTH SHIPPING CO. (AVIATION) LTD.	21.4.59	T	
		HUNTING CLAN AIR TRANSPORT	31.5.60	T	
		BOAC	1959-61	L	
		EAAC	1959-61	L	
		BEA	1959-61	L	

No. 79 *(continue)*

REG	C/N	OPERATOR	D/D		VARIANT
G-APNB	13426	BUA	Merged 1960		
		DONALDSON INTERNATIONAL	10.67	P	
		LLOYD INTERNATIONAL	10.67	L	
		DONALDSON INTERNATIONAL	16.1.69	R	
		AIRLINE ENGINEERING SERVICES	6.10.71	P	

Withdrawn from use at Luton and used by Airline Engineering Services for spares. Broken up in November 1971.

No. 80

REG	C/N	OPERATOR	D/D		VARIANT
CU-P668	13432	CUBANA DE AVIACION	16.12.58		318
CU-T668		CUBANA DE AVIACION	12.58	NR	
G-APYY		EAGLE AIRWAYS	25.3.60	L NR	
		CUNARD EAGLE AIRWAYS	1.9.60	L	
CU-T668		CUBANA DE AVIACION	19.9.61	R RR	
OK-MBA		CESKOSLOVENSKE C.S.A.	10.61	L NR	
CU-T668		CUBANA DE AVIACION	5.64	R RR	

Withdrawn from use and stored at Havana, Cuba. 1991 scrapped.

No. 81

REG	C/N	OPERATOR	D/D		VARIANT
CU-P669	13433	CUBANA DE AVIACION	6.2.59		318
CU-T669		CUBANA DE AVIACION	2.59	NR	
CU-T114		AEROCARIBBEAN	5.84	P NR	

Unlikely to fly again. In store at Havana, Cuba.

No. 82

REG	C/N	OPERATOR	D/D		VARIANT
CU-P670	13437	CUBANA DE AVIACION	15.5.59		318
CU-T670		CUBANA DE AVIACION	May 1959	NR	
		CESKOSLOVENSKE C.S.A.	1963	L	
		CUBANA DE AVIACION	1963	R	

Withdrawn from service and stored at Havana, Cuba. Later scrapped.

No. 83

REG	C/N	OPERATOR	D/D		VARIANT
CU-P671	13515	CUBANA DE AVIACION	26.8.59	P NR	318
CU-T671		CUBANA DE AVIACION	Aug. 1959	NR	
OK-MBB		CESKOSLOVENSKE C.S.A.	Nov. 1963	L NR	
CU-T671		CUBANA DE AVIACION	Jan. 1969	R RR	

Stored at Havana, Cuba to be preserved in Cubana livery.

No. 84

REG	C/N	OPERATOR	D/D		VARIANT
G-18-8	13516	BAC			324
CF-CPD		CANADIAN PACIFIC AIRLINES	16.10.59	NR	
G-ARKA		BRISTOL AIRCRAFT LTD.	12.2.61	R NR	
		CUNARD EAGLE AIRWAYS	8.3.61	L	
		BRISTOL AIRCRAFT LTD.	10.3.64	R	
		CUNARD EAGLE AIRWAYS	10.3.64	L	
		BRITISH EAGLE	1.12.67	P	
		CCT AIRCRAFT LEASING	21.3.69	P	
		TELLAIR AIRWAYS	24.3.69	L	
HB-ITF		TELLAIR AIRWAYS	(NTU)		
G-ARKA		AIRLINE ENGINEERING	June 1971	P RR	

Scrapped at Baginton, Coventry in October 1971.

No. 85

REG	C/N	OPERATOR	D/D		VARIANT
CF-CPE	13517	CANADIAN PACIFIC AIRLINES	13.11.59	L	324
G-ARKB		BRISTOL AIRCRAFT LTD.	11.4.61	R NR	
		CUNARD EAGLE AIRWAYS	1.5.61	L	
		BRISTOL AIRCRAFT LTD.	10.3.64	R	
		CUNARD EAGLE AIRWAYS	10.3.64	L	
		BRITISH EAGLE	23.12.64	P	
		CCT AIRCRAFT LEASING	11.4.69	P	
		TELLAIR AIRWAYS	11.4.69	L	
HB-ITG		TELLAIR AIRWAYS	(NTU)		
G-ARKB		AIRLINE ENGINEERING	6.71	P RR	

Scrapped at Baginton, Coventry in October 1971.

INDEX

A6-HMS *58*, 125, 129 130
CF-CPD 20, 35, 101, 124, 129 130
CF-CPE 20, 35, *101*, 124, 129, 130
CF-CZA 20, 35, *92*, 124, 129, 130
CF-CZB *93*, 124, 129, 130
CF-CZC *93*, 123, 124, 129, 130
CF-CZD 20, 35, 93, *94*, 124, 129, 130
CF-CZW 20, 35, *94*, 124, 129, 130
CF-CZX 20, 35, *94*, 124, 128, 130
CU-P668 35, *96*, 125, 128, 130
CU-P669 35, 97, 98, 125, 128, 130
CU-P670 35, *98*, 125, 128, 130
CU-P671 35, *98*, 125, 129, 130
CU-T114 *97*, 128, 130
CU-T120 61, 129, 130
CU-T121 *64*, 129, 130
CU-T668 96, 97, 128, 130
CU-T669 *7*, *97*, *98*, 125, 128, 130
CU-T670 98, 125, 128, 130
CU-T671 *98*, 125, 129, 130
EC-BFJ *88*, 123, 126, 128, 130
EC-BFK 81, 123, 129, 130
EC-BFL 90, 91, 123, 125, 129, 130
EC-BSY 86, 123, 128, 130
EC-WFJ 88, 123, 128, 130
EC-WFK 81, 123, 129, 130
EC-WFL 90, 123, 129, 130
EI-BAA *73*, 122, 128, 130
EI-BBH 60, *61*, 122, 125, 128, 130
EI-BBY *57*, 123, 126, 129, 130
EI-BCI *55*, 122, 128, 130
EI-BDC *55*, 122, 123, 125, 128, 130
EL-LWG *62*, 126, 129, 130
EL-LWH 54, 126, 128, 130
G-ALBO 5, 13, *15*, *16*, *20*, 35, 37, *38*, 123, 126, 128, 130
G-ALRX 13, 16, 35, 36, *38*, *39*, 40, 126, 128, 130
G-AMYK 78, 129, 130
G-AMYL 79, 129, 130
G-ANBA 4, 16, *19*, 35, *39*, 40, 123, 124, 126, 127, 128, 130
G-ANBB 16, *19*, *40*, 123, 124, 126, 128, 130
G-ANBC 16, 17, 25, 26, *40*, 41, 52, 123, 124, 125, 128, 130
G-ANBD 17, 25, 26, *41*, 123, 124, 128, 130
G-ANBE *42*, 123, 124, 125, 126, 128, 130
G-ANBF *42*, 123, 124, 126, 128, 130
G-ANBG *43*, 123, 124, 128, 130
G-ANBH 17, 26, *27*, *28*, *44*, 123, 124, 126, 128, 130
G-ANBI *44*, 123, 124, 125, 126, 128, 130
G-ANBJ 44, *45*, 123, 124, 126, 127, 128, 130
G-ANBK *45*, *46*, 123, 124, 126, 127, 128, 130
G-ANBL *17*, *46*, 123, 124, 127, 128, 130
G-ANBM *46*, 123, 124, 126, 127, 128, 130
G-ANBN *47*, 123, 124, 125, 126, 128, 130
G-ANBO 16, 35, *48*, 123, 124, 125, 126, 128, 130
G-ANCA 18, 35, *69*, 82, 126, 128, 130
G-ANCB 35, 69, 70, 123, 128, 130
G-ANCC 35, 69, 70, 123, 125, 127, 128, 130
G-ANCD 35, *72*, 122, 123, 124, 125, 126, 127, 128, 130
G-ANCE 35, *73*, 122, 123, 124, 126, 127, 128, 130
G-ANCF *19*, 35, *74*, 75, 123, 124, 125, 126, 127, 128, 130
G-ANCG 74, *75*, *83*, 123, 124, 128, 130
G-ANCH 75, 76, 123, 124, 125, 126, 127, 128, 130
G-ANCI 83
G-ANCJ 84
G-ANGK 91, 129, 130
G-AOFA 78, 129, 130
G-AOFB 79, 129, 130
G-AOFC 79, 129, 130
G-AOFD 80, 129 130
G-AOFE 81, 129, 130
G-AOFF 81, 129, 130
G-AOFG 82, 129, 130
G-AOFJ 84, 128, 130
G-AOVA 18, 35, 36, *78*, 123, 124, 125, 126, 127, 129, 130
G-AOVB 20, 35, *79*, 124, 125, 129, 130
G-AOVC 35, *79*, 80, 124, 125, 129, 130
G-AOVD 35, 80, 124, 129, 130
G-AOVE 35, 81, 124, 126, 129, 130
G-AOVF 4, 36, *81*, *82*, *120*, 122, 124, 125, 126, 129, 130
G-AOVG 35, 36, *82*, 83, 123, 124, 126, 129, 130
G-AOVH 35, 36, *83*, 124, 126, 127, 128, 130
G-AOVI 35, 36, *84*, 124, 126, 127, 129, 130
G-AOVJ 35, *84*, 85, 124, 125, 128, 130
G-AOVK 35, *85*, 123, 124, 125, 128, 130
G-AOVL 35, *85*, 124, 126, 128, 130
G-AOVM *11*, 35, 85, 86, 124, 127, 128, 130
G-AOVN 35, *86*, 122, 124, 126, 128, 130
G-AOVO 36, *87*, 124, 125, 128, 130
G-AOVP 35, 36, *87*, 88, 123, 124, 125, 126, 128, 130
G-AOVR 35, 36, *88*, 123, 124, 128, 130
G-AOVS 35, 36, *88*, *89*, 123, 124, 125, 126, 127, 128, 130
G-AOVT 7, 18, 35, 36, 88, *89*, 90, 123, 124, 126, 128, 130
G-APLL 43, 123, 124, 126, 128, 130
G-APNA 20, 35, *95*, 123, 124, 125, 126, 128, 130
G-APNB 20, 35, 96, 123, 124, 125, 126, 128, 130
G-APPE 18, 35, 41, *52*, 126, 128, 130
G-APPF 18, 52, 126, 128, 130
G-APPG 18, 35, 52, 126, 128, 130
G-APYY *96*, 97, 125, 128, 130
G-ARKA *101*, 123, 124, 125, 127, 129, 130
G-ARKB *101*, *103*, 123, 124, 125, 127, 129, 130
G-ARWZ *91*, 123, 124, 129, 130
G-ARXA *91*, 123, 124, 126, 129, 130
G-ASFU 92, 124, 128, 130
G-ASFV 90, 124, 129, 130
G-ASTF *94*, 124, 129, 130
G-ATGD *92*, 123, 124, 127, 129, 130
G-ATLE *93*, 126, 127, 129, 130
G-ATMA 94, *95*, 122, 124, 126, 128, 130

G-ATNZ *94*, 124, 126, 129, 130

G-BDLZ *60*, 122, 123, 128, 130

G-BDUP *61*, 122, 123, 129, 130

G-BDUR *64*, 122, 123, 129, 130

G-BEMZ *58*, 60, 122, 123, 125, 127, 129, 130

G-BEPX *62*, *63*, 122, 123, 129, 130

G-BHAU *56*, 127, 128, 130

G-BRAC *55*, *89*, 127, 128, 130

G-14-1 74, 123, 128, 130

G-14-2 75, 123, 128, 130

G-18-1 69, 123, 128, 130

G-18-2 70, 123, 128, 130

G-18-3 72, 123, 128, 130

G-18-4 74, 123, 128, 130

G-18-8 101, 123, 129, 130

G-41 *76*, 128, 130

HB-ITB *90*, 125, 129, 130

HB-ITC *91*, 92, 125, 128, 130

HB-ITF 101, 129, 130

HB-ITG 103, 129, 130

LV-GJB 74, 127, 128, 130

LV-GJC *75*, 127, 128, 130

LV-JNL *79*, 122, 129, 130

LV-PNJ 79, 122, 129, 130

LV-PPJ 74, 127, 128, 130

LV-PPL 75, 127, 128, 130

N6595C 72, 126, 128, 131

N6596C 73, 126, 128, 131

N6597C 74, 126, 128, 131

N6598C 75, 126, 128, 131

N6599C 75, 126, 128, 131

OK-MBA *97*, 125, 128, 130

OK-MBB *98*, 125, 129, 130

OO-YCA *53*, 127, 129, 130

OO-YCB *57*, 127, 129, 130

OO-YCC 59, 127, 128, 130

OO-YCD 63, 127, 129, 130

OO-YCE 54, 127, 129, 130

OO-YCF 61, 129, 130

OO-YCG 62, 127, 129, 130

OO-YCH 54, 126, 127, 128, 130

PK-ICA 47, 126, 128, 130

PK-ICB *47*, 126, 128, 130

VX-442 13, 38, 126, 128, 130

VX-447 13, 38, 126, 128, 130

VX-454 13, 130

WB-470 38, 126, 128, 130

WB-473 38, 126, 128, 130

XA-MEC 18, *69*, 128, 130

XA-MED 18, *70*, 128, 130

XL-635 35, *53*, 127, 129, 130

XL-636 *53*, 127, 129, 130

XL-637 *54*, 127, 128, 130

XL-638 35, 39, *54*, 127, 128, 130

XL-639 35, 54, 55, 127, 128, 130

XL-640 35, 55, 126, 127, 128, 130

XL-657 35, *56*, 126, 127, 129, 130

XL-658 57, 127, 129, 130

XL-659 *57*, 127, 129, 130

XL-660 35, *58*, 122, 127, 129, 130

XM-489 35, *59*, 127, 128, 130

XM-490 59, *60*, 125, 127, 128, 130

XM-491 35, *60*, 127, 128, 130

XM-496 35, 61, 123, 127, 129, 130

XM-497 61, *62*, 127, 129, 130

XM-498 18, 35, 62, 127, 129, 130

XM-517 18, 35, 62, 63, 126, 127, 129, 130

XM-518 18, *63*, 127, 129, 130

XM-519 18, 64, 123, 127, 129, 130

XM-520 18, 35, 64, 127, 129, 130

XN-392 18, *52*, 122, 127, 128, 130

XN-398 11, 18, 125, 127, 128, 130

XN-404 18, *53*, 122, 127, 128, 130

XX-367 *77*, *86*, 122, 128, 130

4X-AGA 20, 35, *90*, 125, 129, 130

4X-AGB 20, *90*, 125, 129, 130

4X-AGC 20, 35, *91*, 125, 129, 130

4X-AGD 20, 35, 91, 92, 125, 128, 130

4X-AGE 72, 123, 125, 128, 130

5X-UVH 92, 122, 128, 130

5X-UVT 92, 122, 129, 130

5Y-ALP 92, 122, 129, 130

5Y-ALT *91*, 92, 128, 130

5Y-ANS 94, 95, 122, 126, 128, 130

5Y-AYR *72*, *73*, 122, 123, 125, 127, 128, 130

5Y-AZP 74, 122, 128, 130

7708M 38, 128, 130

9G-AAG *76*, 125, 128, 131

9G-AAH 78, 125, 129, 131

9G-ACE *55*, *64*, 125, 127, 129, 131

9Q-CAJ *62*, 63, 123, 129, 131

9Q-CAZ *82*, 125, 129, 131

9Q-CBT 54, 125, 126, 131

9Q-CDT *62*, 124, 125, 126, 129, 131

9Q-CGP 58, *59*, 126, 129, 131

9Q-CHU 56, 126, 128, 131

9Q-CHY 62, 86, 124, 126, 128, 131

9Q-CKG 54, 125, 126, 128, 131

9Q-CMO 61, 127, 128, 131

9Q-CPX *52*, 125, 128, 131

9Q-CUM 64, 126, 131

9U-BAD *56*, 125, 129, 130

Charlie Fox in open storage at the Brooklands Museum. Work on her restoration is progressing well. The main wing and fuselage centre section are being worked on at RAF Quedgelay and is looking impressive. (Graham Cowell)

The objectives of the Trust are directed wholly to the preservation and exhibition of Britannia aircraft, their parts, documents, articles and related information about their construction and operation.

The main thrust of the Trust's efforts is to raise funds and co-ordinate volunteer work programmes to assist with the preservation and restoration of Britannia aircraft in the United Kingdom.

The Trust already owns Britannia G-ANCF – "Charlie Fox" which has been donated by Proteus Aero Services, who acquired the aircraft some years ago and has been stored dismantled since 1988 at the Brooklands Museum, Weybridge. Work recently started on a long term restoration programme in conjunction with the Bristol Aero Collection, with a view to rebuilding the aircraft for display by the Collection at Filton.

The Trust would like to hear from Companies and individuals who are interested in supporting its efforts, be they in the form of financial assistance, donation of parts and memorabilia, historical information or volunteer workers to assist in the administration of the Trust or with the various Britannia restoration and preservation programmes.

Please reply to: 4 Vale Road, Exmouth, Devon EX8 2LZ

REGISTERED CHARITY No. 1004012

BYE-BYE